A+ Jumpstart™:
PC Hardware and Operating Systems Basics

Faithe Wempen

SYBEX®

San Francisco ◆ London

Associate Publisher: Neil Edde

Acquisitions and Developmental Editor: Heather O'Connor

Editor: Kathy Grider-Carlyle

Production Editor: Liz Burke

Technical Editor: Michelle Roudebush

Book Designer: Maureen Forys, Happenstance Type-O-Rama

Graphic Illustrator: Tony Jonick

Electronic Publishing Specialists: Maureen Forys, Kate Kaminski, Happenstance Type-O-Rama

Proofreaders: Dave Nash, Nancy Riddiough, Laurie O'Connell

Indexer: Ted Laux

Cover Designer: Archer Design

Cover Illustrator/Photographer: Archer Design

To Margaret, for the usual reasons.

Acknowledgments

Great big thank-yous to the wonderful staff at Sybex for taking my work from rough manuscript to finished book, especially my editors Heather O'Connor, Liz Burke, and Kathy Grider-Carlyle. I just can't say enough nice things about Sybex as a publishing company; writing a book for them is a great experience. Thanks also to Tony Jonick who turned my pen-and-ink scratchings into the line drawings you see here and to Michelle Roudebush for making sure I got all the facts straight.

Contents

Contents

Contents

Contents

Contents

Introduction

Welcome to my favorite hobby—personal computing! I love tinkering with computers so much that I've turned it into my full-time business. I find working with computer hardware really fascinating, and I hope that by the end of this book, I will have passed some of that enthusiasm along to you.

Judging from the title, you can probably guess the primary purpose of this book: to help people prepare for CompTIA's A+ exams. But unlike many other study guides, which assume you are already a working PC technician, this book starts at the very beginning. That makes it a great first book to pick up in your journey toward A+ certification.

Many people who sign up for A+ certification classes end up dropping out because the material is over their heads. Most good A+ certification courses—the kind that really go into the needed depth on each topic—are not for beginners! They're for people who are already working as PC technicians and want the certification to demonstrate the proficiency that they—for the most part—already possess. If you aren't already experienced with PC terminology and procedures, this book can bring you up to the level of the other students in the class, so you won't get lost or intimidated.

Introducing CompTIA's A+ Exams

A+ certification is administered by a company called CompTIA. This same company also administers several other certifications, including Network+ and iNet+.

To become A+ certified, you must pass two separate exams. You can take them both on the same day or spread them out, and you can pass them in any order. They are

A+ Core Hardware Service Technician   This exam tests your knowledge of PC hardware—including theory, safety, terminology, assembly, and troubleshooting.

A+ Operating System Technologies   This exam tests your knowledge of Microsoft Windows (NT 4, 2000, 95, and 98), including installation, startup, device interaction, file management, and troubleshooting.

Most people find the hardware exam tougher because they have less day-to-day experience with it. People who enjoy computers tend to fiddle around with Windows quite a bit, so they already know a lot of what's covered on the operating system exam. Fewer people take the time to fiddle around with hardware.

In addition, the hardware exam requires that you know quite a lot of specifications about various hardware types, and that kind of information doesn't normally come up in an average person's experience. This book, therefore, spends about 2/3 of its space on hardware. I have also included lots of pictures of various pieces of hardware, because not everybody reading this book will have access to a PC they can tear apart and examine.

You take the exams on a computer, with multiple-choice questions appearing onscreen. The testing software is mouse-based, so you click the answer you think is right and then click Next to move on to the next question.

Both exams are adaptive, which means they throw different questions at you based on your answers to previous ones. For example, if the testing software asks you a question about networking and you get it right, you probably won't get any more networking questions. But if you get it wrong, you might get several more questions about networking. This makes it hard to avoid the areas that you're weak in, and it forces you to study everything! The good part is that adaptive exams are usually shorter than nonadaptive ones. If you answer all the questions correctly, you could finish an exam in only 15 minutes or so.

To register to take an exam, visit Prometric (www.2test.com) or NCS/VUE (www.vue.com/comptia). Each exam costs $132, but volume discounts for 50 or more vouchers are available for corporations. If you take an A+ certification class, it might include the vouchers as part of the course fee. Then you go to a testing center in your area and take the exam at a testing workstation.

Who Needs A+ Certification?

A+ certification is useful for anyone who wants to work in the PC support industry. This could include people who do any of the following in their daily jobs (or want to):

- ◇ Fix broken computers
- ◇ Build new PCs from scratch
- ◇ Troubleshoot Windows problems
- ◇ Set up new PCs
- ◇ Install hardware upgrades
- ◇ Advise users about hardware and software purchases
- ◇ Train people to use Windows and applications

A+ certification is not meant to be a "master" level designation; it is supposed to measure the amount of competency gained by having six months of experience. At this time, there is no higher-level certification program for PC technicians, although there are specialized certifications such as Microsoft Certified Systems Engineer (MCSE) that focus on Windows and networking.

The average PC end user does not need A+ certification, any more than the average person who drives a car needs to be a mechanic. Other certifications are more suitable for end users, such as IC^3 for basic computer and Internet proficiency and Microsoft Office User Specialist (MOUS) for Microsoft business applications.

How to Study for Certification

Start with this book! But don't stop there. To pass the A+ examinations, and to be a really top-notch PC technician, you need the following as well:

In-depth study guides   When you are ready for more details, check out the *A+ Complete Study Guide* or the *A+ Complete Study Guide, Deluxe Edition*, also published by Sybex.

Hands-on experience   There is no substitute for real-world experience in this business! Offer to fix the PCs of your friends, relatives, and coworkers for free, just for the practice. Take your own PC apart and put it back together. Go to auctions and buy stacks of old, untested computers, and set up a little lab in your garage for trying to make them work.

Test preparation courses   Many companies out there offer complete A+ certification classes with both lecture and hands-on portions. Taking one of these can really help cement the concepts you'll read about in this book, and you can go into much greater depth on each topic.

Practice tests   Look around on the Internet; there are lots of practice exams for A+. Some are totally free; others have some questions available free and have more available if you pay. Sybex provides an inexpensive and easy way topractice A+ exam questions with the *A+ Complete Virtual Test Center*.

Reference books   Remember, A+ certification isn't the end—it's just the beginning of your career as a PC technician. You will want to keep abreast of the latest trends in the industry, as well as gain more in-depth knowledge, by consulting reference books on PC hardware that may have nothing to do with certification per se. One excellent one is Sybex's *Complete PC Upgrade & Maintenance Guide* by Mark Minasi.

Book Features

This book contains 19 chapters, each of which tackles a particular class of hardware or type of Windows task. Each chapter starts out with a summary of the topics covered and ends with ten review questions you can use to test how well you understood and absorbed the material in the chapter.

Within each chapter, you'll find lots of pictures, along with boxed notes, tips, and cautions that point out additional helpful material. You'll also find important definitions spotlighted in the margins, and these definitions are collected in a comprehensive glossary at the back of the book.

Let's Get Started!

Okay, enough of the preliminaries—I'm eager to get started, and you probably are too. So turn the page and let's begin preparing for A+ certification.

Chapter

1

Safety and Preventive Maintenance

E xploring the inside of your PC can be educational and fun. Before you dive in though, you'll need to be aware of some potential perils to both your well-being and the PC's. In this chapter, you'll learn the safe ways of interacting with PC hardware, including:

 Avoiding electric shock

 Disposing of PC-related hazardous materials safely

 Preventing electrostatic damage to a PC

 Avoiding electromagnetic interference

 Preventing PC problems caused by power fluctuation

 Cleaning a PC and its associated parts

Preventing the PC from Hurting You

Cathode Ray Tube (CRT)
The technology behind the box-type display monitors sold today. It consists of a vacuum tube that sends electron rays to charge photosensitive phosphors on the monitor screen. The phosphors light up, creating the display picture.

Let's start with this topic because your safety as a human being comes before the safety of the equipment—or at least it should!

Electricity Precautions

Most of us take electrical precautions in daily life as a matter of course. Things such as not operating electrical items near water and not sticking your finger in a wall outlet are no doubt everyday life skills for you, since you have survived to reach adulthood. All those common sense warnings about electricity apply when you're working on PCs as well.

The biggest danger comes not from the PC itself, but from the monitor. The traditional type of PC monitor (known as a **CRT**) contains a large capacitor in the back that can store up to 30,000 volts—more than enough to kill a person. Further, it maintains its charge even after the monitor has been unplugged from the wall outlet for many months. Because of this, you should not attempt to work on your own monitor, nor should you remove the monitor's cover. If you ever do remove the cover, don't touch the thing that looks like a suction cup; that's the high-voltage anode.

Inside the PC itself, nothing has enough voltage to kill, but the power supply can deliver a nasty 110-volt shock if you tamper with it. The power supply is the metal box inside the PC with a tangle of colored wires emerging from it. This metal box is sealed, but it has some screws that enable you to disassemble it. Don't.

When working on a PC, you should always unplug it first. This is as much to protect the PC itself as to protect you. No matter what the reason, it's a good practice.

NOTE

Some people leave the PC plugged in so its power cord will act as a grounding wire to avoid electrostatic discharge (ESD) damage; but as you'll learn later in the chapter, there are better ways of preventing ESD that don't involve leaving the PC plugged in.

As another precaution when you're working on PCs, try to work with one hand at a time, rather than both hands at once. That way electricity is not as likely to travel through your body to complete a circuit. Finally, try to have someone else around when you're working on anything electrical. That way, someone will be there to call for the ambulance if you hurt yourself.

Don't let all this scare you off! Working on PCs is not particularly dangerous, and your chances of getting an electrical shock are actually quite remote if you just use ordinary care.

Proper Working Attire

As a PC technician, you will probably spend some time crawling around underneath desks hooking up cables, so dress comfortably in clothes that allow you to bend. As is the case with appliance repairpersons, everyone will appreciate it if you wear a belt and avoid low-riding pants.

Avoid jewelry made out of conductive materials, and avoid any jewelry that might get caught on something. That means no dangling earrings, no necklaces, no bracelets, and no watches.

Safe Hazardous Materials Disposal

PCs can not only hurt you directly, but they can also hurt your environment. Several parts inside a PC require special disposal procedures:

Batteries   A motherboard has a very small battery; a notebook PC has a big one. These batteries can contain lead, lithium, nickel-cadmium, and/or mercury—all of which can seep into groundwater in a landfill.

Toner cartridges   These cartridges from laser printers can contain traces of leftover toner, which can cause lung problems if breathed. Depending on the model, you might be able to sell your old cartridges to a company that remanufactures them.

Monitors   These big plastic shells take up a lot of space in a landfill, and they also contain phosphorous, mercury, and lead coatings on the back side of the monitor glass.

Circuit boards   These contain small amounts of lead in the soldering.

Cleaning chemicals   Some cleaning solvents used for PCs can pollute groundwater and soil.

If your community has a hazardous waste disposal facility, take the above materials there. Check the Environmental Protection Agency (EPA) website at www.epa.gov if you do not know where to go.

Avoiding Hurting the PC

It's much easier to hurt the PC than it is for the PC to hurt you. In many cases, you won't even realize you've harmed it until it stops working or starts acting all squirrelly.

The Evils of Electrostatic Discharge

Electrostatic discharge (ESD) is another name for static electricity, the same stuff that shocks you after you've scuffed your feet across the carpet on a low-humidity day.

Computer components are extremely sensitive to ESD. It takes about 3,000 volts of ESD for a human to feel it, but only about 300 volts (or even less) to weaken or even ruin a circuit board. This means you can cause major damage to a PC without any evidence of it at all—until you turn it on and it doesn't work anymore. The damage might not show up immediately; an ESD shock can weaken a component such that it fails a day or a month later, or it can make it malfunction in intermittent, unexplainable ways.

To prevent ESD damage, you need to keep the charge equalized between you and the PC. The best way to do that is to wear an antistatic wrist strap. It has a wristband at one end and an alligator clip at the other; attach the clip to the PC's metal frame. If you don't have a wrist strap available and need to work on a PC, an alternative is to touch the chassis or power supply frequently as you work on the PC, to keep equalizing that charge.

The second part of preventing ESD is to **ground** yourself. One way is to keep the PC plugged in as you work on it, because its power cord connects to a grounding plug in the wall outlet, and then touch the PC chassis periodically as you work. However, as discussed earlier, for your own safety this is not a good idea. When what's best for you and what's best for the PC conflict, your safety should prevail. A better way is to buy an antistatic mat that comes with a grounding plug, and then plug it into the wall outlet. Stand on the mat as you work, or place the mat on the work surface next to the PC. Connect your wrist strap to the grounding mat, instead of to the PC frame.

You can also minimize the chances of ESD damage by wearing appropriate clothing. Rubber-soled shoes are better than leather ones, cotton socks are better than nylon, and fabrics that generate static electricity are a no-no. You can also help the situation by keeping the humidity up in the room in which you're working; a portable humidifier can make all the difference.

Electrostatic discharge (ESD)
An electrical shock that occurs when two objects of uneven charge come in contact with one another. Otherwise known as static electricity.

Ground
To bleed off electrical charge to a safe location where it can dissipate, such as to the earth itself.

4

When storing circuit boards, don't just stack them in a box; place each board in a separate ESD-protected storage bag. You have probably seen such bags before—they look like plastic bags, but they have a coating on the inside that inhibits static. Most circuit boards you buy come in them, and you can also buy extras at your local computer store.

Some PC technicians scoff at ESD damage and don't take any of these precautions. They claim that they've never damaged anything with ESD, and it's all a bunch of hooey. However, as I mentioned before, not all ESD damage is immediate and obvious, so how would they know for sure? I have personally ruined more than one motherboard by failing to take ESD precautions, so let me assure you that this danger is real.

Electromagnetic interference (EMI) The corruption of a signal by the magnetic field of another nearby electrical device.

Understanding Electromagnetic Interference (EMI)

Perhaps you learned in science class that electricity generates a magnetic field. When current travels through a cable, a magnetic field builds up around that cable. When two cables run close together, one can interfere with another. This is **electromagnetic interference**, or EMI. EMI causes no permanent damage to components; when you remove the electrical flow through the cable, the interference ceases.

EMI can manifest itself in a number of ways. On a cable carrying data, you might get garbage characters in your data. For example, in a printer cable the printout might contain extra characters or have odd formatting. On a cable carrying power, you might get power spikes and sags.

To avoid EMI, try to use shielded cables whenever possible. A shielded cable contains a sheath around the outside that prevents a magnetic field from passing through. Using shorter cables can also minimize EMI, and keeping cables separated physically from one another helps as well.

The Hazards of Magnets

Hard disks and floppy disks are coated with metal particles, and the write head on the drive magnetizes them to store the data. So you can imagine what happens to the data on the disk when the disk is exposed to a magnet, right? All kinds of headaches.

Most people wouldn't be so blatant as to stick a magnet inside a PC, although there's always the occasional doofus who affixes a floppy disk to his filing cabinet with a magnet. But magnets are not always obvious. Watch out for the following magnetic sources, and keep them well away from your disks:

Magnetic tools   A lot of hand tools, such as screwdrivers, are magnetized so that they can be used to pick up screws. Never use magnetized tools when working on a PC! It's a good idea to buy a set of tools designed for PC work, because you can be sure they aren't magnetized.

Unshielded speakers   Speakers contain rather powerful magnets. If your PC has a sound card into which you plug a set of speakers, make sure you use speakers designed specifically for PCs, because they're more likely to be magnet-shielded.

Telephones   Some telephones contain magnets. Keep disks away from telephones, just to be on the safe side.

TIP

The magnets in unshielded speakers can distort the image on your monitor if the speakers are too close to it. If you notice distortion on the sides of the display, try moving the speakers farther away from it.

Preventing Power Fluctuations

A PC's power supply requires a constant source of 110-volt AC power. It's able to tolerate minor fluctuations, so a little more or a little less won't hurt anything. But there are limits to this tolerance, and anything outside those limits can cause problems.

Surge Suppressor

To protect your PC against **power surges** and **spikes**, invest in a surge suppressor. This is a power strip that takes the hit when a surge or spike occurs, channeling off any excess power so it doesn't reach the electrical devices plugged into it. The effectiveness of a surge suppressor is measured in **joules**.

Power Conditioner

A **power sag** can cause the PC to restart itself, such that you lose all your unsaved data; it can also cause whatever is in memory at the moment to become corrupted. The problem resolves itself when the PC restarts.

A surge suppressor does nothing to prevent power sags. To do that, you need a power conditioner. Such a device stores power in a battery, and it supplements the AC wall current whenever it is insufficient. You don't usually find power conditioners for sale in computer stores; this function is normally combined with that of an uninterruptible power supply (UPS).

UPS

A UPS protects against power failures that cause the PC to be unexpectedly shut down, and it can also act as a power conditioner and surge suppressor. You plug your devices into it, and the battery supplements or replaces the AC current whenever it is insufficient. A UPS is larger than a regular surge suppressor because of its rather large battery, and it is also very heavy because of the battery.

There are two kinds of UPSes: *online* and *standby*. An online UPS charges the battery from the wall current and then uses the battery power all the time to power the attached devices. This is the better and more expensive kind. A standby UPS charges the battery but lets the AC wall current flow directly through to the devices as long as wall current is available. When it's not available, the unit quickly switches the devices over to the battery. This is the more common type sold in stores, and it is much cheaper.

Power surge
A power surge occurs when the power supply gets too much power. It can cause the PC to reset, the power supply to burn out, or circuit boards to go bad. A power spike is like a surge only more so. Power spikes are even more likely to permanently damage hardware.

Joule
A unit of electrical energy. Surge suppressors are rated in joules, such as 800 or 1,300 joules.

Power sag
Occurs when the power supply doesn't get enough power. It's also called a brownout. You may have experienced this in your home when the lights dim and buzz for a moment but don't go out completely.

Cleaning a PC

Computers attract a lot of dust, both inside and out. Outside it's just a nuisance, making for a less pleasant working environment. Inside, dust can prevent components from being cooled properly, causing overheating and causing them to go bad faster.

Cleaning Supplies

Using the right cleaning supplies is important. You don't want to use heavy-duty solvents on components, nor do you want to do anything that will cause a short circuit. (For example, don't get water on a circuit board.) Here are some safe, useful supplies to have on hand:

- Compressed air in an aerosol can, preferably with an extension straw that can direct the air precisely
- Clean, lint-free soft cloths
- Paper towels
- Warm water with a small amount of very mild detergent (such as dish washing liquid), or a cleaning fluid designed for cleaning computer equipment
- Antistatic spray-on cleaner specifically designed for computer equipment
- Moist towelettes specifically designed for computer monitors
- Cotton swabs
- Alcohol (not rubbing alcohol)

Cleaning a Circuit Board

Circuit boards accumulate dust. To remove the dust, blow it off with canned air. Avoid putting any kind of wet substance on a circuit board, because it can cause short-circuiting if the liquid is not completely dried when you power up. If you must use a liquid, use pure alcohol (not rubbing alcohol, which contains water).

WARNING

Canned air comes out very cold, so don't blow it on yourself if you can help it. Because it does make whatever it touches very cold, some PC technicians use it to cool off an overheated chip on a circuit board.

Avoid touching any of the chips or resistors on a circuit board because you might damage them; handle it only by its edges.

Cleaning the Inside of the PC

Big dust bunnies can grow inside a PC; you'll be shocked the first time you open up an old PC. Fish out the large pieces by hand. Then blow the dust off everything with canned air. But hold your breath! All that dust will be floating around in the air, and you'll be hacking and coughing. If you can blow it out outdoors, that's all the better.

TIP

If your CPU has a heat sink or fan on it, there's probably a lot of dust accumulated in the little nooks and crannies of it. Make sure you get all that crud out too.

Cleaning a Monitor

Always turn the monitor off before cleaning it. Then wipe the screen with special glass cleaner designed specifically for computer monitors and a soft lint-free cloth. You can buy premoistened towelettes for cleaning monitors if you prefer.

NOTE

Nothing bad is likely to happen if you clean the monitor with the power on, but it never hurts to play it safe. A long time ago I saw a store employee fry a monitor by spraying glass cleaner on it while it was running, and that image has stayed with me ever since. Besides, it's much easier to see the spots and dirt on the monitor when it's turned off.

Don't use regular glass cleaner on a monitor because it contains ammonia and can potentially harm the anti-glare coating used on some monitors. Don't use soap because it can leave a residue.

Clean the plastic parts of the monitor with a clean damp cloth and a mild soap solution. Make sure the cloth is just barely damp—not wet! Damage can result if you drip water down inside the vent holes on the monitor.

Cleaning a Keyboard

A keyboard can get pretty filthy, because it's always being touched. To clean one, first make sure the PC is off. (You don't necessarily need to unplug the keyboard from the PC.) Then do the following:

1. Turn the keyboard upside down and shake it. This clears the debris out from under the keys.
2. Wipe the keycaps with a damp cloth and mild soapy water.
3. Use a folded moistened paper towel to reach in the cracks between the keys. Be careful not to drip water under the keys.
4. Allow the keyboard to dry before using it.

If you ever spill liquid on the keyboard, turn off the PC right away, shake the keyboard upside down to get rid of the bulk of the liquid, and then clean it and let it dry thoroughly. If the liquid contained sugar, and it went down below the keys, you probably won't be able to get it clean; just buy a new keyboard. Some people have had success washing a keyboard in a dishwasher (on the top rack, with no heated drying), so if you're going to throw the keyboard away anyhow, you might try it.

WARNING

Don't try to remove the individual keys on a keyboard for cleaning. You'll find it very difficult to get it reassembled.

Cleaning a Mouse

Like the keyboard, the mouse gets very dirty because people have their hands on it. And that's just the top of it—the bottom also gets dirty from picking up debris and dust from the mouse pad.

When the mouse ball picks up dirt, it conveys it inside the mouse as it rolls. Over time, the rollers inside the mouse can get so dirty that they don't work well anymore. The sensors inside the mouse that tell it how much the rollers are moving can also become impaired. When a mouse is dirty, the pointer often jumps or stutters across the screen.

To clean a mouse:

1. Turn the mouse on its back, and rotate the plastic plate that holds the mouse ball in place.

2. Turn the mouse over again. The ball and plate should fall into your hand.

WARNING

Don't clean the mouse ball with alcohol, because it dries out the rubber.

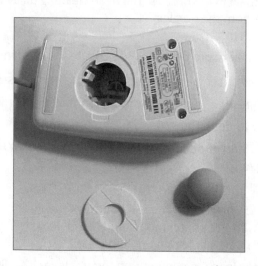

3. Clean the ball with soap and water; then dry it with a lint-free cloth.

4. With a cotton swab and alcohol, clean the rollers and contact points inside the mouse. Let the alcohol evaporate completely before reassembling the mouse.

5. Replace the ball and the plastic plate, and rotate the plate to secure it.

Cleaning a Printer

Different types of printers have different cleaning procedures. If any portion of the discussion of the printer's parts doesn't make sense to you here, wait until you've learned more about printers in Chapter 12, "Printing Basics."

Cleaning an Inkjet Printer

Wipe the outside casing of an inkjet printer with a damp cloth and mild soapy water. It won't necessarily make the printer perform any better, but it'll make for a nicer office environment.

The only parts of the inside that need cleaning are the inkjets, and you don't clean them manually; instead you use a utility built into the printer to clean them. When printouts seem to be missing one color or another in a certain area, or there are gaps in the printout, it's probably a dirty inkjet nozzle problem.

NOTE

How do the inkjet nozzles get dirty? Well, the ink in an inkjet printer is liquid, and if you don't use the printer frequently, it dries out, and bits of dried ink remain in the nozzles. The head cleaning utility flushes out any dried-up ink from the nozzles.

On most printers there are two ways to activate the cleaning utility:

You can press a sequence of buttons on the printer itself.

You can choose a command from the printer's Properties box in Windows.

Here's how to do it from Windows.

1. Choose Start ➢ Settings ➢ Printers. (In Windows XP, it's Start , Printers and Faxes.)
2. Right-click your printer and choose Properties.
3. Click the Utilities tab. The tab you want may not be named Utilities; it varies with the printer model and driver. However, you're looking for a tab with a Head Cleaning option on it.
4. Click the Head Cleaning button (or whatever it's called for your printer) and then follow the onscreen prompts.
5. Use the Nozzle Check feature (or similarly named feature for your printer model) to print a test that checks to make sure the print heads are clean.

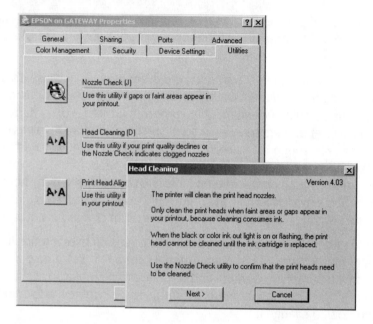

You can also use compressed air to blow any paper dust out of the inside of the printer.

Cleaning a Laser Printer

Laser printers use toner rather than ink. Because toner is a dry substance (made up of a mixture of plastic resin and iron oxide), it doesn't clog things up the way liquid ink does. However, toner is a loose powder that can get all over your clothes and workspace if you don't handle the cartridges with care.

If you do happen to spill some toner, use a slightly damp paper towel to clean it up as best you can. If you get it on your clothing, the best way to get it out is with a magnet. Because toner is half iron, it's very magnetic.

Several parts of a laser printer can accumulate toner on them, making them less effective over time. Until you learn about the inside parts of a laser printer (in Chapter 12), this discussion might not make much sense to you, but remember it for later.

The parts to clean on a laser printer include:

Corona wires   These are individual wires strung horizontally across the inside of the printer. Most printers have two: the primary corona and the transfer corona. The latter is inside the toner cartridge on some models. Check the printer's manual to find out whether you can clean them. If you can, clean them with a cleaning tool especially designed for that purpose, or use an alcohol-dipped cotton swab if you don't have one. Be very careful not to break them. On some printers, corona wires are not present at all or not user-accessible.

Drum   You should never, *ever* touch the drum directly, because it's easy to scratch, and a scratched drum leaves a scratched image on every printout. Instead, use the printer's built-in cleaning utility program if there is one. Many Hewlett-Packard LaserJet printers have such a utility. The procedure involves running a sheet of paper through the printer so that a heavy layer of toner adheres to the paper, and then running the same sheet through again to pick up excess toner from the drum. If your printer doesn't have such a utility, you don't need to clean the drum. Some models include the drum in the toner cartridge, so that it's replaced with each new toner cartridge; on such printers drum cleaning is not an issue.

Cleaning pad   On some printers, a felt pad cleans off excess toner. It's mounted on a hard plastic strip. If your printer model uses a felt pad, a new one will be included with the toner cartridge and will need to be replaced at the same time as the cartridge. Look in the printer's manual to determine the location of the pad and how to change it.

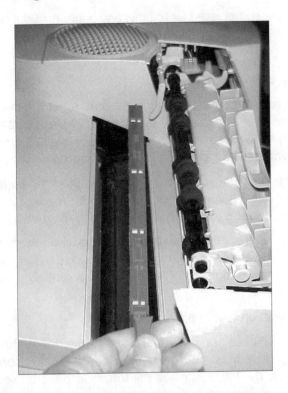

Inside plastic parts   If any paper debris or dust is on the open plastic areas inside a printer, you can wipe it off with a slightly damp cloth.

Review Questions

1. What parts of a computer system need special disposal to protect the environment?

   _____

Terms to Know
❑ CRT
❑ ESD
❑ Ground
❑ EMI
❑ Power surge
❑ Joule
❑ Power sag

2. What does ESD stand for?

   _____

3. What precautions can you take to avoid ESD damage?

   _____

4. What are some ways to avoid EMI?

   _____

5. True or False: A magnet can damage a keyboard.

   _____

6. True or False: A standby power system supplies power to attached devices through its battery only when the wall current is insufficient.

   _____

7. A surge suppressor's ability to prevent power surges is measured in

   _____.

8. True or False: To clean a circuit board, use a water-dipped cotton swab.

   _____

9. What would be a symptom of a mouse that needed to be cleaned?

   _____

10. How do you clean the inkjet nozzles on a printer?

   _____

Chapter

2

A Look Inside a PC

Now that you've gotten your safety briefing, you're ready to start checking out your PC. We'll start with the parts that are accessible from the outside, and then we'll move inside for an overall introduction to the inner parts. Later chapters will look at each of these parts in detail, but here you'll see the big picture.

This chapter covers:

 Identifying the parts visible from the outside

 Opening the case

 Identifying the parts on the inside

What You See from the Outside

On the front of a typical PC, you can see the following features:

Power button   Turns the PC on/off (duh!).

Floppy drive   Accepts 3.5-inch floppy disks, which for a long time were the only viable means of transferring files between PCs.

CD-ROM drives   Accepts CD-ROM discs, and if the drive is capable of it, might also write to writeable CDs and/or read DVD discs.

Power light   Illuminates when the PC is on; remains on all the time. Usually green.

Hard disk light   Illuminates when the hard disk is being accessed. Flashes while the hard disk reads or writes; goes out when there is no disk activity. Can be either red or green. Might not be operational at all on some home-built systems.

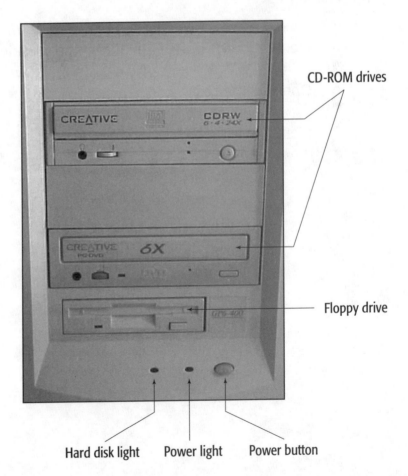

CD-ROM drives

Floppy drive

Hard disk light   Power light   Power button

From the back, you can see:

Fan vent   Draws in air from the outside to cool the components inside. The fan runs constantly whenever the PC is on.

Power cord connector   Accepts a standard three-prong power cord.

Voltage switch   Most power supplies have a switch that enables them to operate at different voltages depending on the voltage of the wall outlet. In the United States, standard voltage is 110-volt (the switch may read 115-volt, but that's basically the same thing). In Europe, it's 200-volt.

Power supply   The fan vent, voltage switch, and power cord connector are built into the power supply, which is a separate metal box fastened to the case from the inside. From the outside, it looks like a part of the PC's case.

Removable panel for additional fan   Some cases have extra vents; if the optional fan is not installed, a metal plate covers them as shown here.

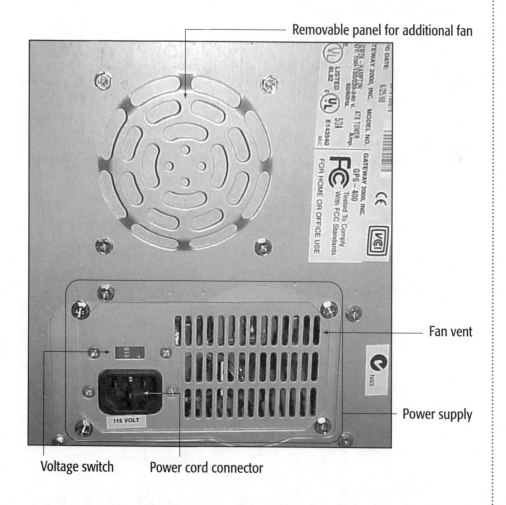

Removable panel for additional fan

Fan vent

Power supply

Voltage switch   Power cord connector

Built-in ports   Ports that come with the PC that are used for plugging in keyboard, mouse, and other standard devices. We'll look at these in more detail momentarily.

Expansion ports   Ports that are added in expansion slots on the motherboard and are not part of the base PC itself (for example, a video card or modem). We'll look at these more closely in a moment as well.

Your PC probably has a tangle of wires plugged into the back, as you saw in the preceding figures. With all those wires, sorting out what's what can be difficult. Here's a closer look at the built-in ports:

Keyboard port   On an ATX system (which is shown here), the keyboard port is a **PS/2 port**. On an AT system, the keyboard port is a larger round plug. You can buy different keyboards with the different connectors, or you can buy a plug that converts between them; the keyboards themselves are identical except for the plugs. You'll learn about AT and ATX systems in Chapter 3, "A Closer Look at the Motherboard."

Mouse port   The mouse also plugs into a PS/2 port on most systems. On some older systems, there is no mouse port; on these systems, you must use a mouse that plugs into the serial port (which will be explained in a moment) instead. Even though the keyboard and mouse may both use PS/2 ports, the ports are not interchangeable. Notice in the following figure that there are pictures of a keyboard and a mouse next to the ports to help you avoid confusing them.

USB ports   These small rectangular slots accept Universal Serial Bus (USB) cables. Many types of devices use USB interfaces, including scanners, digital cameras, and printers.

PS/2 port

A small round port used for connecting some keyboards and mice. The name derives from a model of IBM PC that used this type of connector. The PS/2 computer is long obsolete, but the plug type is still around.

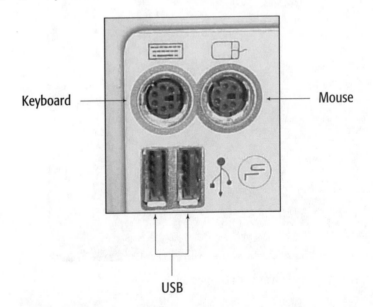

Keyboard —   — Mouse

USB

Serial ports   Some systems have one of these; others have two. They are typically 9-pin **male D-sub** connectors. The nine pins are arranged with five pins in one row and four pins in the other. Some older systems have one 9-pin serial port and one 25-pin serial port. The 25-pin type is just an elongated model with more pins, and you can buy converters that switch between 9-pin and 25-pin formats if you happen to need the connector to be a different size than it is. Serial ports used to be used for many devices, but today the USB type of connector is more popular. You might connect an external modem to a serial port or a mouse (if your system does not have a PS/2 mouse port) or the cradle for a handheld computer such as a PalmPilot.

Parallel port   This is a 25-pin **female** D-sub connector. The 25 pins are arranged with 13 pins in one row and 12 in the other. Printers are by far the most common device to use a parallel port, although some models of scanners are parallel as well.

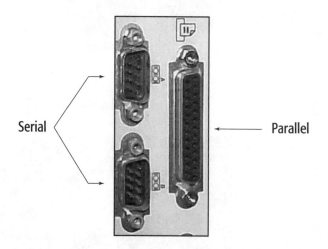

Serial   Parallel

Male
In computer jargon, a male connector is one that has pins rather than holes.

D-sub
A type of connector with asymmetrically arranged pins or holes in multiple rows. The outer ring looks sort of like a capital *D*, which is where the term D-sub comes originates.

Female
A female connector is one that has holes rather than pins.

Sound connectors   On some PCs, the sound connectors are built-in; on other systems, they're on a separate sound card in an expansion slot. Here they're built-in. There are three identical round plugs—output for speakers, input for a microphone, and input for other devices.

Joystick connector   If the PC has a separate sound card, the joystick port will be on that expansion card. If sound is built in, as shown here, it'll appear with the built-in ports. A joystick connector is a 15-pin female D-sub connector with two rows: one with 8 holes and one with 7.

In addition to the built-in ports, your PC has an area of rectangular holes covered by metal panels. Each of these panels corresponds to an expansion slot in the motherboard. When an expansion card is plugged into a slot, its ports stick out of that hole. In the following figure, there are two expansion cards: a video card and a network card. On some budget systems, the video port is among the built-in ones; on higher-end systems, you can expect to find a separate video card.

You can tell what type of card it is by the connectors. A video card has a 15-pin female connector with three rows of pins (the only D-sub connector type to have three rows rather than two); a network card has an **RJ-45** connector.

RJ-45
A type of connector that looks like a wider-than-normal telephone plug. Used for network cables and ISDN phone lines.

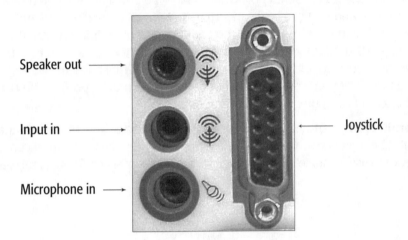

Speaker out

Input in

Microphone in

Joystick

Video (to monitor)

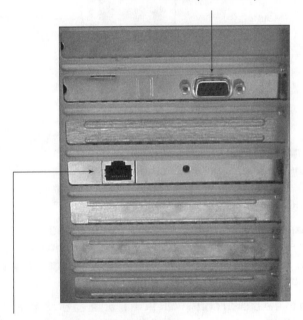

Network interface (to network hub)

Removing the Cover

There are many PC case designs, and each case's cover comes off a little differently. Major PC manufacturers have been using unusual case designs—especially in the last several years—so you may sometimes need to resort to reading the PC's manual to determine how to remove the cover.

On standard PC cases, however, you can usually figure things out by looking for and removing screws that are around the edges of the PC and appear to be holding on the case. For example, there are several screws in the following illustration, but only one of them passes through both the back of the PC and the cover.

Cover Screw

NOTE

Make sure you put the screws somewhere safe, so you'll have them when it's time to reassemble.

After removing any screws holding the cover, slide or lift it off. On some models, you might need to slide it a few inches and then lift.

Some of the nicer and more modern cases don't use screws, or they use thumbscrews that don't require a screwdriver. Some of the new Dell PCs, for example, have buttons to push on the top and bottom of the case; when you push both buttons simultaneously, the case pops open. On others cases, the cover does not come completely off; instead, you remove a side panel for access.

A First Look at the Inside

When you remove the cover, you'll find a complex system of circuit boards and cables inside. Don't let this intimidate you. In the following sections, we'll break down each area and see what it contains.

Drives   Motherboard

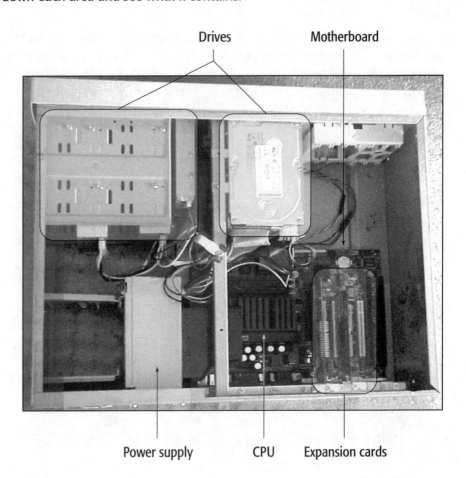

Power supply   CPU   Expansion cards

Motherboard

Let's start with the large circuit board on the floor of the case—the motherboard. It's called the motherboard because all other components plug into it, and so are "children" of it. Other names for it include main board, system board, and planar board.

NOTE

AT and ATX are two **form factors** of motherboards. You'll learn about them in Chapter 3. For now, just keep in mind that things are laid out a little differently on one versus the other. I'll point out the differences as we go along.

Form factor
The size and shape of a device. Most commonly applied to motherboards, but it can also apply to other devices that come in a variety of sizes.

It can be difficult to see the whole motherboard because of all the components installed on it, so here's a picture of a bare motherboard removed from the case. (It's a slightly different model from the one shown in the preceding figure.)

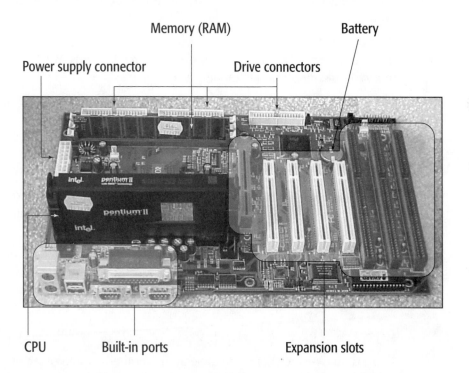

Memory (RAM)   Battery

Power supply connector   Drive connectors

CPU   Built-in ports   Expansion slots

Power supply connector   A group of wires runs from the power supply to the motherboard. An ATX motherboard uses a single connector with holes (shown here). An AT model has two adjacent connectors with six pins each.

Built-in ports   These are the same built-in ports that were peeking out of the back of the computer when you took the external tour. As you can see, they're built directly into the side of the motherboard on this ATX model. On an AT motherboard, the ports are not physically built-in, but instead attach to the motherboard with cables. You'll see the difference in Chapter 3.

CPU   The Central Processing Unit, or CPU, is the engine that drives the entire operation. It performs all the math calculations, processing millions of calculations per second.

Battery   The battery provides a small amount of constant power to the motherboard, so items that always need to be on (such as the system's date/time clock) can stay that way even when the PC is unplugged.

Expansion slots   These are the slots into which expansion circuit boards fit. Three types are shown here. The single gray one in the center is an AGP slot for a video card. (Actually, it's brown on most motherboards.) The white ones are PCI slots, and the black ones are ISA slots. Not all motherboards have all these slot types. You'll learn about the slot types in Chapter 3.

Memory (RAM)   RAM stands for Random Access Memory; this is the main memory on the PC. Most RAM today comes on mini circuit boards. You'll learn about memory in Chapter 5, "Understanding Memory."

Drive connectors   **Ribbon cables** run from the drives to the motherboard, and they connect into these sets of pins.

Central Processing Unit (CPU)

The **Central Processing Unit (CPU)** does the math calculations for the entire PC. Modern CPUs can process many millions of instructions per second; in Chapter 3, you'll learn about the types of CPUs and their specifications.

CPUs have two main shapes: pin grid array (PGA) chips and Single Edge Contact (SEC). The latter are sometimes called Single Edge Connector, but both refer to the same thing. The type you need depends on the type of motherboard you have.

NOTE

There is no direct relationship between the motherboard form factor (AT versus ATX) and the type of CPU it uses.

A **PGA** chip is flat on the top; on the bottom it has many tiny pins. Each pin fits into a hole in a socket in the motherboard. Here's a PGA model, both front and back sides.

And here's an **SEC** model:

Circuit board

SEC
Single Edge Contact cartridge. A type of CPU mounted on a circuit board inside a plastic casing.

An SEC CPU is a chip too, but it's mounted on a circuit board and then the circuit board is encased in a plastic cartridge. You plug an SEC CPU into the motherboard by inserting the circuit board into a slot. There are mounting braces on the motherboard to help hold the cartridge upright.

In actual use, a CPU will almost always have a cooling device attached to it. There are two main types of cooling devices: fans and heat sinks. A fan is just what the name says—a small electric fan that cools the CPU. Here's a PGA CPU mounted on a motherboard with a fan on top of it:

Fan

CPU

A **heat sink** is a porcupine-like block that channels heat away from the CPU. Some CPUs use a combination of both—a heat sink block with a fan mounted in the center of it.

RAM

Random Access Memory (RAM) acts as short-term storage for the PC while it processes data. RAM keeps track of what programs and data files are open, what should appear on the screen at any given moment, and lots more. Writing to and from RAM is very fast—much faster than writing to and from a hard disk. RAM is volatile, which means whatever is stored there is only stored temporarily; when you turn off the PC, RAM's content is erased. In Chapter 5, you'll learn why this is so, and you'll learn lots of other important details about RAM.

Physically, RAM on a motherboard looks like a small rectangular circuit board, about 5.25 inches long. The type shown here is a Dual Inline Memory Module (DIMM).

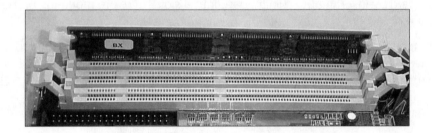

There is also an older, shorter kind called a SIMM (Single Inline Memory Module) that you might encounter in older PCs.

Drives

CD-ROMs, floppy disks, and hard disks are all nonvolatile storage. In other words, whatever you place on a disk stays there, even after you shut off the PC. That's why it's important to save your work to disk before shutting down the PC—because until you save, the data exists only in RAM.

Disk drives are encased in metal boxes to keep them from being damaged. Some drives are separate from their disks, and you can remove one disk and insert another; CD-ROM and floppy drives are like that. Other drives integrate the disk and the drive in a single package, as with a hard disk.

NOTE

Because a hard disk cannot be removed from the hard drive, the terms *hard disk* and *hard drive* have come to be synonymous.

All drives have at least two connectors on the back: one for power and one for data. The data connector accepts a ribbon cable, which then attaches to a drive connector on the motherboard. Here's the back of a hard disk:

Data connector   Power connector

NOTE

Hard drives (and CD-ROM drives) use two types of interfaces: Integrated Drive Electronics (IDE) and Small Computer Systems Interface (SCSI). Most motherboards include IDE connectors, but not SCSI connectors; you must add an expansion card for SCSI device use. Most IDE hard drives are cheaper than SCSI drives too, so the vast majority of systems have only IDE hard drives. SCSI drives tend to be faster and have advantages in situations where there are many hard drives on the same system, such as on file servers. The drives shown in this chapter are IDE drives. You'll learn more about drive types in Chapter 8, "Focus on Hard Disks."

A floppy drive uses a different size of power connector than a CD-ROM or hard drive, and it also uses a slightly shorter data connector:

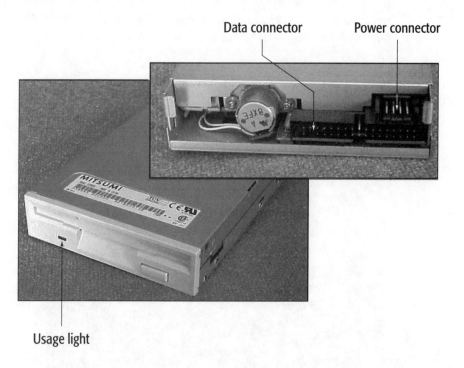

Notice in the preceding figure that the front of the floppy drive has a light on it; it illuminates when the PC is reading or writing the disk. CD-ROM drives have them too. Hard disks don't, because they are not accessible from the outside. However, as you saw near the beginning of the chapter, a hard disk can be attached to a light on the front of the computer case itself so that the light indicates when it is in use.

Expansion Boards

Expansion boards are circuit boards that fit into expansion slots on the motherboard, adding some new or improved capability. Examples include modems, network interface cards, sound cards, and video cards. Here's a network interface card (NIC), for example.

Fits into motherboard

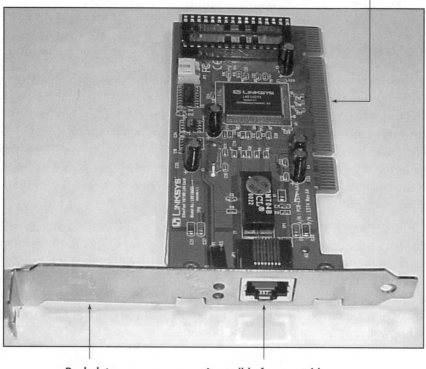

Backplate   Accessible from outside

Notice that in addition to the circuit board, a metal backplate fastens the card to the PC case, and any ports that need to be accessible are on that backplate.

NOTE

The terms "board" and "card" are used interchangeably in the PC industry; both refer generically to any circuit board. You might hear an item called an expansion board, a circuit card, or any combination of those words; they're all the same thing.

The expansion board interacts with the motherboard according to the conventions of the type of slot into which it plugs. As you saw earlier, there are several different slot types on most motherboards, and each slot type has its own pathway to the CPU, called an expansion bus. In Chapter 3, which covers motherboards, we'll look at the various types of expansion slots in great detail, including their specifications and advantages/disadvantages.

Power Supply

The power supply is essential because the motherboard cannot use 110-volt AC electricity. It requires a much lower voltage (around 3v to 12v), and it requires direct current (DC). The power supply takes in the electricity from the wall outlet, converts it, and sends the appropriate voltages to each device attached to it. Each different colored wire supplies a different voltage or performs a unique monitoring or management task. For example, all the red wires supply +5v current, and all the black wires are for grounding purposes. Other voltages supplied include +12v, −12v, −5v, and +3.3v.

The power supply mounts inside the back wall of the PC case, so that its fan and plug stick out the back. Inside, a tangle of colored wires emerges from the power supply, leading to various types of connectors. In Chapter 11, "A Few Other Essential Components," you'll learn about the types of power supplies, the types of connectors, and the voltages they supply. The following figure shows a power supply removed from the case, but in real life you will probably buy the case and power supply as a set, with the power supply already installed.

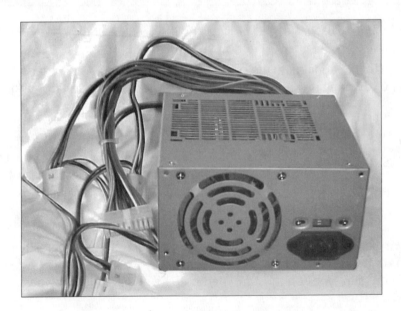

Review Questions

1. Which of these items is not externally accessible: IDE connector, USB port, or voltage switch?

   _____

2. You try to plug a PS/2 keyboard into your PC, but the connector on the PC is too large. How can you remedy this?

   _____

3. If you don't have a PS/2 port for a mouse on your PC, what type of mouse should you get?

   _____

4. You have one male 25-pin D-sub connector and one 25-pin female D-sub connector on the back of your PC. Which is the parallel port?

   _____

5. A friend wants to connect a joystick to his PC, but he does not have a joystick port. What type of expansion card could he add to the system that would provide one?

   _____

6. You have a 15-pin D-sub connector on your PC with three rows of pins. What device should be plugged into it?

   _____

7. What does RAM stand for?

   _____

8. Which of the following are nonvolatile storage? CD-ROM, hard disk, floppy disk, and RAM. (Choose as many as apply.)

   _____

9. What's the difference between a floppy disk and a floppy drive?

   _____

10. What functions does the power supply serve?

    _____

Terms to Know

- ❑ PS/2 port
- ❑ Male
- ❑ Female
- ❑ D-sub
- ❑ RJ-45
- ❑ Form factor
- ❑ Ribbon cable
- ❑ CPU
- ❑ PGA
- ❑ SEC
- ❑ Heat sink
- ❑ RAM

Chapter

3

A Closer Look at the Motherboard

I n the last chapter, you were introduced to the motherboard in an overview sort of way; here we'll take a closer look at what a motherboard does, why it's important, and what different kinds of motherboards exist.

This chapter covers:

 Form factors

 Buses

 CPU slots or sockets

 RAM slots

 Expansion slots

 Drive connectors

 BIOS and CMOS chips

 Working with the BIOS setup program

Motherboard Form Factors

Form factor refers to the size and shape of a device, as you learned in Chapter 2, "A Look Inside a PC." Let's begin this chapter by talking about the two form factors that a motherboard can have, because many details later in the chapter will depend on which form factor of motherboard you have.

The AT Motherboard

The older of the two form factors is AT, which stands for Advanced Technology. Its name comes from a very old PC, the IBM AT. It was the first PC based on the 80286 CPU, which we'll talk more about in Chapter 4, "Understanding CPUs." For many years, AT was the most popular motherboard form factor.

Size-wise, there are actually several AT motherboard subtypes. The original was 12"×13". Eventually, as computers became smaller, a smaller version of the AT motherboard was introduced called Baby AT. It measured only 8.5"×13", or about the size of a sheet of legal paper. Later models of Baby AT mother-boards were even smaller—8.5"× 9.5". Today, all AT motherboards are actually Baby AT boards; the full-size models are obsolete. Here's one of the modern 8.5"×9.5" models:

A Closer Look at the Motherboard

TIP

You can tell an AT motherboard at a glance because the expansion slots on it run parallel to the long edge of the board. (In the preceding figure, there is only a 1-inch difference between the lengths of the two sides, so you need to look close.) On an ATX motherboard (the second kind, which we'll discuss in a moment), the expansion slots run parallel to the short edge.

Notice where the CPU sits in relation to the expansion slots. It sits behind them. When the motherboard is mounted into a case, the expansion slots point toward the back, and the CPU points toward the front.

An AT motherboard also has an AT style of keyboard connector, rather than the PS/2 style you saw in Chapter 2.

An AT motherboard has an AT style of connector for the power supply as well. It has 12 pins sticking up out of it.

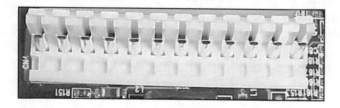

Power supply units come in two styles too: AT and ATX. An AT-style power supply has two motherboard connectors, labeled P8 and P9; these fit down over the 12 pins—six pins each. These must be oriented so the black (ground) wires on each plug points toward the center; if you switch them, you can ruin the motherboard.

NOTE

There's an apocryphal story in the industry that the AT power supply plug to the motherboard is in two pieces because the original designer didn't have a large enough connector, so he rigged it temporarily with two separate connectors and the design caught on so fast they didn't have time to fix it before it became the industry standard.

An older AT power supply will have the power switch for the PC built into the power supply itself. The switch is mounted on the inside of the case with screws; when you replace the power supply on an AT system, you must detach the switch from the case. Newer models have four plastic-coated leads on an AT power supply instead of the actual switch, and instead of removing the whole switch from the case when you need to replace the power supply, you detach the leads and hook up the new ones.

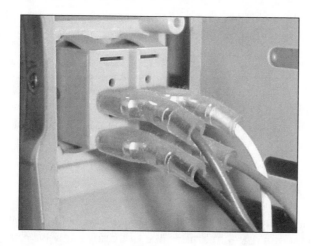

An AT motherboard has one more difference—instead of the built-in PS/2 mouse, parallel, and serial ports you saw in Chapter 2, the motherboard has connectors for these devices. When you buy an AT-style motherboard, it comes with the ports pre-mounted on backplates; you connect the cables to the motherboard and then mount the backplates on the case.

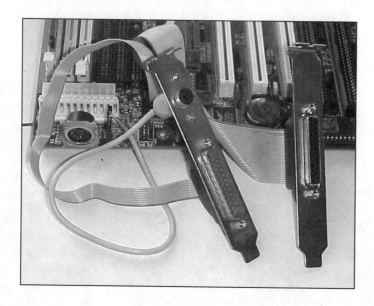

TIP

The 25-pin male port shown here is a serial port; recall from Chapter 2's discussion that serial ports sometimes have 25 rather than 9 pins. The 25-pin female port shown here is a parallel port.

The ATX motherboard is the more modern type, and it will eventually replace the AT style altogether because of its many advantages. However, in your work as a PC technician you will likely continue to encounter AT motherboards for years to come.

The ATX Motherboard

An ATX motherboard is the type you'll find in almost all of the new PCs sold today, including all the mainstream brands like Dell and Gateway. You can still buy AT motherboards at computer parts stores, though.

An ATX motherboard, which is 12"×7.5", is larger than an AT. The expansion slots run parallel to the narrow edge, which means the wide edge of the board runs across the back of the PC case when installed.

Notice the position of the CPU on the ATX motherboard; it's next to the expansion slots. This enables the CPU to sit closer to the power supply fan, providing improved cooling.

Notice also that the ports are all built into the motherboard on an ATX model, so no connectors and cables are required to hook up the parallel, serial, and mouse ports. The keyboard connector is the smaller, PS/2 style rather than the large round plug on the AT.

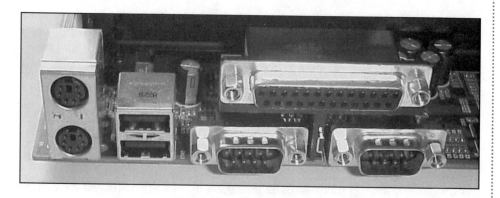

The power supply connector on an ATX is a 20-pin female connector. Because it's all one piece, there is no possibility of getting the plugs switched accidentally as there is on an AT.

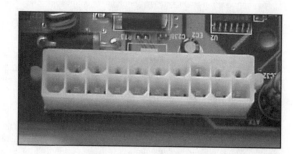

One other feature of an ATX power supply is that the power switch isn't permanently attached to the power supply; it's attached only to the case itself. A wire runs from the power switch in the case directly to the motherboard, and when you press the power button, an electrical signal tells the motherboard to start up.

This is significant (and a very good thing!) for a couple of reasons. One is that it's much easier to replace a bad power supply when you don't need to fuss with removing the switch from the case. The other reason is that because the motherboard controls the power on/off state, not the power supply, you can use software to start up the PC. For example, ATX motherboards can "wake on LAN," which means that when the network interface card receives a request from the network, it can start up the PC to answer it.

What Makes Up a Motherboard?

The motherboard is the "boss" of the system, handling dozens of administrative functions including starting things up, directing traffic, and interfacing with external devices. In the following sections, we'll look at various parts of the motherboard to see what they accomplish.

Buses: The Circuits in "Circuit Board"

A motherboard contains many chips and connectors. How do they communicate with one another? The secret's in the circuits.

All those tiny lines of metal thread zig-zagging across a circuit board are pathways (a.k.a. **buses**) that carry data. Data is sent via electrical pulses: a +5v signal stands for a 1 and no signal (that is, a +0v signal) stands for a 0. As you probably know, computers use binary numbers, so 1s and 0s are the only digits it needs.

You can think of a bus as a "highway" for data. One bus is differentiated from another by the number of lanes of traffic it can carry and by its maximum speed at which the data can travel.

The **system bus** is the bus that transports data among the processing portions of the system. It's the fastest, widest bus on the whole PC, and necessarily so because almost every bit of data in the whole computing process must pass through it. The speed of the system bus is either the same as that of the CPU (measured in megahertz, or MHz) or a fraction of it. Newer systems are more likely to have CPUs that operate at multiples of the system bus. For example, on a system with a 1GHz CPU, you might have a system bus of 100MHz (1/10th of the CPU speed). On modern motherboards, the system bus is 64 bits in width, which means it can handle up to 64 bits of data simultaneously.

The motherboard has other bus types, but let's postpone their discussion for a bit. They're associated with the expansion slots on the motherboard, and those items deserve their own section later in the chapter.

System bus
The bus that carries data between the CPU and memory. Also called the external bus. "External" refers to the fact that the bus is outside the CPU; the CPU also has its own internal bus.

CPU Slot or Socket

As you learned in Chapter 2, there are two basic types of CPU: pin grid array (PGA) and single edge contact (SEC). A motherboard will support one or the other, but not both.

A motherboard that supports a PGA CPU will have a square socket with lots of little holes in it, as shown here. There have been various versions of such a socket over the years, and each version has a number. The one shown below is called Socket 7. It's a staggered pin grid array (SPGA) socket, because the concentric circles of pins are offset from one another. Manufacturers do this so they can fit more pins on the back of a chip without increasing the overall chip size. Earlier PGA CPUs did not have staggered pins.

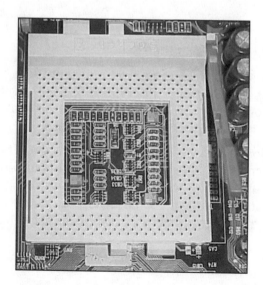

The socket has a lever to its right; you lift the lever to install the CPU and then lower it to secure it. This type of socket is called zero insertion force (**ZIF**) because you don't have to apply any pressure to secure the CPU in the socket.

Not all PGA sockets are ZIF, as you will see in Chapter 4; ZIF sockets started being used with the later i486 models.

A motherboard that supports a SEC CPU will have a slot, similar to the expansion slots but oriented differently, into which the cartridge fits. The motherboard will come with plastic brackets that you install on both ends of the slot to help hold the CPU cartridge in place. This is not a ZIF socket because you have to apply some pressure to insert the cartridge fully.

ZIF

Zero insertion force. A type of socket into which you can insert a chip without applying any pressure to it. ZIF sockets are advantageous when you're working with a chip that has many "legs" or pins because it reduces the chance of bending one of them.

RAM Slots

All motherboards have two or more slots for random access memory (RAM). As mentioned in Chapter 2, modern RAM comes on small circuit boards that you plug into the motherboard. When we discuss RAM in Chapter 5, "Understanding Memory," you'll learn all about the various types of it.

For our discussion of the motherboard, the only thing you need to know about RAM is that it comes in different physical sizes. Most motherboards made in the last five years have slots for 168-pin Dual Inline Memory Modules (DIMMs). The "pins" are not actually pins in the same sense as on the ports and on PGA CPUs; they're more like metal tabs that lie flat against the circuit board.

Pins

Motherboards that use 168-pin DIMMs typically have three RAM slots:

Older motherboards that use 72-pin SIMMs (Single Inline Memory Modules) or 30-pin SIMMs will often have more slots.

Why? It has to do with memory addressing. The older types of RAM could not handle as much data at once, so multiple pieces of RAM were needed to accomplish the same end result that a single stick of 168-pin DIMM can accomplish. We'll get into that in Chapter 5.

Expansion bus
The bus used by ISA expansion slots. Slow and old; soon to be obsolete.

> **NOTE**
>
> The little circuit board of RAM on which the memory chips are mounted is sometimes called a "stick" in PC technician slang.

Expansion Slots

You saw back in Chapter 2 that motherboards have expansion slots into which you can plug expansion boards that add new features like modems, network interfaces, and sound support.

To better understand the expansion slots, let's revisit the concept of buses. Remember, a bus is a pathway that carries data from place to place on the motherboard. Each slot type has a different type of bus.

Expansion Bus (ISA)

The system bus carries data between the CPU and the RAM. Another type of bus is the **expansion bus**. It's a much slower bus than the system bus, and it is used to carry data between Industry Standard Architecture (ISA) expansion slots and the system bus. The width of the expansion bus is between 8 and 32 bits, depending on the system. Its speed is between 3MHz and 12MHz. Think about that for a moment—if the system bus runs at 100MHz, an ISA bus of only 12MHz (at most) has real traffic jam potential.

NOTE

On very old motherboards you'll see a few shorter ISA slots and a few longer ones. The shorter ones were 8-bit slots. Because you can use an 8-bit expansion card (if you can even find one anymore) in either an 8-bit or 16-bit slot, later motherboard designs made them all 16-bit slots.

Local I/O bus
A bus for connecting certain types of high-speed expansion slots to the system bus.

Local I/O Bus

Motherboard makers knew that they needed to make a faster expansion slot in order to avoid bottlenecks caused by the slow ISA bus, so they arrived at the idea of a **local I/O bus** (sometimes just called *local bus*). The local I/O bus is much like the system bus in that it works in synch with the CPU and has a more direct pathway to it.

Several types of expansion slots have used a local I/O bus throughout PC history. The oldest was the VESA local bus (VL-bus). VESA was an international video standards committee, and the VL-bus was the bus they created. It used a normal ISA slot with an extender at the end, and the circuit boards that plugged into it had to be very long. This bus was popular on 486 PCs, but fell by the wayside by the time Pentiums were introduced. The VL-bus ran at up to 33MHz.

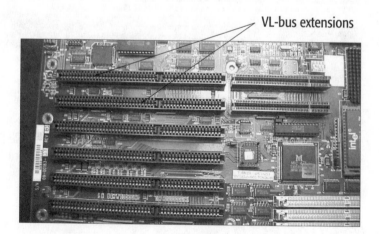

VL-bus extensions

NOTE

The nice thing about VL-bus slots was that you could use them as ISA slots in a pinch. You can't do that with any other slot types, including any of the expansion slots on modern motherboards.

The Peripheral Connect Interface (PCI) bus improved upon the VL-bus by providing an entirely separate slot and making the connector much smaller. PCI slots can run at up to 66MHz. PCI expansion slots are now standard on virtually every motherboard.

As system speeds increased, manufacturers found that the video card was often not able to keep up with the system's demands. For this reason, a new type of local I/O bus expansion slot was created called Accelerated Graphics Port (AGP). An AGP slot's speed is typically the same as the system bus speed, so there are no lag-behind problems with the vide+o.

The following figure shows both an AGP (top) and a PCI slot (bottom). Notice that the AGP slot is made of brown plastic (in the photo, it appears gray); the AGP is white. The AGP slot is also offset farther toward the center of the motherboard, and the ridge that separates one section of pins from another is in a different place.

NOTE

Motherboards typically have only one AGP slot. If you want two or more video cards, the other cards must be PCI models. (Some people like to hook up two monitors to the PC at the same time, and you would need two video cards to do that.)

Drive Connectors

Most motherboards have two Integrated Device Electronics (**IDE**) connectors and one floppy drive connector. The IDE connector is a 40-pin male connector for plugging in a ribbon cable that connects to an IDE device such as a hard drive or CD-ROM drive.

IDE

Integrated Device Electronics. A type of drive connector provided on the motherboard for interfacing with hard drives and CD-ROM drives.

A floppy connector is a 34-pin version of the same; it uses a slightly smaller ribbon cable to connect floppy drives.

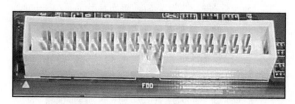

Each ribbon cable can support up to two drives, so the end result is that the motherboard directly supports up to four IDE drives and two floppy drives. If you have more drives than that, you must buy an expansion board that adds more drive connectors.

Ribbon cables have a red stripe on one edge; the cable must be plugged into the motherboard such that the red stripe aligns with pin 1 on the connector.

How do you tell which is pin 1? Some motherboards have a tiny "1" printed near one end of the connector. In the figures shown above, a little triangle at one end serves the same purpose. You'll learn more about connecting drives in Chapter 7, "Introduction to Disk Drives."

Battery

Not all motherboards have batteries anymore, at least not in the identifiable, removable sense; some of the newer ones have built-in batteries that never need changing. (Well, never is a long time, but they do have an extremely long life, and the PC will be long obsolete by the time they wear out.)

However, most of the PCs you work on will have a little silver disc battery, much like a giant version of a watch battery. It's held flat against the motherboard with a metal clip, and you can replace it when needed.

Some older systems have a different kind of battery, one that looks like a little root beer barrel candy (or a tiny oil drum) with a wire passing through the center. Such batteries are not typically removable, so you must disable them (the motherboard usually has a jumper or switch that does it) and then attach an external battery pack to do the job. Thankfully, most of the systems that used this awkward system are now long obsolete, but here's a picture of one:

Chipset
The set of chips built into the motherboard that collectively control its operation.

You can tell that a motherboard's battery needs to be replaced when the system clock starts losing time. When the battery is completely drained, the CMOS (Complimentary Metal Oxide Semiconductor) chip will no longer hold its data, and every time you start up the PC, you'll need to reset any non-standard settings you've configured in the BIOS setup program and reset the system date and time. (More on the BIOS setup program shortly.)

Chipset

The motherboard's **chipset** is just what it sounds like—a set of chips. When you look around on the motherboard, you see square and rectangular chips mounted here or there, each with a bit of cryptic writing on it. This set of chips controls how the motherboard behaves.

You can't do anything with them—they're all permanently soldered to the motherboard. However, when you're troubleshooting a system problem that involves the motherboard, someone might ask you what chipset you have. The answer is written on one of those chips. But which one?

Here's one clue: Intel is a major manufacturer of chipsets, so if one of the chips says Intel on it, along with some letters and numbers, those letters and numbers are probably the chipset number you're seeking. Modern motherboards using the Intel chipset will typically have a number beginning with "8" as the chipset model number, such as 810, 815, 845, etc. Here are a couple of examples of chipset model numbers from motherboards.

Jumper
A cap that fits over a pair of pins, changing the electrical flow through a circuit board.

NOTE

On a motherboard that has built-in sound, video, or other capabilities, you'll find chips for each of those built-in items on the motherboard. Don't confuse these with the chipset for the motherboard itself.

Jumpers

Some motherboards can operate in different modes or with different options depending on what CPU, memory, or other components are installed. On such motherboards, you'll find **jumpers**.

A jumper is a little plastic/metal cap that fits down over two tiny metal pins. When the cap is over the pins, electricity can pass between those pins, "jumping" them. When the cap is not over the pins, electricity cannot pass. This change in the electrical flow through the circuit signals to the motherboard that a different setting is in effect.

Here's a bank of jumpers. Each set of pins (up/down) has a jumper cap that is either on (over both pins) or off (over only one of the pins). When the jumper is over only one pin, it's functionally the same as if it were not there at all.

Other times there will be a set of more than two pins, and the jumper's setting depends on which of the pins it covers. For example, in the following figure there are three possible settings: over pins 1 and 2, over pins 2 and 3, or no jumper at all.

Determining what a particular jumper is for can be tricky. Sometimes a description will be printed on the motherboard. Usually, however, a jumper is named something like J1 or JP3, and a table in the motherboard manual tells what that jumper actually does.

Sometimes on a really old circuit board you may encounter a set of switches instead of jumpers. (They're sometimes called DIP switches; DIP stands for Dual Inline Package.) Switches are more expensive to manufacture, so that's why they aren't more common. Here are some switches:

BIOS and CMOS

You learned about the purpose and functionality of the BIOS and CMOS chips in Chapter 2. Recall that the BIOS chip stores the data that the motherboard needs to start things up when you press the power button. That data is permanently written onto that chip; turning the power on/off does not affect it, nor does removing the motherboard's battery.

The BIOS chip usually has a sticker on it that identifies its manufacturer. The most common ones are Award, Phoenix, and AMI. If you'll look closely at the BIOS chip, you'll see that it's removable. The little legs on the sides are wedged down into sockets, but they're not welded in place. This enables you to update the BIOS by physically replacing the chip if you ever need to do so.

The CMOS chip, on the other hand, stores any exceptions to the BIOS rules that you have defined through the BIOS setup program. The CMOS chip relies on the motherboard's battery to retain its content. If you ever need to replace the battery, all BIOS settings will revert to what is on the BIOS chip itself, and you will need to reenter any settings you have changed.

On modern motherboards there is no separate CMOS chip; its functionality is incorporated into a single EEPROM chip that stores the permanent BIOS defaults plus all the exceptions set up in the BIOS Setup program.

Working with the BIOS Setup Program

The BIOS setup program is your access point for viewing and changing BIOS (basic input-output system) settings. When the PC is starting up, watch for a message onscreen that tells you what key to press to enter the BIOS setup program. It may be F1, F2, Delete, Esc, or some other key. (It depends on the BIOS manufacturer and the motherboard chipset.)

```
PhoenixBIOS 4.0 Release 6.0
Copyright 1985-2000 Phoenix Technologies Ltd.
All Rights Reserved




CPU = Pentium III  933 MHz
640K System RAM Passed
95M Extended RAM Passed
256K Cache SRAM Passed
Mouse initialized




Press <F2> to enter SETUP
```

Once you're in the BIOS setup, you will probably see a screen like this:

```
                        PhoenixBIOS Setup Utility
   Main    Advanced    Security    Power    Boot    Exit

                                              Item Specific Help
     System Time:            [13:37:44]
     System Date:            [02/08/2002]
                                              <Tab>, <Shift-Tab>, or
     Legacy Diskette A:      [1.44/1.25 MB  3½"]   <Enter> selects field.
     Legacy Diskette B:      [Disabled]

   ▶ Primary Master          [None]
   ▶ Primary Slave           [None]
   ▶ Secondary Master        [CD-ROM]
   ▶ Secondary Slave         [None]


     System Memory:          640 KB
     Extended Memory:        98303 KB
     Boot-time Diagnostic Screen:  [Enabled]




   F1   Help   ↑↓ Select Item   -/+    Change Values    F9   Setup Defaults
   Esc  Exit   ←  Select Menu   Enter  Select ▶ Sub-Menu  F10  Save and Exit
```

A Closer Look at the Motherboard

We're looking at a Phoenix BIOS here, but there are other brands. Some look similar to this; some look radically different. There's a whole class of BIOS setup programs that are graphically based, for example, and you can use a mouse in them. They all have the same basic settings, though.

When working with a BIOS setup program, the first thing to do is check for onscreen instructions, because they all work differently. Notice in the preceding figure, for example, that there is item-specific help on the right side of the screen. It tells us that we can advance from the current field (the Hours portion of the time) to the next part (which would be the Minutes portion) by pressing Tab. At the bottom of the screen, there are general instructions that apply to the whole setup program. From this we learn that the up/down arrow keys will move among items on a page, and that the right/left arrow keys will move between menus (pages).

We also learn that items with an arrow next to them open submenus when you select them and press Enter. For example, notice that Primary Master is set to none. That should probably be our hard disk, so we would press the down arrow key until Primary Master is selected and then press Enter to open a submenu for it:

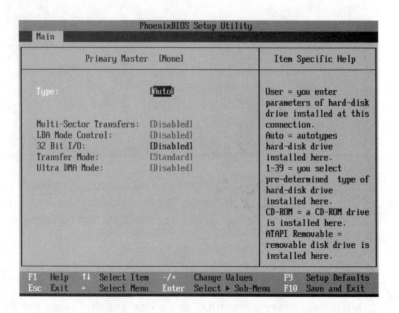

From here we see that the type is set to [Auto], which is the correct setting for allowing the BIOS to autodetect the drive. So if our drive doesn't appear, it's likely that the problem lies with the drive itself, not the BIOS. Notice also that some settings aren't as bold as others; the gray settings are not user-changeable. They're for information only. Only the 32-bit IO setting is changeable.

If you want to change the setting, you can press the plus or minus key to scroll up or down through the available settings. (That information appears at the bottom of the screen in case you forget.) This particular BIOS program works that way—others might have a different means of changing settings. You must pay attention to the onscreen instructions to know for sure.

To return to the main menu, you press Esc. Esc always takes you out of a submenu.

If you press Esc from one of the main menus, it jumps to the Exit menu. From here, you can choose to save your changes or discard them. In most BIOS setup programs, pressing F10 is a shortcut for exiting and saving changes. (Notice that this information is at the bottom of the screen in case you forget it.)

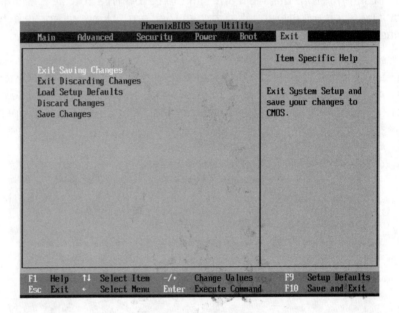

That, in a nutshell, is how you get around in a BIOS setup program. There's a lot more to the individual settings, of course. We'll introduce other features as they become appropriate when we talk about individual system components later in the book.

TIP

If you ever make some BIOS setup changes that cause the PC to stop responding, use the Restore Defaults command to wipe out all your settings and return to the defaults specified by the BIOS chip itself. In the BIOS program we've been looking at here, you would press F9 to do it; in other BIOS programs, you might need to press some other key.

Review Questions

1. Which motherboard form factor has the expansion slots running parallel to the long edge?

   _____

2. Which motherboard form factor has built-in parallel and serial ports on the side of the board?

   _____

3. With which motherboard type would you use a power supply that has two motherboard power connectors labeled P8 and P9?

   _____

4. Which motherboard type has the larger keyboard plug: AT or ATX?

   _____

5. What is a bus?

   _____

6. Why are ISA devices less desirable than PCI devices?

   _____

7. Which type of CPU slot or socket on the motherboard uses ZIF?

   _____

8. A DIMM slot in a typical motherboard accepts memory with how many pins?

   _____

9. If you were to buy a new motherboard today, which expansion slot types is it likely to have?

   _____

10. What does a tiny "1" or arrow signify at the end of an IDE or floppy drive connector on the motherboard?

    _____

Terms to Know

- ❑ Bus
- ❑ System bus
- ❑ ZIF
- ❑ Expansion bus
- ❑ Local I/O bus
- ❑ IDE
- ❑ Chipset
- ❑ Jumpe

Chapter

4

Understanding CPUs

This chapter covers that very important chip: the Central Processing Unit (CPU). In here you'll find out how CPUs do their work, what distinguishes one CPU from another in terms of features, and what the variations are in CPU size and shape within the two broad categories of PGA and SEC.

This chapter features the following sections:

 How a CPU works

 Types of CPU packaging

 A history of CPU features

How a CPU Works

CPU stands for Central Processing Unit, often shortened to just "processor" or "microprocessor." The CPU's sole job is to perform mathematical calculations. Data comes in, data gets processed, and data goes back out again. The CPU is sort of like Rain Man; it's great at what it's great at (math), but it's limited. It doesn't figure out what to do with that data; it just crunches the numbers, many millions of them per second. The PC relies on the operating system to be the sensible guy who figures out what needs to be calculated and why.

External data bus
The bus that transfers data from outside the CPU to inside and then back out again.

Register
A work area inside the CPU that holds a numeric value while the CPU performs a calculation upon it.

Low-order bits
The first four bits in a byte (reading from right to left), representing data to be processed.

High-order bits
The second four bits in a byte (reading from right to left), representing the instructions for processing the data.

> **NOTE**
>
> The following sections contain more technical theory than you will need to work on PCs in real-life; I'm telling you all this stuff only because I think you might find it interesting and because some of it might come up on the A+ exam if you decide to take it.

How Data Is Processed

Data comes in and goes out of the CPU on the **external data bus**. It's called external because it enables data that's outside the CPU (external to it) to get inside. Each of the pins on a CPU carries an electrical charge. Data enters and exits the CPU by patterns of electrical pulse passing through these pins.

Once inside the CPU, the data is stored, arranged, and calculated in work areas called **registers**. For example, if the CPU were adding 5+1, the numbers 5 and 1 would be held in registers while the CPU was preparing the answer.

When data comes in and is placed in a register, a part of that data is the number to be processed and a part of it is a code representing the operation to be performed on it. For example, suppose you send the CPU a byte of data (eight bits). The first four bits represent the data (**low-order bits**) and the second four represent the instruction for processing (**high-order bits**). So, for example, if the CPU received 10011100, it would treat 1001 as data and 1100 as an instruction. (The CPU actually reads from right to left, so the number it receives would be backward to that: 00111001. However I've written it from left-to-right in this book because that's what we English-reading humans expect.)

A byte uniquely represents a single alphanumeric character, so how can we say that suddenly only the first four bits are for data? Well, at this micro level of detail, we aren't dealing with alphabet characters—only numbers. If we're working only with numbers, four digits are more than enough to describe them. This code of low-order and high-order bits that the CPU understands is known as the

machine language. Each CPU has its own machine language, although new generations of CPUs usually have machine languages that build upon the core set of commands from the previous CPUs.

> **NOTE**
>
> Have you ever wondered why a given model of motherboard supports only certain CPUs? Machine language is the reason. The motherboard's CPU socket, and the external data bus associated with it, must be able to send commands to the CPU using the correct machine language.

Data Processing Speed

Data doesn't just flow freely into and out of the CPU at any speed it wants; there's a very orderly cadence to the process. That tempo is set by the **system crystal**, which is a timekeeping unit similar to what's in a modern wristwatch (except it ticks much faster). Each tick of the system crystal is a **clock cycle**, and data movement occurs in rhythm with this ticking. The system bus operates at the same speed as the system crystal. On modern motherboards, such as the one shown here, 100MHz and 133MHz are common system crystal speeds.

Each CPU has a rated speed at which it can reliably operate, measured in megahertz (MHz). This speed represents the number of clock cycles per second that the CPU can handle. This is known as the CPU's **internal speed**.

It is the system crystal, however, not the CPU, that determines the speed at which the PC operates. A CPU will work reliably on a motherboard with a slower system crystal than its own top speed, but it will run at the crystal's speed. (This is called underclocking.) If you operate a CPU with a crystal that pushes it faster than its own rated speed, that's called **overclocking**. It can result in faster system performance, but it can also cause overheating and instability. The actual speed at which the CPU operates as directed by the system crystal is its **external speed**. Some motherboards have a jumper that sets the system crystal speed; others can detect the CPU installed and automatically adjust the system crystal speed.

Machine language
The set of codes that the CPU understands for accepting numbers and instructions for calculating them.

System crystal
A quartz oscillator on the motherboard that sets the pace for movement of data into and out of the CPU.

Clock cycle
One "beat" or "tick" of the system crystal's oscillator.

Internal speed
The maximum speed at which a particular CPU can operate.

Overclocking
Operating a CPU at a higher clock speed than the speed for which it is rated.

External speed
The system crystal speed, which controls the CPU's speed.

"But wait a minute," you are probably thinking. "Today's PCs run a lot faster than 133MHz. How do they do that?" The secret is that they use a clock multiplier.

On 386 computers and earlier, the internal and external speeds were the same, but on later PCs a technology was developed that made it possible for the CPU to execute two or more instructions per clock tick. This is known as clock doubling (or tripling, or quadrupling, etc.), and the multiplier by which the internal speed exceeded the external speed is the **clock multiplier**. The clock multiplier need not be a whole number. For example, a 1.6GHz CPU mounted on a motherboard with a 133MHz external speed would use a multiplier of 12.5.

Interaction with RAM

Because the storage space inside the CPU is very limited, the CPU relies extensively on RAM for holding data close at hand until the CPU is ready to process it. RAM is a waypoint for almost all information that enters and exits the CPU, so the pathway between those two objects is critical. The subsection of the system bus that directly connects the CPU and the RAM is called the **address bus**.

Besides the main RAM that you can physically see and install on a motherboard (see Chapter 3, "A Closer Look at the Motherboard"), there are additional pockets, or caches, of memory into which a CPU can stash data temporarily. Chapter 5, "Understanding Memory," talks about the various types of RAM and how they store data, and you'll learn about these extra memory caches later in this chapter when we talk about the differences between various types of CPUs.

Clock multiplier
The number of times by which the internal speed exceeds the internal speed.

Address bus
The portion of the system bus that transports data between the CPU and RAM. Also called *frontside bus*.

Types of CPU Packaging

Remember from Chapters 2 and 3 that there are two broad categories of CPU packaging: PGA and SEC. Within each of these, however, there are many variations.

As mentioned earlier, a particular motherboard works with only a fixed set of CPUs. Part of that is the machine language; the other part is the physical size and shape of the CPU slot or socket. In this section, we'll look at the physical sizes and shapes.

Pre-PGA CPUs

Back in the earliest days of computing, the PGA socket had not yet been invented. CPUs instead came in a rectangular package called a Dual Inline Pin Package (DIPP). The chip looked sort of like a bug—it had a long rectangular body with "legs" on both sides:

These legs fit down into socket holes in the motherboard, but you had to apply quite a bit of pressure to make them go in, and bent/broken legs were a common occurrence. These chips were used for the original 8086 CPUs and also for the 80286 CPUs.

The next generation of CPU used a square chip, a precursor to the PGA chip you'll see in the next section. This chip had little legs on all four sides that stuck out like fringe, and the legs were soldered permanently to the motherboard. Here's an example.

This type of chip was used for all 80386 CPUs and most i486 CPUs.

PGA CPUs

A PGA CPU has a grid of pins on the bottom of a flat chip. PGA CPUs are physically differentiated from one another by the number and arrangement of the pins on their underside.

PGA chips are removable, but with early models you had to use a chip-puller tool to pry them out. Here's an example:

These were followed by the first Zero Insertion Force (ZIF) sockets, which as you saw in Chapter 3, have a lever that holds/releases the CPU so that no pressure is required to insert or remove them.

The socket sizes and types are numbered. Table 4.1 shows the types of PGA sockets, the number of holes they have, and the CPUs that fit into them. Notice that some CPUs appear for more than one socket; that's because motherboard technology advanced from the beginning of that CPU type's life to the end.

NOTE

An OverDrive chip, mentioned in Table 4.1, is a chip that enables a CPU upgrade. You'll learn about it later in the chapter.

Table 4.1: PGA Sockets

Socket	Pins	CPUs
Socket 1	169	486 SX/SX2, 486 DX/DX2, DX4 OverDrive
Socket 2	238	486 SX/SX2. 486 DX/DX2, DX4 Overdrive, 486 Pentium OverDrive
Socket 3	237	486 SX/SX2, 486 DX/DX2, 486 DX4, 486 Pentium OverDrive, AMD 5x86
Socket 4	273	Pentium 60/66, OverDrive
Socket 5	320	Pentium 75-133, OverDrive
Socket 6	235	486 DX4, 486 Pentium OverDrive
Socket 7	321	Pentium 75-233+, MMX, OverDrive, AMD K5, AMD K6, Cyrix M1/11
Socket 8	387	Pentium Pro, OverDrive
Socket 370	370	Celeron/Pentium III
Socket PAC418	418	Itanium
Socket A	462	AMD Athlon, AMD Duron
Socket 603	603	Pentium 4
Socket mPGA-478	478	Pentium 4

Early PGA sockets used regular concentric rings of pins. For example, here's a Socket 3 model.

Later models, however, had a hard time fitting enough pins on the chip without making the chip too large, so they staggered the rows of pins so more would fit. This was called a staggered pin grid array (SPGA). Here's an example:

Just because a PGA chip is physically compatible with a particular socket is no guarantee that it will work in that motherboard. Compatibility also depends on the motherboard's chipset (which determines the machine language it speaks) and on the voltage that the CPU requires (usually 5v or 3.3v). For example, some Pentium-class motherboards use a Socket 7 socket but use a split-voltage scheme that runs the CPU internally at a lower voltage (2.8v) while it communicates with the rest of the components at 3.3v. A CPU that requires a split-voltage motherboard will not work in earlier motherboards that have a Socket 7 socket. A motherboard containing a socket that can accommodate any Socket 7 CPU, whether split voltage or not, is called a Super Socket 7.

The Pentium II CPUs used an SEC design (described in the following section), but don't imagine that the PGA style died out at that point—far from it. Both the Pentium III and Pentium 4 use a type of PGA slot too.

Slot 1
A motherboard slot that accepts an Intel SEC cartridge CPU.

SEC CPUs

One of the problems with PGA CPUs, from Intel's point of view, was that competitors could make CPUs that would work in motherboards designed for Intel CPUs. To prevent this with the Pentium II, Intel trademarked the type of slot it fits into, calling it **Slot 1**, such that no other CPU manufacturers could develop compatible CPUs. (Later there was also a Slot 2, a slightly larger version that was used with a few high-end CPUs.)

You've already seen an SEC CPU in earlier chapters; it's a cartridge with a circuit board edge sticking out of the bottom. That's the "single edge" in the name Single Edge Contact:

There have been other variants of the SEC CPU besides the Slot 1 type, but most of them don't look any different from the outside than the Pentium II model just shown. For example, early versions of the Pentium III used an SEC cartridge design with internal improvements. It required a slightly different motherboard slot called SECC-2.

Intel's primary competitor, AMD, also came out with its own SEC-style CPU, the Athlon. It was physically compatible with a Slot 1 slot but was not pin-compatible. In other words, the Athlon CPU could not be used in a motherboard designed for a Pentium II, but motherboard manufacturers could create motherboards for the Athlon using the same parts that they used for Pentium II motherboards. AMD called theirs **Slot A**.

Intel's Celeron CPU, a popular low-cost alternative to the Pentium II, also used a Slot 1 compatible design. However, instead of having the plastic outer cartridge, the Celeron's circuit board was bare, allowing users to strap fans directly onto the CPU chip as with a PGA CPU. The result was a sort of hybrid PGA and SEC effect, with a PGA socket and cooling fan mounted on a circuit board at a 90-degree angle to the motherboard. This type is called a Single Edge Processor Package, or SEPP. The latest CPUs today (Pentium III and Pentium 4 and beyond) have gone back to a PGA design, for two main reasons. One is the cost—it's much cheaper to produce PGAs. The other is motherboard design—the PGA packaging takes up much less space.

Slot A
A motherboard slot that accepts an AMD SEC cartridge CPU.

A History of CPU Features

Now that you know about the shapes and sizes of CPUs, let's look at the evolution of the features.

8086/8088 CPUs

One of the first viable CPUs developed for a personal computer was the Intel 8086. It used the DIPP packaging you saw earlier in the chapter. The problem with the 8086 was that it was ahead of its time. It was a 16-bit processor that ran on a 16-bit motherboard, but 16-bit motherboards did not exist at that time—only 8-bit did. Therefore, the 8086 was never widely used.

So what does a company do when they have a great product that nobody wants to buy? They dumb it down. And that's exactly what Intel did. They came out with an 8-bit version called the 8088. IBM chose it for use in the original IBM PC, the first widely used personal computer. The 8088 had two 16-bit registers and one 20-bit register, and it used a 20-bit address bus. It came in speeds ranging from 4.77MHz to 10MHz.

80286 CPUs

The next generation of CPUs was the 80286, or 286 for short. This chip was used in the IBM AT (Advanced Technology) personal computer. It had a 16-bit register, 16-bit external data bus, and 24-bit address bus. (By that point, 16-bit motherboards were available.) Clock speeds ranged from 8MHz to 20MHz.

Here's where all the hassles with backward-compatibility began, troubles that are still plaguing the industry today. The 286 had some advanced features that made it much better than the 8088; but in order to use them, the computer had to be switched to **protected mode**, which was incompatible with all the programs written for the 8088. Therefore, 286 computers also could function in **real mode**, which provided backward-compatibility. In real mode, the 286 functioned essentially as a high-powered 8088.

The 8088 could use only 1MB of RAM, but in protected mode the 286 could use up to 16MB, provided you were using an operating system that could support that much memory. (MS-DOS couldn't. Some versions of UNIX could, as could the early IBM OS/2 operating system.) Protected mode also offered the ability to switch back and forth between two or more running programs simultaneously

Protected mode
A mode of operation for an 80286 CPU that enables it to take advantage of advanced features not available in the 8088 CPU.

Real mode
A mode of operation for an 80286 CPU that makes it compatible with applications written for the 8088 CPU.

loaded in memory. The 286 CPU performed basic math functions very well, but it struggled somewhat with more complex math. A 287 **math coprocessor** chip was available as an add-on for people who used their computers for activities involving advanced math.

80386 CPUs

The 80386 (or 386 for short) was a 32-bit chip, with all the buses and registers running at 32-bit. Clock speeds ranged from 16MHz to 40MHz. Like the 286, it could run in protected mode, but the 386 actually had two different protected modes available: **286 protected** and **386 protected**. In 386 protected mode, it supported some new features, including virtual memory and virtual 8086.

Starting with the 386, Intel began using an "I" at the beginning of the number, creating a trademarkable name. So we begin to see "I386" or "i386" on Intel brand CPUs.

Virtual memory made it possible to use part of a hard disk to simulate extra RAM. This allowed a computer able to run programs that required more RAM than it physically had. **Virtual 8086** made it possible to multitask—that is, run several programs at once—by creating multiple virtual 8086 processors and running a separate program on each one. Even though each processor could run only a single program at a time, collectively a 386 system could run several programs at once.

Not all motherboards at that time were 32-bit, because 32-bit motherboards were still rather expensive. Therefore, a variation on the 80386 chip was introduced called the 386SX, which was just like a regular 386 but had a 16-bit external data bus and a 24-bit address bus. It offered most of the benefits of a 386, but it could work on a motherboard designed for a 286.

With the 386 family, Intel faced its first serious competition from other CPU makers. AMD and IBM both produced 386-type CPUs, and in fact AMD produced the fastest 386 chip available: a 40MHz model. Intel's own 386 CPUs ran at a maximum of 33MHz.

80486 CPUs

With the 486 line, Intel solidified the naming convention of using an "I" with the number. All Intel 80486-based CPUs are called i486. (Notice the small *i*. On the 386, it was a capital *I*.) The competitors, however, such as AMD and Cyrix, still referred to theirs as "486" or "80486."

The i486 was a 32-bit all-around chip (32-bit external data bus, registers, and memory address bus), and it contained a built-in math coprocessor and an 8KB

Math coprocessor
An extra chip that provides additional registers with which the CPU can process complex math calculations more quickly and efficiently.

286 protected mode
An operating mode for an 80386 CPU that emulates an 80286 CPU.

386 protected mode
An operating mode for an 80386 CPU that takes advantage of the 80386's advanced features, but is incompatible with programs written for earlier CPUs.

Virtual memory
Using the hard disk to simulate RAM.

Virtual 8086
Using a single CPU to simulate multiple 8086 CPUs so several tasks can run concurrently.

L1 cache. It also contained some new functions and commands that reduced the amount of instruction that had to be sent to the CPU, thereby improving overall throughput. The 486's ranged from 25MHz to 133MHz.

The 486 systems were the first to have separate speeds for the internal and external bus. Recall that when the CPU is faster than the motherboard's bus, a multiplier is used to allow the CPU to execute multiple instructions per clock cycle. Early attempts at this were called clock doubling because they multiplied it times 2; the later 486s used 4x multipliers.

Recall from the previous section that the difference between a 386 (a regular one, or DX) and a 386SX was the bus width. With 486 systems, however, the difference between a 486DX and an SX is that a 486DX has a built-in math coprocessor, while the 486SX does not.

Pentium CPUs

Intel released the original Pentium in 1993. Early Pentiums had an internal speed of between 60MHz and 200MHz, and they had an external speed of between 60MHz and 75MHz.

The Pentium CPU had a 64-bit external bus, split into two dual-pipeline 32-bit data buses that enabled the CPU to process two separate sets of instructions at the same time. The two pipelines were not equal; the main pipeline (U) was fully functional, while the secondary pipeline (V) could handle only simple commands.

The Pentium also added two 8KB caches: one write-back (for data) and one write-through (for program execution). You'll learn about those cache types in the next chapter, when we talk about memory.

Another improvement implemented in the Pentium was branch prediction, a scheme in which the cache tries to "hedge its bets" by storing both sides of a Yes/No branch. For example, suppose a line in a program says "If X=1, go to line 100 in the program. If not, go to line 200." With branch prediction, both line 100 and line 200 would be loaded into the cache, so either way the needed data would be readily available.

Later Pentiums (1996 and after) added a new feature called multimedia extensions (**MMX**). The MMX addition helped the CPU with graphic-intensive applications such as games, but only those that were specifically written to take advantage of MMX. MMX was much hyped, even though there were not many applications that could use it.

Here's a Pentium CPU. I've taken it out of its socket and flipped it on its back so you can get a better look. Notice that the CPU itself is the smaller chip on the

Cache
A temporary holding area for data that needs to be kept close at hand for reuse.

L1
Stands for Level 1. A cache that holds data that is waiting to enter the CPU. Sometimes called a front-side cache.

MMX
Stands for Multimedia Extensions. Built-in CPU functions that applications designed for MMX can take advantage of to streamline the processing of graphics-intensive commands.

underside; that larger chip is just a ceramic holder for it that helps dissipate heat. This is the case with most PGA chips.

L2
Stands for Level 2. A cache that holds data that is waiting to leave the CPU. Also called a backside cache.

Pentium Pro CPUs

The Pentium Pro was Intel's attempt to produce an improvement to the Pentium. It included quad pipelining and an on-chip **L2** cache.

One other improvement the Pentium Pro offered was dynamic processing. This allowed it to run commands out of queue order whenever it was stalled waiting on something else to happen, optimizing overall throughput.

The Pentium Pro was optimized for 32-bit operating systems and worked great with them, but with a 16-bit operating system like MS-DOS it was actually slower than a regular Pentium. It did not support MMX. These drawbacks made it unpopular in consumer-level PCs, and they ultimately led to its demise.

Pentium II, III, and 4 CPUs

The last several years have brought newer and better versions of the Pentium. They're light years ahead of their ancestors in performance, but the technology behind them is less interesting to study because at this point they're just improving on existing technologies. The designers are making everything progressively smaller, faster, and lower voltage (so it runs cooler), and they're coming up with better ways to use caches and to support multimedia.

The Pentium II is basically a fast Pentium Pro with MMX added. Pentium II CPUs have an internal speed ranging from 233MHz to 450MHz, and they run on external buses of either 66MHz or 100MHz. Like the later split-voltage Pentiums, they have an internal voltage of 2.8v and an external voltage of 3.3v. The Pentium II uses the Slot 1 cartridge.

The Pentium III adds some processing improvements, including Streaming SIMD Extensions (SSE) that add new instructions for improved imaging and improved handling of streaming audio and video. It also adds support for higher-speed motherboard buses of up to 133MHz. It also takes the core voltage down to as low as 1.7v in some cases, decreasing the amount of heat generated. Pentium III speeds range from 450MHz to 1133MHz (that is, 1.133GHz). The Pentium III uses a FC-PGA design. FC stands for "flip chip," and it refers to the fact that the core CPU chip faces up, away from the motherboard, for better cooling. In the following figure, I've left the CPU facing up, so you can see the CPU mounted on top of it.

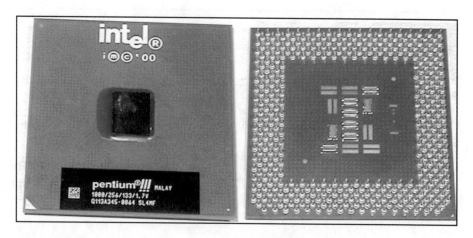

The Pentium 4 (yes, it's really a 4 and not a Roman numeral IV) has a whole suite of new features. They include a 400MHz system bus, which is accomplished by using quad-pipelining to deliver four channels of data simultaneously over a 100MHz system bus. The Pentium 4 also features a more compact, efficient design made possible by recent advances in manufacturing technology. The manufacturers can now make the circuitry as small as 0.13 microns! It also features various types of advanced L1 and L2 caches that combine to virtually eliminate any backlogs for entering or exiting data. At this writing, the Pentium 4 is available in speeds up to 2.2GHz. It uses either the Socket 603 or the Socket mPGA-478.

Review Questions

1. What are the work areas inside the CPU called?

2. What item on the motherboard controls the speed at which the system bus runs?

3. What is overclocking?

4. Which bus connects the CPU to RAM?

5. What type of CPU packaging preceded PGA?

6. Intel's SEC cartridges fit into Slot 1 slots. What type of slot do AMD's SEC cartridges use?

7. What two operating modes did 80286 CPUs have?

8. What were two advantages of the 80386 CPU over earlier models?

9. Of the L1 and L2 caches, which holds data waiting to exit the CPU?

_____

10. Why was the Pentium Pro unpopular with consumers?

_____

Terms to Know
- ❏ Real mode
- ❏ Math coprocessor
- ❏ 286 protected mode
- ❏ 386 protected mode
- ❏ Virtual memory
- ❏ Virtual 8086
- ❏ Cache
- ❏ L1
- ❏ L2
- ❏ MMX

Chapter 5

5

Understanding Memory

If the CPU is the biggest piece in the computing puzzle, memory follows it closely in second place. The CPU needs memory to operate, and it gets it from a variety of sources in the computer. The main memory that most people think of immediately is the RAM mounted on the motherboard, but there are several other types of memory as well. You'll learn the ins and outs of all the types in this chapter, including:

 Read Only Memory (ROM)

 Random Access Memory (RAM)

 Static versus dynamic RAM

 RAM packaging

 RAM speed, capacity, and features

 Installing and removing memory

Types of Memory

"Memory" is a very generic term. It means any chip or other circuitry that stores data as its primary function. In everyday use, the term memory has come to be synonymous with Random Access Memory (RAM), but there are actually two types: RAM and ROM.

Read-Only Memory (ROM)

ROM
Stands for Read-Only Memory. A memory chip that can be read but not written to.

Read-Only Memory is just what it sounds like: a memory chip that is read-only. You can't change what's on it (except by special means, which I'll discuss in a moment). **ROM** is used in situations where the data is essential to system operation and does not change on a day-to-day basis. We've already talked about one example of ROM—the BIOS chip on the motherboard. Another example is the operating system on a PDA (Personal Digital Assistant).

As I mentioned in Chapter 3, "A Closer Look at the Motherboard," sometimes an older BIOS can cause problems because it doesn't recognize some new device or feature. In such cases, it's useful to update the BIOS. On older systems, the only way to update the BIOS was to replace its ROM chip with a different ROM chip. However, newer motherboards include ROM variants that enable you to change what's on the chip with specialized software.

There are several types of ROM. The differences between them are primarily in if and how they can be modified.

Programmable ROM (PROM)   A ROM chip that cannot be modified in any way.

Erasable Programmable ROM (EPROM)   A ROM chip that can be erased and rewritten with ultraviolet light. This is also called Flash ROM because of the flash of light used to erase it.

Electrically Erasable Programmable ROM (EEPROM)   A ROM chip that can be erased and rewritten with an electrical charge. This is the most common type of ROM used for BIOS chips.

NOTE

EPROM and EEPROM are both referred to as Flash ROM, even though only the EPROM is modified with light.

To update an EEPROM, you download a utility and an update file from the motherboard manufacturer or get a floppy disk containing it. You boot from a floppy containing the utility, which sends the specialized electrical pulses to the

EEPROM to tell it to prepare for an update. The utility sends the contents of the update file to the EEPROM and then tells it that the update is over so it can close down again and return to being a read-only chip.

NOTE

On some newer motherboards, the BIOS setup program has its own EEPROM access utility built-in, so that when you make changes in BIOS setup it writes them directly to the EEPROM.

Random Access Memory (RAM)

Most of the memory in a PC is **RAM** rather than ROM—Random Access Memory. "Random access" refers to the fact that data is not stored in any particular order. One area of RAM storage is just as easy to access as any other, unlike on a cassette tape where you must rewind and fast-forward to hit a particular spot.

Static and Dynamic RAM

There are two broad types of RAM: dynamic and static.

Dynamic RAM (DRAM) is what most people mean when they talk about RAM; it's RAM that loses its data whenever there is no electrical charge flowing through the system. Inside a DRAM chip is a grid of tiny capacitors, each of which can store an electrical charge for a few milliseconds before it must be refreshed. When a particular capacitor has a charge, it represents a 1 value. When it does not, it represents a 0. Because of this need to be continually refreshed, DRAM retains the data placed into it only as long as the PC is turned on. When electrical power is removed, everything in DRAM reverts to an uncharged (0 value) state. That's what we mean when we say RAM is volatile.

Static RAM (SRAM) retains whatever it holds until it receives instructions to change. You can think of it as a series of switches—the switch is on until you flip it off, or it is off until you flip it on. No electricity is required to maintain its state. SRAM is used mostly for caches that assist the CPU by acting as temporary storage, as you learned in Chapter 4, "Understanding CPUs." SRAM is very fast because it has low overhead—it does not need to expend any effort in retaining its data. In theory, a computer could use all SRAM, but it would be very expensive.

The most common usage for SRAM is in the caches that support the CPU. These SRAM caches are necessary because of the speed limitations of DRAM. Because DRAM is slower than the CPU, sometimes there are delays when moving data between DRAM and the CPU. To minimize the performance hit, most CPUs have

RAM
Random Access Memory. Memory that you can both read from and write to.

Dynamic RAM
RAM that requires constant electricity to retain its data. Abbreviated as DRAM.

Static RAM
RAM that retains its data until new data is received. Abbreviated as SRAM.

one or more caches built into the CPU package. The CPU can save and retrieve data from the cache quicker than it can do so from RAM, so the CPU can stash data that it probably will need again in the near future (say, in the next few millionths of a second) in the cache rather than in DRAM for a performance boost. The L1 cache is on the front side (conceptually, not physically); it holds data waiting to enter the CPU. The L2 cache is on the back side; it holds data waiting to leave the CPU and travel to DRAM.

Because SRAM is rather specialized, whenever you see "RAM" you can usually assume that the reference is to DRAM. In the rest of this book, I'll call it RAM.

How RAM Stores Data

RAM stores data in rows and columns, much like a spreadsheet, and each intersection of a row and column is a unique address containing one bit (containing either a one or a zero).

Just like a spreadsheet, a RAM chip's memory space has a vertical size and a horizontal size. Its **width** is the number of cells across, and its **depth** is the number of cells down. (This concept of width will become important later when we talk about memory banks.)

The operating system uses RAM's "spreadsheet" as a holding tank for itself, for open applications, for open data files, and for many other purposes. The operating system keeps track of what is stored where, and it then signals to RAM to deliver the content of a particular memory address to the CPU at the needed time.

Memory addressing in a PC is referred to in hexadecimal ("hex"), which you may remember is a numbering system with a base of 16. A hexadecimal number can have digits *0* through *9* plus the letters *A* through *F* in it. Memory addressing is done in hex rather than decimal because everything is in multiples of 8 or more, and a base-16 numbering system fits the requirements very well.

Where RAM Is Physically Located

The system's main DRAM comes on mini circuit boards called **DIMMs** (Dual Inline Memory Modules) or **SIMMs** (Single Inline Memory Modules) that fit down into slots in the motherboard, as you saw in Chapter 2, "A Look Inside a PC." These are commonly referred to as **sticks** of RAM. You'll learn more about them in the Packaging section later in this chapter.

There are other types of DRAM in a system too. For example, a video card typically has its own RAM, usually somewhere from 4MB to 64MB of it. This RAM may be soldered permanently to the video card, or it may exist as removable

---

RAM width

The number of bits that the RAM can simultaneously accept. Analogous to a row on a spreadsheet.

RAM depth

The number of rows that the RAM can simultaneously store. Analogous to a column on a spreadsheet.

DIMM

Dual Inline Memory Module. A modern type of RAM packaging with 168 pins.

SIMM

Single Inline Memory Module. An older type of RAM packaging with either 72 or 30 pins.

Stick

A small circuit board on which is mounted multiple RAM chips. SIMMs and DIMMs are both sticks.

DIPP chips. (Recall from Chapter 4 that a DIPP is a rectangular chip with legs on two sides, looking somewhat like a centipede.)

Cache on a Stick
A type of SRAM that serves as an external CPU cache, found mainly on older systems.

Depending on the age of the system, there may be other pieces of RAM on the motherboard as well. For example, in some early systems that did not incorporate a cache in the CPU packaging, a separate cache module was available that plugged into a slot on the motherboard. These were called **Cache on a Stick**, or CoaST.

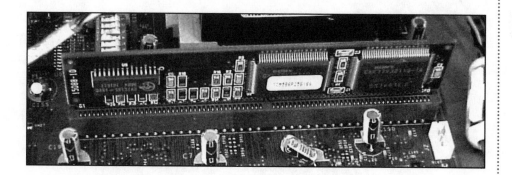

Understanding the Differences in RAM

There are lots of different types of RAM on the market today, and even more types if you look at the RAM in older systems. The following sections provide an overview to help you make sense of them.

RAM Banks and Packaging

Recall from the earlier discussion in this chapter that a RAM chip has a width. Sometimes more than one RAM chip is mounted on a stick (that is, a SIMM or DIMM), giving that stick a width. For example, if you mount eight 1-bit RAM chips on a SIMM, you get an 8-bit SIMM.

The width of a bank of RAM must match the PC's address bus width. Nowadays, a single physical piece of RAM can function as a bank all by itself because of advances in RAM packaging (for example, a 64-bit piece of RAM in a system with a 64-bit address bus), but in older PCs this was not always the case.

Eight-bit SIMMs are the older, 30-pin variety. There are not always physically eight chips on one of these SIMMs, because some chips may be able to handle more than 1 bit.

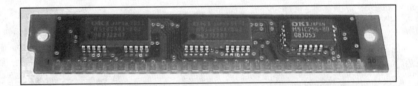

Whenever you see slots for 30-pin SIMMs on a motherboard, they're always in groups of four. All four slots are needed to comprise a single bank.

Thirty-two-bit SIMMs are the 72-pin variety. The number and arrangement of chips may vary; here are several different 72-pin SIMMs:

On a motherboard with a 32-bit address bus, a single 72-pin SIMM can make up a bank by itself. On a motherboard with a 64-bit address bus, two SIMM slots together make up a bank. (Systems using an i486 and higher CPU usually have a 64-bit address bus.) Here's a motherboard that contains both 30-pin and 72-pin SIMM slots:

On the above motherboard, there are three banks. The four 30-pin slots are a single bank, and each of the two 72-pin slots are a bank.

Here's a 64-bit DIMM. Each one stands alone in a single bank.

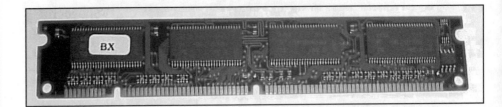

On some systems made during the transition period between SIMMs and DIMMs, you might find both SIMM and DIMM slots. On such a system, the SIMM slots are in banks of two, and each DIMM is a separate bank. On newer motherboards there will be only DIMM slots.

WARNING

In systems with multiple slots per bank, you must be careful to place identical sticks of RAM in each slot of a bank. Different banks can have different RAM, but within a bank they must all be the same capacity and speed and have the same special features (if any).

Parity Checking

Because RAM was not completely reliable in the earlier days, a system of error checking was developed called **parity**. Memory with parity checking had an extra 1-bit chip that functioned as a cross-check to make sure the data was being stored correctly. A parity check compares the number of 1 values stored in a particular byte with the number of 1 values found when accessing that byte. If the values are the same, the data is assumed to be correct. If the values are not the same, a parity error occurs and you see an error message.

Here are a couple of sticks of memory—one parity and one non-parity. Count the number of chips; the parity model has an extra one. (It wouldn't be quite as obvious if the SIMMs didn't have eight and nine chips.)

Parity
An error checking mechanism in RAM that uses an extra bit to ensure data accuracy.

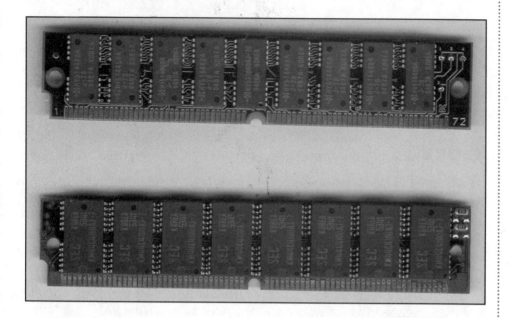

Parity makes RAM more accurate, but it also adds overhead. Parity-type RAM was popular in earlier days when RAM was not very accurate or dependable, but these days it is not needed, and most systems do not require parity-type RAM. (Some systems are flexible and allow it to be used but do not require it.)

RAM Capacity

Recall again that RAM has a width and a depth. Multiplying the two together gives you its capacity. For example, you might find an old 30-pin SIMM that's marked 4×8-70. That means it is 4 megabits (1,048,676 bits) in depth and 8 bits in width, and 70 nanoseconds in speed. Multiplying those two numbers together produces 33,667,632 bits. Divide that by 8 to determine the number of bytes, and you get 4,194,704 bytes. So it's a 4MB stick of RAM.

The width and depth measurements used to be important in older systems, where you could not assume a particular width. However, with the advent of 72-pin SIMMs, all SIMMs had a 32-bit width so the width measurement was no longer much of an issue. On 72-pin SIMMs, you will commonly see ×32 or ×36 in the measurement, as in 4×32 or 4×36. Both represent the same amount of memory, but the ones with ×36 are parity memory, and therefore have an extra 4-bit width for the parity chip. You can assume that a 168-pin DIMM is 64 bits in width. Parity chips are not used in DIMMs.

TIP

When working with 72-pin SIMMs, you can determine capacity by multiplying the first number times 4. The designations 8×32 and 8×36 are both 32MB; 16×62 is 64MB.

FPM

Fast Page Mode. An older type of RAM in which the speed does not correspond to the system bus speed. Speeds are measured in nanoseconds.

SDRAM

Synchronous Dynamic RAM. RAM in which the speed is the same as the system bus speed. Speeds are measured in megahertz (MHz).

Speed

Each SIMM or DIMM has a speed. Early speeds were measured in nanoseconds of delay between the request for data to be retrieved from RAM and the actual supplying of that data, with lower numbers being better. For example, 60ns RAM was faster than 80ns RAM. You had to be careful to buy RAM that was at least as fast as your motherboard required and careful not to mix speeds in the same bank. This type of RAM was called Fast Page Mode (**FPM**).

Today, most systems use Synchronous Dynamic RAM (**SDRAM**), which operates at the same speed as the system bus. You need to match the RAM speed to the motherboard bus, so for a motherboard with a 100MHz bus, you need 100MHz RAM, known as PC100. On a motherboard with a 133MHz bus, you need PC133 RAM. SDRAM comes packaged only in 168-pin DIMMs.

WARNING

Not all 168-pin DIMMs are SDRAM, although the ones sold today are. Some of the older ones may be EDO or FPM.

Technology

One reason it can be difficult to select RAM for a motherboard is that there have been many different schemes for improving RAM performance over the years. Some of them have remained popular; others have gone the way of the dinosaur. The following sections explain a few of them.

Extended Data Out (EDO)

Extended Data Out is a type of RAM in which the capacitors need to be refreshed less often, so there is less overhead involved in its operation. It's impossible to tell by looking at a SIMM or DIMM whether or not it's EDO; you must rely on its labeling.

EDO RAM was popular in the late 486 and early Pentium period. Most Pentium class motherboards that used 72-pin SIMMs could take advantage of EDO RAM; most 486 motherboards could not. The only definitive way to tell is to consult the motherboard manual. EDO is an obsolete standard today, because of the introduction of SDRAM.

Error Correction Code (ECC)

ECC is a quality-control mechanism in the RAM, much like the old parity bit in some SIMMs. The motherboard must be capable of using ECC in order to take advantage of the feature. It makes the system more expensive, so it's not in widespread use on consumer-grade PCs.

RDRAM RIMMs

A whole new type of memory called Rambus DRAM, or RDRAM, has been in the works for the last few years at Intel. It's very fast (with a top speed of up to 800MHz), but it is also very expensive. RDRAM comes in its own proprietary packaging, so it doesn't fit into standard DIMM slots. The slot that it fits into is called a RIMM.

Most PCs do not use RDRAM because it is so expensive. However, almost all PC manufacturers these days have a high-end line of computers, mainly designed for use as servers, with motherboards that accept RDRAM.

DDR SDRAM

A lower-cost competitor to RDRAM is Double Data Rate (DDR) SDRAM. It processes two operations each clock cycle, so it can operate at twice the speed of the system bus. It also fits into regular 168-pin DIMM slots, even though it actually has 184 pins on the DIMM itself.

Even though it's not as fast as RDRAM, it costs much less, so many PC manufacturers are using it in their consumer-grade PCs. However, Intel is still the processing leader, and Intel makes RDRAM, so DDR SDRAM will probably never be the single dominant standard.

Virtual Memory: The Un-Memory

Paging file
The file on the hard disk that stores the data in virtual memory. Also called a swap file.

As you learned in Chapter 4, virtual memory is not really memory at all, but rather a way of simulating memory using unused space on a hard disk. It allows an operating system such as Windows to hold more programs and data in RAM at once than it is physically capable of (given the system's actual RAM capacity). Microsoft Windows uses virtual memory extensively, especially on systems with only a small amount of RAM.

Virtual memory works by creating a reserved area on the hard disk and then temporarily storing part of the RAM's content there. The reserved hard disk area (known as the **paging file**) acts as an overflow tank for data in RAM that has not been accessed recently but still needs to remain in RAM, freeing up the actual RAM to store something else. When a program calls for the data that has been farmed out to virtual memory, the operating system does a swap, moving something out of real RAM and moving the called-for data from the hard disk back into RAM again.

Virtual memory is divided up into "pages" of a fixed size, and swapping between RAM and virtual memory is sometimes called paging.

TIP

Because a hard disk is much slower than RAM, virtual memory is much slower than real RAM. Therefore, systems that lack sufficient RAM and use virtual memory to hobble along are very poor performers. Such systems can almost always be dramatically improved by adding more RAM.

Windows manages virtual memory automatically, and its default settings are usually as good as any you could come up with on your own. But should you ever need to adjust virtual memory, you can do so in Windows.

In Windows 2000, follow these steps:

1. Right-click My Computer, and choose Properties.
2. Click the Advanced tab, and then click the Performance Options button.
3. In the Performance Options dialog box, click the Change button.
4. In the Virtual Memory dialog box, choose a drive to contain the paging file and an initial and maximum size for it.

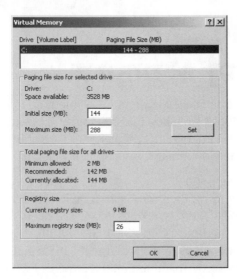

5. Click OK three times to close all dialog boxes.

In Windows 9x, the steps are slightly different:

1. Right-click My Computer and choose properties.

2. Click the Performance tab.

3. Click the Virtual Memory button.

4. To configure the settings manually, choose the Let Me Specify My Own Virtual Memory Settings option button and then enter a location, minimum, and maximum.

5. Click OK as needed to close all dialog boxes.

Installing and Removing Memory

PC technicians are often called upon to install memory in a PC. The biggest challenge is not the actual installation but selecting and buying the correct sticks of memory. As you've learned in this chapter, there are many different kinds, and within each kind there are multiple speeds, capacities, and other specifications.

The best way to determine what kind of memory a PC needs is to consult the manual for it (or for its motherboard if it's a built-from-scratch model). That documentation should tell what type of memory you need. For example, you might find that an old motherboard with 72-pin SIMM slots requires non-parity FPM RAM with a speed of at least 60ns and that it can take 16, 32, or 64MB SIMMs. With a newer system, you might find that it requires PC100 SDRAM DIMMs of 32, 64, or 128MB each.

After you know the specs, check the motherboard to see what is already installed. If all the memory slots are filled already, you will need to remove some of them and add higher-capacity sticks.

SIMMs

To remove a SIMM, you need to pull back the little metal clips on both ends of the slot simultaneously to release it.

Then tilt the SIMM back to a 45-degree angle and lift it out. Be careful to touch the SIMM only by the edges.

To insert a SIMM, reverse the process. Slide the SIMM into the slot at a 45-degree angle, and then tilt it up to 90 degrees with your fingers.

DIMMs

To remove a DIMM, push down on the levers at both ends of the DIMM (simultaneously or not, it doesn't matter). When you push down, the DIMM pops out of its slot. Then just lift it out.

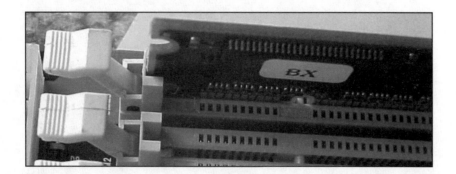

To insert a DIMM, make sure you have it oriented correctly; check the metal pins at the bottom, and notice that the breaks in them are offset to one side.

Breaks

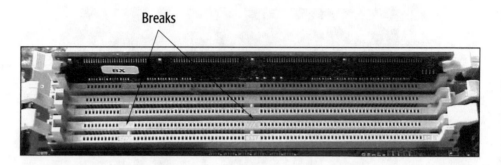

Then firmly press the DIMM down into the slot, pressing only on the top edge. You may need to see-saw it from side to side. When the DIMM is fully inserted, the levers will be completely upright and the little plastic bump on the levers will fit into an indent in the side of the DIMM.

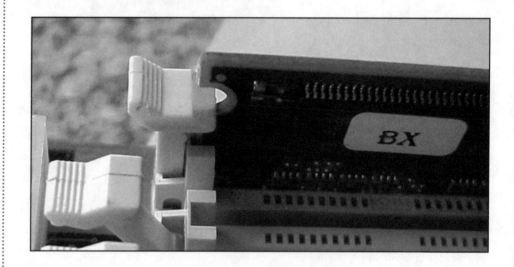

Review Questions

1. What's the difference between ROM and RAM?

   _____

2. Is the regular RAM in a PC dynamic or static?

   _____

3. Are the L1 and L2 caches built into a CPU package dynamic or static?

   _____

4. Why did some older systems require more than one stick of RAM to make up a single memory bank?

   _____

5. Which has more pins: a SIMM or a DIMM?

   _____

6. Which is physically longer: a stick of parity memory or a stick of non-parity?

   _____

7. What is the bit width of a stick of DIMM RAM?

   _____

8. What is the capacity of a SIMM that's marked 8×36?

   _____

9. What's the capacity of a SIMM marked PC100?

   _____

10. Which one runs at the same speed as the system bus, FPM or SDRAM?

    _____

Terms to Know

- ❏ ROM
- ❏ RAM
- ❏ Dynamic RAM
- ❏ Static RAM
- ❏ RAM width
- ❏ RAM depth
- ❏ DIMM
- ❏ SIMM
- ❏ Stick
- ❏ Cache on a Stick
- ❏ Parity
- ❏ FPM
- ❏ SDRAM
- ❏ Paging file

Chapter

6

How Video
Cards and
Monitors Work

Well, the tough stuff is behind us now—all that techie detail about the motherboard, memory, and CPU. Now we'll explore how the PC communicates with you onscreen. In this chapter, you'll learn about:

 The video subsystem

 Resolution and color depth

 Video card memory

 What makes one video card better than another

 How a CRT monitor works

 How an LCD monitor works

 How to adjust display settings in Windows

 How to troubleshoot display problems

The Video Subsystem

The **video card** and the **monitor** together form the video subsystem. These two items work closely together, with the limitations of one affecting the performance of the other.

The video card plugs into an expansion slot in the motherboard and provides a 15-pin male D-sub connector for the monitor. (This is sometimes notated as HD15 on a monitor.) Notice in the following figure that there are five holes per row; this is different from the other D-sub type connectors you've seen in earlier chapters where there were different numbers of pins/holes in each row. Notice also that the middle row is offset from the others.

The monitor has a D-sub connector that plugs into the video card, but depending on the monitor there may not actually be 15 pins. In the following figure, for example, notice that the second pin from the left in the second row is missing, giving this connector a total of only 14 pins. So don't assume a pin is broken off and the connector is damaged if you see fewer than 15 pins on a monitor connector.

On most PCs, the video card is an expansion card plugged into the motherboard. However, some economy-models PCs have built-in video support on the motherboard, so a separate video card is not required. On such systems, there is a connector on the motherboard to which you attach a cable. That cable runs inside the PC to a normal 15-pin video connector that mounts on the back of the case. From the outside, it looks like a video card, but inside there's nothing there but the cable.

Video card

An expansion board that adds a port into which a monitor can be connected. Also called *video board* or *video adapter*.

Monitor

A display panel that shows the results of the PC's activities or processing.

Some high-end monitors don't use the standard 15-pin connector; instead, they use separate **BNC** connectors for red, green, and blue. (Obviously, this requires a special, high-end video card too.) You will seldom see this type of monitor connection on an ordinary PC, but you might find it on a large screen in a video teleconferencing center, for example.

Display Resolution

The monitor's screen is made up of individual dots called **pixels**. Each pixel can be a different color from the one adjacent to it. The video card tells the monitor which pixels to light up and what colors to make them. It sends new information about each pixel to the monitor hundreds of times a second, making any animation on the screen look smooth and seamless.

The monitor has a maximum number of pixels it can display across and down. This is known as its maximum **resolution**, and it's described with two numbers: width times height. For example, my monitor's maximum resolution is 1900×1200. The video card has its own maximum resolution. The monitor and video card must agree upon the resolutions that they can both support as a team.

You don't need to run the monitor at its maximum resolution. It will work nicely at any resolution up to and including its maximum. You can switch among resolutions by making the change through the operating system. For example, in Windows you set display properties that tell the video card what resolution to instruct the monitor to use. You can run Windows at any resolution from 640×480 (**Standard VGA**) on up to your monitor's physical maximum—provided your video card has enough memory (we'll get into that later in the chapter).

The higher the resolution you choose, the smaller everything appears onscreen in a graphical interface like Windows. That's because each item on a Windows screen is a fixed number of pixels, so if the pixels are closer together, the object looks smaller. To fill in the extra space, Windows expands the Desktop on which everything sits, so a high-resolution display will have much emptier Desktop behind the icons and windows than a lower resolution display.

Color Depth

In addition to resolution, a particular video mode also has a **color depth**. The color depth is the maximum number of unique colors that the display will support in that mode.

BNC
Stands for British Naval Connector. The type of connector used on coaxial cable (the kind used with cable TV). Some dictionaries show BNC as an abbreviation of different words, including Bayonet-Neill-Concelman or Bayonet Nut Coupler.

Pixel
A dot with a separately described color from the surrounding dots on the display.

Resolution
The number of pixels across and down in a particular video display mode.

Standard VGA
VGA stands for Video Graphics Array; it's the standard for basic operation of all modern monitors. Standard VGA is 640×480 pixels of resolution and 16 colors.

Color depth
The number of unique colors that a particular video mode supports.

Color depth is measured in bits. For example, 4-bit color supports 16 unique colors. A four-digit binary number has 16 possible combinations; therefore, the video card needs to send four digits for every pixel to the monitor. With 16-bit color, you get 256 unique colors, but the video card must send 16 digits to the monitor for each pixel. To calculate the number of colors in a particular bit depth, take 2 to the nth power, where n is the number of bits. For example, 2^8 is 256. Table 6.1 lists some common color depths and the maximum number of unique colors in each.

Table 6.1: Color Depths

Bits Required to Describe Each Pixel	Maximum Number of Colors
4	16
8	256
16	65,536
24	16,777,216
32	4,294,967,296

Video Cards

The monitor itself doesn't have any computing abilities, nor memory, nor any ability to communicate with the PC. All it does is turn little dots of light on and off. It's basically just a glorified Lite-Brite. The video card is the brain of the operation. The next few sections look at the video card and its features and capabilities.

Video Card Memory

Remember how we talked about memory addressing in a PC being stored in a big spreadsheet-like table? Well, the video card has its own memory and its own grid of memory addresses that keep track of what color each individual dot on the display should be at any given moment. This table is constantly updated by the operating system, and at the same time the table content is constantly sent to the monitor so it can update the image onscreen. The more video memory, the more data it can store.

Most video cards sold today have at least 8MB of memory on them; some have up to 64MB. This memory is for the video card's use only; the PC in general cannot access it. It's a different kind of memory, too—both physically and in terms of how it works. The RAM on a video card is typically in a DIPP package (remember, that's the one that's a rectangular chip with legs on two sides; it looks like a centipede). The chip might have lettering that says how much RAM it represents, but more likely it will just have the manufacturer's name on it.

Some of the older video cards were memory-upgradeable, meaning there were expansion sockets for extra RAM on them. Most of today's video cards don't have this feature, however, so it's important to choose a video card that comes with an ample amount of memory. "Ample" can mean different things depending on the applications you plan to run, as explained in this section.

One way to determine the amount of video memory is to watch the screen as the PC starts up. For a brief second or two at the very beginning of the boot process, a message will appear on the screen reporting the video card manufacturer and model and the amount of video memory.

If you miss that message, you can also utilize Windows to find out how much video memory you've got. To do so, right-click the Desktop and choose Properties. Then click the Settings tab, the Advanced button, and then the Adapter tab. On this tab you'll find information about the video card, including the memory size.

Video memory is important because it enables you to run higher resolution and color depth combinations. On some video cards, having more memory can also result in better video card performance, but we'll get into that in the section "What

Makes One Video Card Better Than Another?" later in the chapter. For now, let's just look at the resolution/color depth equation.

As you saw earlier in this chapter, the number of pixels in a particular resolution can be determined by multiplying the number across by the number down. So, for example, a display resolution of 800×600 has 480,000 unique pixels. With 8-bit color (256 colors), 8 bits are needed to describe each pixel. Eight bits is a byte, so you need 480KB of video memory to support that combination. Because that's less than half a megabyte, and because the average video card these days has at least 8MB of RAM, almost all video cards should be able to support that combination.

However, the required memory starts to add up when you begin working with higher color depths and resolutions. Table 6.2 shows some examples of the amounts of memory required for some common color depth and resolution combinations.

3D video acceleration

Memory buffers on a video card that give it better performance when displaying graphically intense programs that draw images with depth perspective.

Table 6.2: Video Memory Required for Color Depth and Resolution Combinations

Resolution	Color Depth	Video Memory Required (Approximate)
640×480	4-bit (16 colors)	154KB
800×600	8-bit (256 colors)	480KB
800×600	16-bit (65,536 colors)	960KB
1024×768	16-bit (65,536 colors)	1.6MB
1024×768	24-bit (16.7 million colors)	2.4MB
1280×1024	24-bit (16.7 million colors)	3.9MB
1280×1024	32-bit (4.3 billion colors)	5.2MB

As you can see in Table 6.2, even very high resolution and color depth combinations don't require 8MB of RAM. So why do most video cards these days come with 32MB or more? One reason is that some of the extra memory can serve as a cache, speeding up the video card's performance. Another reason is that in some cases, having more memory on the video card can enable the use of a wider local bus between the video card's chipset and the video card's memory.

The main reason to have more video memory, however, is to support **3D video acceleration**. No, it doesn't show spooky special effects like 3D glasses at the movies. (Don't feel bad; that's what I thought the first time I heard it too. I was disappointed.) Rather, a video card with 3D acceleration is one that is optimized for running programs that have graphics with depth perspective, such as games that enable a character to move through what seems like a 3D space. It's like the difference between looking at a drawing of a flat square and looking at a drawing of a cube. Such programs require additional memory for three buffers that store video data and quickly transfer it in and out of the main video memory space to help improve the speed at which one graphic can morph into another. They're called the front buffer, the back buffer, and the Z buffer, although you'll probably never need that information. (Well, okay, it might impress someone at a cocktail party. Doubtful, though.)

NOTE

The bus into which the video card connects to the motherboard has a certain bus speed and bus width. For example, a PCI video card would have a 32-bit or 64-bit bus operating at 33MHz. The video card also has a bus that runs between the video memory and the video card's chipset. It has its own width (usually 64-bit or 128-bit) and speed. When I talk about the video bus width, I'm talking about the bus on the video card.

All of these buffers add quite a bit to the memory requirements. Table 6.3 shows some of the common resolutions and color depths used in 3D game programs and the amount of video memory required to run them—just so you can get an idea of the amounts we're talking about here. Suddenly 16MB doesn't seem like an excessive amount anymore, does it?

Table 6.3: Video Memory Required for 3D Video Cards with Three Buffers Running 3D Programs

Resolution	Color Depth	Video Memory Required
640×480	16-bit	2.34MB
640×480	32-bit	4.69MB
800×600	16-bit	3.66MB
800×600	32-bit	7.32MB
1024×768	16-bit	5.49MB
1024×768	32-bit	12MB
1280×1024	16-bit	10MB
1280×1024	32-bit	20MB

What Makes One Video Card Better than Another?

If you shop around for video cards, you'll quickly see that some cards cost under $50, and others cost over $500. Why? Here are a few of the reasons.

Memory Type

As pointed out in the preceding section, different video cards have different amounts of memory on them. Not only is the amount of memory important, but also the type of memory.

There have been various types of video RAM over the years, with different prices, speeds, and capabilities. Some of these types have been unique to video cards; others have simply been different packaging of the same kind of memory found on SIMMs and DIMMs. Originally video cards used FPM DRAM, which you may remember from Chapter 5, "Understanding Memory." It was rather slow, but it was cheap. The alternative at that time was to pay big bucks for a video card with Video RAM (VRAM), which was fast but expensive. A variant of it called Window RAM (WRAM) also came and went; it was also fast and expensive. When Extended Data Out (EDO) RAM was popular in PCs, it also began to be used on video cards. You may still find it used on low-end video cards today. It's cheap, but it's not particularly fast.

Most video cards today use SDRAM or DDR SDRAM, which is the same stuff that the PCs themselves use (although of course it's in a different physical package, to fit on the video card). Remember from Chapter 5 that the "S" stands for synchronous; it means the RAM is synchronized with the bus. In this case, however, it's the bus on the video card. DDR SDRAM is double data rate, so it performs two operations per clock cycle and is twice as fast as regular SDRAM; not surprisingly, it's also more expensive.

3D Acceleration

As you learned in the "Video Card Memory" section earlier in the chapter, some video cards support 3D acceleration. This basically means that they use part of their RAM for multiple buffers that store data for quicker graphics handling in programs that have 3D graphics.

To understand 3D animation in terms of the video card, think about an animated cartoon. In the old days, each frame of the cartoon had to be drawn and colored by hand, so animation was very labor intensive. Computers have greatly simplified the process in several ways. One is that animators can create each individual frame on a computer, but the other is that the computer itself can actually create some of the frames automatically with the use of **keyframes**. Let's say you want to animate an object moving from point *A* to point *B*. With computer animation, you could create a still image of the object at point *A* and another one at point *B*, and the computer could fill in all the other frames between them.

Many computer programs that contain lots of animation employ keyframes for their animation, so that the computer program doesn't have to send such a staggering amount of data to the video card through its relatively slow connection. Instead, the program sends only selected keyframes to the video card, and the video card uses its extra memory and processing capabilities to generate all the other frames needed for the animation. It's more complicated than that, because the moving object also needs to have shading, texture, smoothed edges, and so on, but this example gives you the basic idea.

Video cards that are better at helping programs generate 3D animation are more expensive than those that are not so good at it, or that don't have that capability at all. When you install certain 3D games, the setup program might allow you to choose between low-, medium-, or high-definition graphics; if you have a high-end video card, the high-definition graphics will be no problem. However, on a cheaper video card, the high-definition setting might cause the game to play with sputtering and jerking, and you might need to resort to a lower-quality setting.

The programmers who write these 3D games use **application programming interfaces** (APIs) to create the lines of code that tell the video card what to do. This makes it possible for a program to work with many different video cards, rather than being written specifically for one model. The most popular APIs are OpenGL, 3Dfx Glide, Direct 3D, and DirectX. When installing certain applications, a question may appear asking which API you want to use. If in doubt, check the documentation for your video card to find out which ones it supports.

Bus Type

As you learned in Chapter 3, "A Closer Look at the Motherboard," different buses have different speeds and widths. The bus that the video card uses to attach to the motherboard makes a big difference in how quickly data can transfer between them. By using a card that plugs into a high-speed bus slot such as an AGP slot rather than a low-speed one like an ISA, you can dramatically improve the speed at which complex images are drawn onscreen.

The first video cards used the ISA interface, which is limited to 16-bit, 8MHz data transfer. When local bus interfaces became available, video card manufacturers immediately began taking advantage of them. Many 486 PCs used VLB video

Keyframes
A set of still images that represent the start, middle, and end points of an animation; the computer can then generate the additional frames between the points.

API
Application Programming Interface. A set of standards that programmers can use to access the features of a piece of hardware in their programs.

cards, and then when PCI supplanted VLB as the dominant local bus standard, manufacturers switched to PCI.

Today, however, AGP is the standard bus used for video cards. AGP was developed specifically for video cards, and it's the highest speed, highest width bus available. That means that the interface between the PC and the video card is less likely to be the bottleneck point in data transfer. Not all systems have an AGP slot, however, so video card manufacturers continue to make PCI versions of their products too. When shopping for a video card, you will probably have a choice of PCI or AGP.

Video driver
A file that translates instructions from the operating system into commands that the video card understands.

Video Driver

As I mentioned way back in Chapter 2, "A Look Inside a PC," various pieces of hardware in a PC speak different languages. The motherboard speaks machine language; the printer speaks printer language; the modem speaks modem language; and so on. Driver files within the operating system (Windows, for example) translate commands into the languages needed to give instructions to the devices.

The operating system uses a **video driver** to communicate with the video card, and then the video card communicates with the monitor. That's how the operating system controls what should appear on the screen. That's important because it means you can radically change the video performance of your PC by using a different video driver.

The video card works best when you use a driver for it that was specifically designed for that video card model and for the version of Windows that you have installed. Other drivers might work after a fashion, but you'll lose out in features, options, and/or performance quality. We'll talk more about drivers in Chapter 10, "A Look at Some Expansion Cards."

To see which video driver is installed in Windows, and to view its properties, do the following:

1. Right-click the Desktop, and choose Properties.
2. Click the Settings tab, and then the Advanced button.
3. Click the Adapter tab. The name of the video driver appears in the Adapter Type section.
4. To view the adapter's properties, click the Properties button. A Properties box opens for it. You can explore this dialog box to learn details about your video card.
5. To see what files are used for its driver, click the Driver tab, and then click the Driver Details button. A list of the files involved in driving the

video card appears. This list contains not only the actual driver (with a
.sys extension) but also helper files such as .hlp and .dll files.

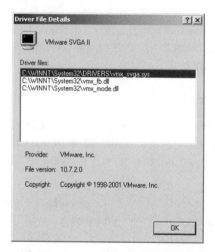

6. When you are done looking at the file list, click OK.

7. If you want to install an updated video driver (for example, if you have
   downloaded one from the manufacturer's website), click the Update
   Driver button. This starts the Upgrade Device Driver Wizard. Work
   through the wizard to specify the location of the new driver.

Updating drivers is described in more detail in Chapter 10.

Monitors

Monitors come in two types: **CRT** and **LCD**. A CRT is a "normal" monitor (the box type), and an LCD is the flat panel type of monitor found on notebook PCs. The following sections explain how each of them works.

How CRTs Work

The most common type of monitor today is the cathode-ray tube, or CRT. It's essentially a large vacuum tube. At the back of the CRT is a long, narrow neck containing a cathode, and at the front is a broad rectangular surface with colored phosphors on it.

When the cathode is heated, it emits negatively charged electrons. Those electrons are attracted to the positively charged front of the CRT, where they strike the phosphors and cause them to light. One or more electron guns inside the monitor direct the electrons precisely, so they don't just fly around aimlessly. A **monochrome** monitor has only one gun; a color CRT has three guns: one each for red, blue, and green.

The guns don't emit colored electrons, of course, so how are the colors formed on the screen? That's a function of the phosphors on the screen. For each pixel on the screen (that is, each uniquely identifiable "dot"), there are three phosphors—one red, one blue, and one green—arranged in a triangle, or triad. Each electron gun works only on dots of a certain color. So, for example, if a certain pixel is supposed to be purple, the red and blue guns will fire at that triad but the green gun won't, and your eye will see purple.

The distance between one color in a triad and the same color in the adjacent triad is the **dot pitch** of the monitor, one measure of CRT quality. A lower number means the dots are closer together, which makes for a better-quality picture. LCD monitors (covered in the next section) are also evaluated in terms of dot pitch.

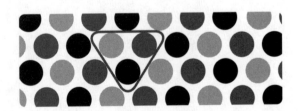

As you can imagine, the potential for misalignment error is great when you are dealing with such small phosphors. Several technologies are available for keeping the electron beams properly aligned. The most common is a **shadow mask**, a thin sheet of perforated metal that sits between the guns and the phosphors.

CRT
Cathode Ray Tube. A type of monitor that uses a large vacuum tube and electrons to light up phosphors on a glass screen.

LCD
Liquid Crystal Display. A type of monitor that sends an electrical charge through liquid crystals to bend their reflectivity, changing the light passing through them.

Monochrome
Consisting of only one color. A monochrome monitor shows a single color on a black or white background (usually black).

Dot pitch
The measurement of the distance between one colored dot in a triad and the same color in an adjacent triad.

Shadow mask
A grid of perforated metal with holes that guide electron placement to ensure that the correct phosphors are illuminated on a CRT.

Each gun directs itself through the designated hole for a particular triad, masking any stray electrons.

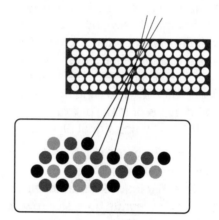

Aperture grille
A system of vertical wires that help guide the electrons so they hit the correct phosphors on a CRT.

Slot mask
A hybrid technology combining shadow mask and aperture grille.

Another technology for accomplishing the same thing is an **aperture grille**, made up of vertical wires between the guns and the phosphors. Still a third method, **slot mask**, is a combination of the two other technologies. In both aperture grille and slot mask, red, green, and blue stripes run the full length of the monitor rather than interspersed dots. The main difference between them is the number and placement of the stabilizing wires.

On an aperture grille or slot mask monitor, *stripe pitch* rather than dot pitch measures the distance from one colored stripe to another stripe of the same color. Stripe pitch is basically the same thing though: lower is better. Entry-level CRTs have a dot pitch or stripe pitch of about 0.28mm, while the highest quality monitors have .22mm or so.

How LCDs Work

The other common display type nowadays is a liquid crystal display, or LCD. You'll find them in laptops and also in flat-panel workstation monitors.

An LCD screen has two polarized filters, and between them are liquid crystals. In order for light to appear on the display screen, it must pass through both filters and the crystals. The second filter, however, is at an angle to the first, so by default nothing can pass through to the display. By applying current to a crystal, you can cause it to twist, which also twists the light passing through it. If the light twists so that it matches the angle of the second filter, it can pass through it and light up an area of the display. On a color LCD, an additional filter splits the light into separate cells for red, green, and blue. Because there is no need for a mask to help direct electrons, there is less dark area between each pixel; that's what gives an LCD display that "saturated" appearance that most CRTs cannot fully duplicate.

Several different technologies exist for directing and controlling an LCD display. They differ primarily in the number of transistors controlling the cells.

The cheapest-to-manufacture type of LCD is a **passive matrix** display. A passive matrix has one transistor for each row and one transistor for each column, much like spreadsheet row numbers and column letters. The transistors emit pulsing charges, and the combination of charges from two sides twists the liquid crystals in that row/column intersection. Because a passive matrix relies on pulsing, each pixel has moments when it is receiving no signal, so passive matrix displays are not as bright as other types of LCD. For example, a laptop with a maximum monitor resolution of 1024×768 has a total of 1,792 transistors.

Double-scan passive matrix displays (DSTN) were developed to help improve the brightness of a passive matrix display without increasing the cost too dramatically. They use the same technology as a normal passive display, but divide the screen into two sections with separate transistor rows/columns for each section. This allows the screen to be refreshed more rapidly.

In contrast, **active matrix** LCD provides a separate transistor for each pixel. Because the pixels don't have to share, pulsing is not required and each cell can be constantly "on." This results in a much brighter display that is visible from any angle, but also in a display that uses a lot more power.

The latest type of active matrix display, **Thin Film Transistor** (TFT), uses multiple transistors for each pixel (up to four), resulting in very high refresh and redraw rates and even higher power consumption.

Monitor Resolution

The monitor, like the video card, has a maximum resolution. A computer is limited to the resolution on which the two can jointly agree.

A low-end CRT might have a maximum resolution of 1280×1024. That means there are 1,280 triads across and 1,024 triads down, for a total of 1,310,720 pixels. More expensive monitors will usually have higher maximum resolutions, up into the 2 thousands. LCD monitors usually have lower maximum resolutions than their CRT counterparts; a high-quality LCD might have a maximum resolution of only 1024×768.

Most monitors can operate in any of a range of resolutions by treating several triads as an individual pixel. On a CRT, this is no big deal, and in fact most people operate CRTs at a lower resolution than the maximum. However, LCD monitors are less adept at simulating lower resolutions than their maximum, so an LCD monitor's display (especially text) can look fuzzy at lower resolutions. In such a case, a high-resolution LCD monitor might actually give display results inferior

Passive matrix
An inexpensive type of LCD display that uses one transistor for each row and each column.

Double-scan passive matrix
An improved passive matrix display that divides the screen into separate sections and has one transistor for each row and column in each section.

Active matrix
A type of LCD monitor that uses a separate transistor for each pixel.

TFT
Thin Film Transistor. A type of LCD display that uses multiple transistors for each pixel, resulting in a very bright and high-quality display.

to those of a less-expensive LCD monitor having a maximum resolution that matches the resolution at which it is being operated.

WARNING

Not all LCD screens can operate in less than their maximum resolution. On some notebook PCs, if you change the resolution in Windows to a lower one than the maximum, a big black ring appears around the outside instead of everything appearing larger on the screen. This is mostly an issue on older notebook PCs. If possible, you should view a notebook PC in the resolution in which you plan to operate it before you buy it.

Refresh rate
The rate at which pixels are refreshed on a monitor, expressed in hertz (Hz).

Interlacing

Some older monitors, or cheaper ones sold today, have electron guns that can't keep up with the refreshing needs to display a decent picture. Rather than spending more money for better electron guns, the manufacturers sometimes use a technique called *interlacing* to make the monitor's picture less flickery. Interlacing refreshes only every other line of the display with each pass, rather than every line. Avoid using monitors that cannot achieve a decent refresh rate (say, 85Hz) at the resolution you want without interlacing. There is little reason to buy an interlaced monitor new today—assuming you could even find one—because monitor technology has advanced over the last few years to the point where interlacing is seldom necessary.

Refresh Rate

As soon as an electron hits a phosphor, it immediately begins to start decaying, so each triad in the display must be refreshed by a re-hit with the electron gun many hundreds of times per second. If pixels aren't refreshed quickly enough, the display flickers, causing eyestrain. The measurement of how many times per second the display is refreshed is its **refresh rate**.

The higher the resolution used, the more challenging it is for the monitor to refresh it at top speeds because of the increased number of unique pixels involved. At a refresh rate of lower than 75Hz or so, a display flickers noticeably, so a high maximum refresh rate is an important feature in a monitor. The maximum refresh rate is typically not expressed as a single number, but rather as a separate number for each of several common resolutions. For example, a monitor might be capable of 120Hz refresh rate at 800×600, but only 85Hz at 1280×1024. To change the refresh rate, see "Adjusting Display Settings in Windows" later in this chapter.

Monitor Driver

The monitor has a driver file in Windows too, but it's not the same as a video card driver. It's only an information file that tells Windows about the monitor's capabilities. Windows uses that information to set limits on the video card's behavior so that it will not push the monitor to do something that it can't do.

Windows doesn't do perfect Plug and Play on monitors, so your monitor may be identified as a Plug and Play monitor by default. That's a generic set of settings. If your monitor is capable of more than those settings specified, your monitor's true capabilities are wasted until you install the driver for your exact monitor model. For example, your monitor might be capable of a higher refresh rate than the maximum setting specified for the generic Plug and Play monitor.

To check the monitor driver installed in Windows, and change it if need be, do the following:

1. Right-click the Desktop, and choose Properties.
2. Click the Settings tab, and then check to see what monitor is reported under the Display heading.
3. If the monitor that appears in the display is correct, you're done; click OK. Otherwise, click Advanced.
4. Click the Monitor tab, and then click Properties.
5. Click the Driver tab, and then click Update Driver.
6. The Hardware Update Wizard runs; choose Install from a list or specific location and then click Next.
7. Click Don't Search, and then click Next.
8. Deselect the Show Compatible Hardware checkbox. A list appears of monitor manufacturers and models. Select yours from the list.

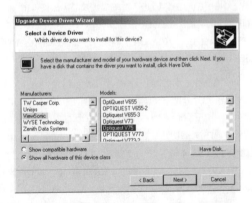

9. Click Next, and then click Finish. Then close all open dialog boxes.

Adjusting Display Settings in Windows

The Display Properties in Windows is your one-stop shop for changing settings pertaining to the monitor and video card. To access Display Properties, right-click the Desktop and choose Properties. Then click the Settings tab for access to the settings affecting your video card and monitor.

Here's an overview of what you can do from the Settings tab in Windows 2000; Windows 9x is similar. Explore these on your own in whatever version of Windows you have.

- ◇ Change the resolution with the Screen area slider and color depth with the Colors drop-down list.

- ◇ Click the Advanced button and then the Adapter tab for information about the video card. From there, click Properties to work with the video card driver or click List All Modes to see a comprehensive list of all the resolution, color depth, and refresh rate combinations that the installed hardware can support.

- ◇ Click the Advanced button and then the Monitor tab to see information about the monitor. Click Properties to change the monitor driver, as you saw earlier, or choose a different refresh rate from the Refresh Frequency drop-down list.

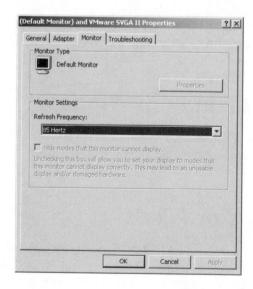

Troubleshooting Display Problems

Here are some common display problems and some ideas for solving them.

No Display at All

If the monitor is completely dark, check the following:

◇ Does the power light on the monitor come on? If not, the monitor is not plugged in, not turned on, or is broken.

◇ Are the monitor's brightness and contrast settings turned up? Is the monitor snugly plugged into the video card, and is the video card snug in the motherboard?

◇ Does swapping out the video card solve the problem? If so, the problem is the video card. Chapter 10 covers installing and removing expansion cards, including video cards.

◇ Does swapping out the monitor solve the problem? If so, perhaps the monitor is physically bad.

◇ Does text appear on the screen at startup and then disappear when Windows tries to load? If so, it's a Windows problem, not a hardware problem.

◇ Does running Windows in Safe Mode solve the problem? If so, it's probably a video driver issue. Safe Mode is covered in Chapter 15, "Starting Up a PC."

Garbled Display in Windows

This is almost always caused by a bad or incompatible video driver. Run Safe Mode (see Chapter 15), and while in Safe Mode, reinstall the video driver (see Chapter 10).

Bad Colors or Pixels

If the display has an overall tint to it (red, green, or blue), the monitor is probably at fault. First, make sure the monitor's cable is firmly seated. A loose monitor cable can cause one of the three colors to cut out. Then try adjusting the controls on the monitor itself. Check for bent pins on the monitor connector too.

If you have a monitor testing program, run it. (You can download one for free from almost any download site, such as CNet.) Some are very sophisticated, allowing you to take a monitor through several resolutions and color depths; others are simply test patterns and solid color screens that you can use to visually check for display flaws such as damaged phosphors. If one of the dots in a triad is faulty, for example, the display will look fine when displaying a pure screen of two of the colors, but you'll notice a black speck when displaying a pure screen of the other color.

Display a pure-white screen and look for **convergence** problems. This will appear as places onscreen with a red, green, or blue tint, and it indicates a problem with the dots in the triads not aligning properly. Some monitors have an adjustment to correct this. If you don't have a utility that will give you a pure white screen, a shortcut is to open a new document in a word processing program and maximize the window. Also look for any individual pixels that are not white; this can indicate a damaged phosphor in that spot.

If possible, display pure red, pure green, and pure blue screens and look for any dropped-out pixels. A monitor testing program usually provides such screens.

If you find damaged phosphors, convergence problems, or uncorrectable screen distortion, you can't do much about it other than recommend that the client buy a replacement. It is possible to make some internal adjustments to some monitors, but that involves removing the cover from the monitor, and on a CRT you've got that big bad capacitor that can potentially kill you, so it's usually just time for a new monitor when problems like that occur.

Black Ring

This one's easy. Some resolutions and refresh rates require that you fine-tune the image size on the monitor. Adjust the controls on the monitor front or back to expand and position the image on the screen so it is centered and as large as possible.

Display Problems with a Specific Application

Sometimes an application (usually a game) that has 3D graphics will have a problem running with certain video cards. If this happens, there are several tools you can use to troubleshoot the situation.

If the game itself has a display troubleshooting feature, start with that. You can also adjust the overall hardware acceleration setting in Windows. By default, it's

Convergence
The ability of the electron guns in a monitor to align precisely on each triad. If one of the guns is slightly off, it will result in a green, red, or blue tinge to the screen, either overall or in certain areas.

set to the highest setting, but turning it down may solve some problems. To access it, right-click the Desktop and choose Properties; then click the Settings tab, click Advanced, and click the Troubleshooting tab.

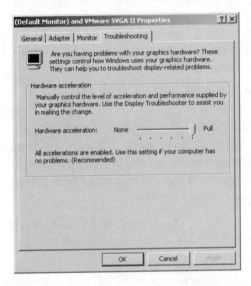

If the problem is related to DirectX (one of those API technologies mentioned earlier), you can use the DirectX troubleshooter to run some tests. To do so, choose Start, Run, type **dxdiag**, and click OK.

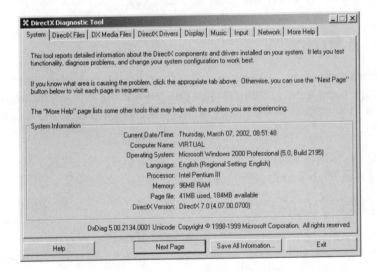

Review Questions

1. Which resolution and color depth is considered Standard VGA?

   _____

2. How many colors are used in 16-bit color?

   _____

3. A store sells video cards with 4MB, 8MB, 16MB, 32MB, and 64MB. You want to be able to run Windows at 1280×1024 with 32-bit color. You don't care about 3D video acceleration. Which video card is the minimum you should consider?

   _____

4. What is an API?

   _____

5. Which bus type results in the best video card performance?

   _____

6. What three colors make up a triad on a CRT's screen?

   _____

7. Of these types of LCD monitors—Thin Film Transistor, active matrix, passive matrix, and dual-scan passive matrix—which results in the brightest, highest-quality display?

   _____

8. Which refresh rate would result in a less flickery display: 60Hz or 100Hz?

   _____

9. What would be appropriate troubleshooting techniques when faced with a monitor that shows no picture at all?

   _____

10. How would you adjust the display to correct a black ring around the outside of the monitor's picture?

    _____

Terms to Know

- ❑ Video card
- ❑ Monitor
- ❑ BNC
- ❑ Pixel
- ❑ Resolution
- ❑ Standard VGA
- ❑ Color depth
- ❑ 3D video acceleration
- ❑ Keyframes
- ❑ API
- ❑ Video driver
- ❑ CRT
- ❑ LCD
- ❑ Monochrome
- ❑ Dot pitch
- ❑ Shadow mask
- ❑ Aperture grille
- ❑ Slot mask
- ❑ Passive matrix
- ❑ Double-scan passive matrix
- ❑ Active matrix
- ❑ TFT
- ❑ Refresh rate
- ❑ Convergence

Chapter

7

Introduction
to Disk Drives

The topic "disk drives" is so big that this book divides it into several chapters. This first chapter is devoted to the theory behind drives—how they work physically, how they organize data, and how they interact with the operating system. In Chapter 8, "Focus on Hard Drives," and Chapter 9, "Focus on Removable Disk Drives," you'll learn about specific drive types and pick up some practical skills for working with them.

This chapter covers the following topics:

    Types of drives

    Physical operation of a drive

    Electromagnetic and optical drives

    How drives organize data

Types of Drives

You're probably already aware of the major types of disk drives a PC can have:

Hard disk   A non-removable electromagnetic drive, encased in a metal box. The disk and the drive are a single unit together and cannot be separated. Used for long-term storage in the PC.

Floppy   Removable electromagnetic disk with a separate drive unit installed in the PC. Holds up to 1.44MB. Used for short-term storage and data transfer between PCs. Becoming obsolete because of other drive types that are faster and hold more data.

LS-120   Just like a floppy drive except it can also accept special LS-120 ("Super-Drive") disks that hold up to 120MB.

ZIP   A hybrid between a floppy disk and a hard disk. Reads and writes to 100MB or 250MB floppy disks encased in a proprietary type of cartridge.

CD-ROM   Removable optical disc with a separate drive unit installed in the PC. Used for distributing software rather than floppy disks because it can hold so much more data (up to 700MB) than a floppy. Read-only; cannot be written to or changed.

CD-Recordable (CD-R)   Removable optical storage that's just like a CD-ROM except it can also write to special CD-R discs. Discs can be written to only once; then they become read-only.

CD-Rewriteable (CD-RW)   Just like CD-Recordable except it also accepts another kind of writeable CD disc (CD-RW) that can be written to and modified multiple times.

DVD   Just like CD-ROM except it also reads Digital Versatile Discs (DVDs), which hold much more data than ordinary CDs.

These drive types can be broken down in two different ways: electromagnetic versus optical and removable versus non-removable. I'll explain the concepts of electromagnetic and optical later in this chapter.

The difference between removable and non-removable is fairly obvious: removable drives are separate from their disks, while non-removable ones are not. Chapter 8 talks about hard drives, which are the most common non-removable drive type. Chapter 9 covers removable drives, of which floppy and CD-ROM are the most common.

How a Drive Operates Physically

Before we start talking about the differences between drives, let's talk about what they all have in common. They all store data.

As you learned earlier in the book, computer data is stored digitally, in bytes. Each byte is an eight-digit combination of 1s and 0s and represents a number, a letter, or a symbol. When data moves through a circuit board, it does so in patterns of electrical pulses: 1 is a pulse and 0 is a lack of a pulse. Disks store data basically the same way. Disks store patterns of magnetic charge or of reflective and less-reflective areas. The read/write heads on the drive convert the transitions between the spots into electrical pulses (1s). The areas in which there is no transition are 0s.

Read/Write Heads

Each drive has at least one **read/write head**. This is like the needle on a phonograph player, in that only the part of the disk that is directly under the head gets used; the rest of the disk just spins waiting to be noticed by the head. It's mounted on an arm, again like a phonograph needle.

Unlike on a phonograph, however, the arm on a disk's read/write head (also called the **actuator**) can jump in and out very quickly, so it can go from the edge to the center to the middle and back again as part of its routine operation rather than sticking with a single spiral track. Because of this ability to jump around, disk storage is called **random access** (just like random access memory except it's a disk instead).

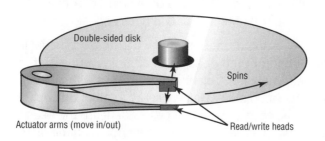

Double-sided disk

Spins

Actuator arms (move in/out)

Read/write heads

Read/write head
The recorder/reader unit on a drive that reads data from the disk and writes data to the disk.

Actuator
The arm on which the read/write head is mounted, which moves the head in and out on the disk surface.

Random access
Able to jump to and access any part of the data just as easily as any other part.

As the name implies, a read/write head serves two purposes: it reads data already on the disk, and it writes new data to the disk. Most disk drives have more than one read/write head. A typical floppy disk has two heads, one on either side of the disk, for example. The disks are double-sided, so data is stored on both sides. A typical hard disk has many more heads; within that hard disk casing are multiple platters, each with a separate read/write head on each side of it. We'll discuss more about hard disks later.

Electromagnetic Storage

Hard and floppy disks store data **electromagnetically**, on disks coated with a very magnetic iron oxide mixture. This magnetic material is used to store patterns of electromagnetic charges on the surface of the disk.

To understand what that means, let's review some electromagnetic basics. Remember from our discussion of EMI earlier in the book that whenever you pass electric current through a wire, it generates a magnetic field around the wire. There's a second part to that: if you reverse the flow of the current, the magnetic field reverses too. The conversion also works the other way as well: not only can electric current generate a magnetic field, but a magnetic field can generate electric current, and you can reverse the current flow by reversing the magnetic field.

On an electromagnetic disk drive, the read/write head is a U-shaped piece of metal wrapped in the center with conductive wire. The ends of the U sit close to the disk surface. When electricity passes into the U-shaped piece (via the wire), it generates a magnetic field, which in turn affects the tiny magnetic particles on the surface of the disk. When the **polarity** of the current changes, the polarity of the magnetic field changes too. Because there are two possible polarities, there are two possible states for each area of the hard disk over which the read/write head passes: on or off (that is, 1 or 0 in binary-speak).

The disk surface is some sort of non-magnetic base material (Mylar for floppies, usually aluminum for hard disks), with a thin covering of iron oxide or some similar magnetic material. A blank disk starts out with all the particles in a random assortment of polarities that cancel each other out. As the read/write head writes to the disk, each particle that passes beneath the head is individually set for one of the two magnetic polarities, depending on the direction (the **flux**) of the magnetic field at that instant.

Electromagnetic
A magnetic field created by electricity.

Polarity
The positive or negative aspect of an electrical voltage. A charge can have either a positive polarity or a negative polarity.

Flux
The direction of the flow of the magnetic field.

120

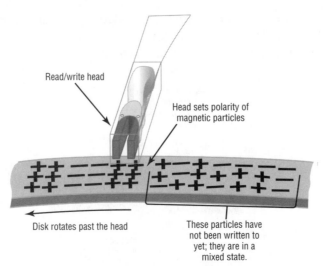

Read/write head

Head sets polarity of
magnetic particles

Disk rotates past the head

These particles have
not been written to
yet; they are in a
mixed state.

Flux transition
A spot where the flux
changes directions.

When the read/write head writes, electrical voltage applied to the head makes
the magnet active and polarity changes in the magnetic field cause different values
to be written. Whenever there is a polarity change, there is a **flux transition**. When
the read/write head reads, it does not actually look for individual magnetized
particles; rather, it looks for flux transitions, and when it finds one, it sends a
small electrical pulse to the circuitry saying "Found one!" The pattern of these
pulses received from the head, in relation to the drive timing, is translated into
data and sent to the CPU.

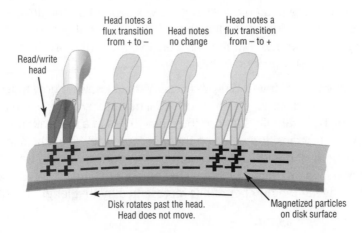

Read/write
head

Head notes a
flux transition
from + to −

Head notes
no change

Head notes a
flux transition
from − to +

Disk rotates past the head.
Head does not move.

Magnetized particles
on disk surface

The minimum amount of physical space between flux transitions is determined by the drive's rotational speed and performance abilities, and the pattern created by these cells is known as the **encoding method**.

Encoding method
The pattern that determines the distance between each bit of data on a disk.

Drive timing
The amount of time that passes between reading one bit and reading the next bit on a drive.

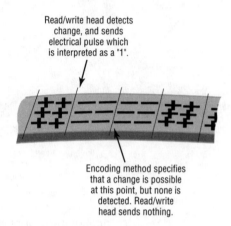

Read/write head detects change, and sends electrical pulse which is interpreted as a "1".

Encoding method specifies that a change is possible at this point, but none is detected. Read/write head sends nothing.

The most popular encoding method for hard disks today is Run Length Limited (RLL), of which there are several variations. On a floppy drive, the disk platter is separate from the drive controller. Floppy disks typically use a different method of encoding, one called Modified Frequency Modulation (MFM).

For example, let's say that the closest together that two flux transitions can possibly be is one "click" (which is really an electrical pulse rather than a sound). The timing between clicks, and the amount of physical real estate on the disk that the read/write head moves per click, will depend on the drive and is known as the **drive timing**. If when reading the disk the drive controller hears *click - nothing - nothing - click*, it knows that there is a bit, two more bits just like it, and then a change to the opposite kind of bit.

As you can imagine, drive timing is critical. Without knowing how much time there should be between clicks, the drive can't tell how many same-value bits in a row are present. For example, suppose there are 10 bits in a row with the same value. There is no flux transition between them because they're all the same. So the drive timing must measure the amount of time during which a transition is not encountered, and then divide that by the amount of time it should take between clicks to arrive at the number of bits represented by that length of "silence."

Optical Storage

Optical storage also relies on binary patterns to store data, but instead of magnetism, it uses light. The surface of a CD-ROM has tiny **pits** in it, and when light bounces off a pit, it reflects back less strongly than when it bounces off an unpitted area (called **land**). So a CD-ROM uses a pit to represent a 1 and a land area to represent a 0.

Land (very reflective)   Pit (less reflective)

CD Surface

The read/write head in an optical drive has two parts: a laser that shines light on the disk surface and a light sensor that measures the amount of light that bounces back. Whenever it detects a change in the amount of reflectivity, it sends a "click" to the operating system, which the operating system interprets as a "1". When it detects no change during a certain time period (depending on the drive timing), it interprets that as a "0".

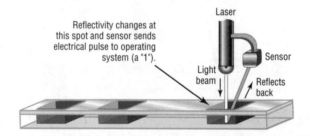

Reflectivity changes at this spot and sensor sends electrical pulse to operating system (a "1").

Laser

Sensor

Light beam

Reflects back

Regular CD-ROM drives are read-only, so the read/write head is actually just a read head. There's no writing. However, a CD-Recordable or CD-Rewriteable drive can also write. CD-Recordable (CD-R) is a one-time writing process for a CD, and it requires a special kind of disc. CD-Rewriteable (CD-RW) is a multi-write process that enables the same CD disc to be written and rewritten many times; it requires its own special kind of disc too.

Pit

An area of an optical disk that is indented, resulting in less light reflecting back from it.

Land

An area of an optical disc that is unpitted, resulting in a full measure of light reflecting back from it.

Recordable CD-ROM

When you make your own CDs, you don't have the manufacturing equipment to create the pitted aluminum layer that exists on a mass-produced CD. Therefore, the recording process must be different.

The recording process for CD-R is made possible by the fact that CD-ROM readers don't actually touch the surface of the disc—they only look at it. As you just learned, a CD-ROM drive bounces light off the surface of the CD, and it reads data depending on the amount of reflectivity it finds there. So a home-recorded CD need not actually have the pits and land areas of a normal CD, as long as it *appears* to have them.

Recordable CDs are coated with metal and then overlaid with photosensitive organic dye. The dye layer reflects back to a CD-ROM drive just as a blank CD would (that is, all land). Then during the recording process, a laser heats the metal and the dye layers in certain spots so that they change their reflectivity to resemble a pit on an aluminum-pitted CD. When a drive reads the CD, the CD appears to have the normal pit and land areas of a commercially produced CD, even though there are not actually any pits.

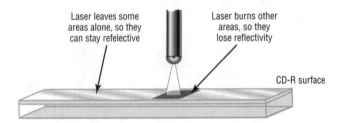

Laser leaves some areas alone, so they can stay refelective

Laser burns other areas, so they lose reflectivity

CD-R surface

A recordable CD-ROM drive can write once to a disk; then that disc cannot be written to any more. The laser on the read/write head has two power settings: one for reading (low) and one for writing (high).

Rewriteable CD-ROM

The CD-RW medium is physically different from a CD-R disc. It is more complex and costs more to manufacture, which is why CD-RW discs cost so much more.

Data is burned into a regular CD-R by heating the dye and metal to change how it reflects in certain spots on the disc. That change is permanent, which is why you can't make changes to the data on a CD-R. A CD-RW disc, in contrast, does not have the traditional dye-and-metal coating. Instead it is coated with a metal alloy (containing silver, indium, antimony, and tellurium, in case you're curious) with reflective properties that change depending on the temperature to which you heat it.

A CD-RW drive has a laser that has three different power settings. The high setting heats the alloy to around 600 degrees Celsius, at which temperature it liquefies. When it solidifies again, it has lost its reflective properties. This imitates a pit. The same spot can be reheated to a lower temperature (around 200 degrees Celsius), causing it to revert back to its original reflectivity, imitating a land area. That's how it rewrites an area. The lowest power setting is used to read the data without changing it.

How Disks Store Data

Now that you know the physical part of how drives store those all-important 1s and 0s, let's look at their internal operations—the way the data is organized.

Tracks, Sectors, and Cylinders

A freshly manufactured disk consists of one or more blank platters covered with random electromagnetic particles or a solid sheet of unpitted land. In order to store data efficiently, there has to be some sort of filing system in which each area has a unique name that can be referred to and accessed. That's where the concepts of tracks and sectors come in.

To prepare a disk for use, you must **format** it. The drive's read/write head does this, as instructed by the operating system. Hard disks, floppy disks, and CD-RW discs must be formatted, but not CD-R discs. That's because a CD-R disc can be written to only once, so if you formatted it, you couldn't write any data to it later.

When a disk is formatted, **tracks** are created on each side of each disk platter. These are small concentric bands, like the rings on a cross-section of a tree.

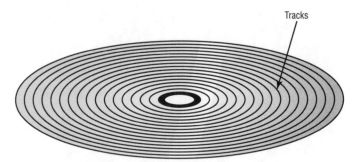

Tracks

Because a track is too large an area to be effective for storage, each track is further carved up into **sectors**. (This name comes from the straight lines that bisect the circle, forming the individual sectors.)

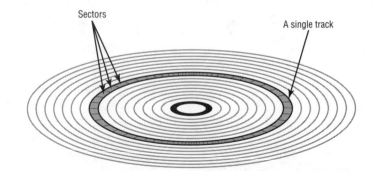

Sectors

A single track

Formatting
Laying down guide tracks for the read/write heads on a disk in a drive.

Tracks
Concentric bands on a disk platter, like the rings on a tree.

Sector
A section of a track created by straight lines cutting across the diameter of the disk platter.

On most hard disks, the number of sectors is not the same for each track. Tracks near the edge of the disk have more physical area, so they are divided into more sectors. Tracks near the center have less area, so they are divided into fewer sectors. This is called *zoned recording*, because different zones on the drive have different numbers of sectors per track. There are usually about 10 zones per drive.

Each sector has a unique identifier that the operating system keeps track of, so when you store data in a particular sector it can be retrieved on your command. Different drive types divide the surface into different numbers of sectors. Floppy disks use between 8 and 36 sectors per track, while hard disks have many hundreds. (The average is 700 for a typical hard disk today.)

Most hard disks have two or more platters. Data that exists on different platters but at the same head position (and the same side of the platters—top or bottom) is said to be on a common **cylinder**. There are no real cylinders in a physical sense; cylinder is simply a convenient way of thinking about the stack of platters. When the read/write heads are at a certain in/out position, all the data that can be read without head movement is defined by a cylinder number, starting with 0.

Cylinder
The same head position on a stack of platters in a multiplatter disk such as a hard disk.

Geometry
A drive's organizational structure, including the number of cylinders, number of read/write heads, and number of sectors.

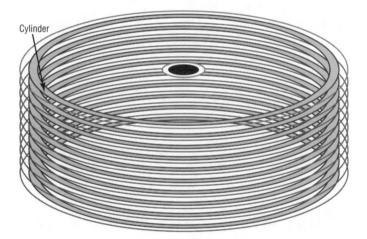

Cylinder

One way to envision a cylinder is to think of a doughnut-shaped cookie cutter slicing through a stack of platters.

The **geometry** of the drive is its organizational structure—the way it breaks down its surface into logical units for storing data. All disks have a geometry, even floppies, but on a hard disk the geometry is more significant because it is not the same for every hard disk. The "big three" for drive geometry are cylinders, heads, and sectors (CHS). There are other factors too, but they're not as significant.

In order for a hard disk to communicate with the computer, the BIOS must be informed about the hard disk's geometry. Modern BIOSes and hard disks can automatically communicate this information between them, but in very old systems you sometimes need to manually enter the drive's geometry stats into the BIOS setup program. Should you ever need to manually enter a drive's geometry specs, you can usually find the information on a label on the outside of the disk.

Partitioning

Partitioning is done only on hard disks, so we'll postpone the discussion of how to do it until Chapter 8. Briefly, though, partitioning prepares the drive by creating one or more formattable areas called **partitions**.

A single physical hard disk (the **physical drive**) can be divided up into multiple partitions, just like a single large building can be divided into multiple rooms by erecting walls. The FDISK utility that comes with MS-DOS and Windows 9x handles partitioning; in Windows 2000 and XP it's handled through Windows Setup or through the Disk Management utility.

Each physical disk has a primary partition, which when formatted becomes the C: drive. One way to set up the system is such that the primary partition takes up the entire physical drive, as shown here:

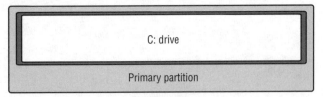

It may also have an extended partition. That extended partition, in turn, may be occupied by a single drive letter (**logical drive**), like this:

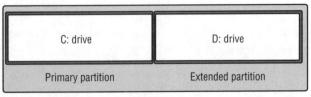

Partition
A formattable section of a physical hard disk.

Physical drive
The entire physical hard disk, encompassing all partitions and logical drives.

Logical drive
A section of a physical hard disk that's identified by a unique drive letter, such as C:, D:, etc.

Or, it may be occupied by multiple logical drives, like this:

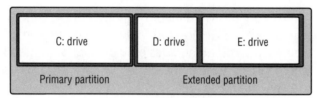

C: drive	D: drive	E: drive
Primary partition	Extended partition	

Physical disk

The primary partition always contains only a single logical drive, however.

FDISK does not allow more than one primary partition per physical drive, but if you partition using some other utility, such as Disk Management in Windows 2000, you can have multiple primary partitions per drive. The difference between a primary partition and an extended one is that a primary partition is bootable.

Even though only a primary partition is bootable, you can still store an operating system on an extended partition's logical drive, as long as the operating system on the primary partition is multi-boot capable. When the computer is starting up, the primary partition will be read first, and the primary partition will contain the instructions for displaying a menu from which you will select an operating system.

Some people like having multiple logical drives because it gives them more storage flexibility; it also enables them to install multiple operating systems on a single PC, each on its own partition. Other people prefer to have a single large logical drive for each physical drive so they don't have to worry about running out of room on one logical drive while another one has space to spare.

Formatting

Before it can be used, a disk must be formatted. (The exception is a CD-R disc, which gets formatted simultaneously as you write to it.) The operating system does the formatting, and thereby ensures that the formatted disk will be readable in that operating system. This used to be a much more critical issue back in the days when there were lots of different operating systems, but nowadays almost all PCs use Windows so a disk could theoretically be formatted using almost any PC and then used on another PC.

On MS-DOS and Windows operating systems, formatting specifies that each sector will hold 512 bytes of data. In addition to the 512 data bytes per sector, some of each sector is occupied by header and trailer identifier information about that sector. You might hear about a drive having a different formatted and unformatted capacity, and that's the reason. A 1.44MB floppy, for example, actually has a raw capacity of 2MB, but only 1.44MB of data can be stored.

Two kinds of formatting must be done to a disk before you can use it for data storage: physical (low-level) and logical (high-level).

When you format a floppy disk, either in Windows or DOS, the Format command performs both physical and logical formatting at the same time. However, with a hard disk, the Format command does only the logical format. The physical, low-level format must be done at the factory or performed by using a special utility from the drive manufacturer.

A low-level format creates the sectors and the gaps between them (which are something like the blank spaces between songs on an audio recording). It also writes all the usable data areas with a placeholder value. You will probably never need to perform a low-level format on a hard disk because they come prefor-matted these days, but should the need ever arise (to repair a disk that has become unreadable, for example, or for security purposes), you should acquire a utility from the drive manufacturer to do it, rather than relying on a generic utility. That's because different drive makers handle low-level formatting differently.

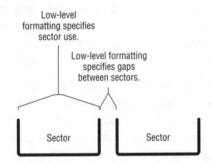

After a hard disk has been low-level formatted, it must be partitioned before it can be high-level formatted. Partitioning a drive allows more than one operating system to exist on a drive, each on its own partition. But even if you have only one operating system to install, you must still create at least one partition.

After partitioning a drive, you can use the Format command (or the Format utility in Windows) to perform a high-level format on the disk. This operation writes some housekeeping features to the disk, such as the boot sector, two copies of a File Allocation Table (FAT), and a root directory. These features allow the operating system to interact with the disk, store files on it, and avoid any defective spots. The following sections explain each of those items in more detail.

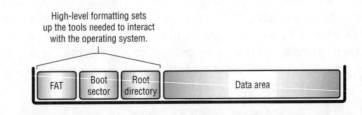

Boot Sectors

Each high-level formatted disk has a **boot sector**, which is a sector near the center of the disk reserved for boot files (that is, startup files). When a disk is bootable, that sector contains instructions for processing the startup routine for the operating system. When a disk is not bootable, that area is empty.

When a PC starts up, it checks the disk drives in an order specified by the BIOS, looking in the boot sector for the files needed to help it load the operating system. (You'll learn more about starting up a PC in Chapter 15, "Starting Up a PC.") If it finds the needed information, it tries to boot from that disk. If it doesn't, it moves on to the next disk on its list.

File Allocation Tables (FATs)

The **File Allocation Table (FAT)** is a table that tracks the content of each sector in the drive's root directory. It's stored on a reserved section of a disk, and the operating system knows where to look for it.

The FAT is important because it provides the operating system with a central point of reference when opening and saving files. It's like a card catalog in a library.

Because each sector holds only 512 bytes, almost all files occupy more than one sector. A file does not necessarily use a group of contiguous sectors. Remember, part of "random access" is that each area is just as easily accessible as any other area, so a file could store its data in little pockets all over the disk just as easily as all in one place. When the operating system calls for the file, the read/write head jumps around picking up the pieces of that file and sends them to the operating system. It knows where to look for those pieces because of the data in the FAT.

When you open a file stored on a disk, it's like a game of telephone: the operating system consults the FAT, and then tells the drive controller to retrieve information from a specific sector. The drive controller tells the actuator arm, which moves the head, which reads the data and sends it back to the controller, which relays it to the operating system. It's the same basic process when you write to a disk.

Because the File Allocation Table is so important, two copies of it are stored on the disk; they are synchronized with one another. If the two copies don't match, a utility such as ScanDisk (or Check Disk in Windows XP) can identify and correct the error. The FAT does not keep track of the location of every file on the whole disk; it's in charge only of the root directory, and any files and folders stored directly therein. Each directory (folder) is then in charge of keeping its own mini-FAT detailing its own content.

Boot sector
A reserved sector on the disk for commands that load an operating system when the PC starts up.

File Allocation Table (FAT)
A table that keeps track of the content of each sector of the disk. The operating system consults the FAT whenever it needs to open or save a file.

Root directory
The top-level or main storage area on a disk, not associated with any particular folder.

Root Directories

Each high-level formatted disk has a **root directory**. The root directory is like the lobby of an office building—when you're there, you're in the building, but not in any particular office. Similarly, when the root directory is active, the drive is active, but not any particular folder on it.

The root directory can contain files and folders. Files stored directly in the root directory are like people standing in the lobby. Folders in the root directory are like office suites. Folders can, in turn, hold files, or they can hold subfolders (which are like individual rooms within a company's office suite).

The root directory is important because the File Allocation Table keeps track only of the root directory's content, sort of like the lobby of a building listing only the names of the companies that have offices in it, not the names of all the individual employees. When a program references a file, it references a complete path to it, such as C:\Windows\win.ini. The operating system sees C: and knows it needs to query the C: drive. The C: drive's FAT sees \Windows and directs the request to the Windows folder. The Windows folder has its own internal listing of its contents and is able to direct the operating system to the win.ini file.

Review Questions

1. What would type of drive is electromagnetic and removable?

   _____

2. True or False: On an electromagnetic disk, positively charged particles are 1s and negatively charged particles are 0s.

   _____

3. When the actuator arm of a drive moves the read/write head in or out, it is moving to a different _____.

4. The same tracks on a set of stacked platters constitute a _____.

5. Ordinary CD-ROM discs store data with patterns of _____ and _____ in the surface of the disk.

6. What does an optical drive have to "see" in order for it to send a "1" bit to the operating system?

   _____

7. How does the laser on a recordable CD-ROM drive write the data?

   _____

8. Which disk types require partitioning before they can be high-level formatted?

   _____

9. Suppose you want to partition a physical drive into four logical drives using FDISK. How many of the logical drives will reside on the extended partition?

   _____

10. Which activity creates the sectors and defines how much space will exist between sectors on a drive?

    _____

Chapter

8

Focus on
Hard Drives

In this chapter, we'll take a look at hard drives: what makes them work, what types of interfaces they use, and how to install and configure one. The topics covered in this chapter include:

 IDE and SCSI drive interfaces

 Measures of hard drive performance

 Physically installing and removing hard drives

 Partitioning a hard drive

 Formatting a hard drive

 Troubleshooting common hard drive problems

Introducing the Hard Drive

A hard disk and the drive mechanism are built together in a single package, so the terms "disk" and "drive" are more or less synonymous. In this chapter, I'll use "hard drive" for consistency.

Inside the hard drive's metal box are a series of rigid aluminum platters coated with a nickel-cobalt or ferro-magnetic material. Each platter is double-sided, and each side of each platter has its own read/write head. As the drive spins, the read/write heads are held slightly off the surface of the disk by air pressure from the spinning. When the computer is off and the platters are not spinning, the read/write heads rest lightly on the platter surfaces.

Because the hard drive's performance depends on the ability to keep the space between the read/write heads and the platters free of dust, hard drives are sealed in a metal casing. You should never attempt to open this casing yourself; such repairs are performed only in special ultra-clean facilities.

Hard drives can store a lot more information than floppies, for several reasons. One is that there are multiple platters. Another is the physical composition of the platters—because they are rigid and coated with a superior surface, they can store more data per inch. Still another is that because the disks are sealed inside a dust-free metal casing, the read/write head can be much smaller and more sensitive.

Hard drives are also much faster than floppies. One reason is the use of the IDE bus instead of the much slower floppy one. Another reason is the superior performance of the read/write heads and the fact that there are multiple platters, not a single large platter, on which to locate data. Today's hard drives can read and write data at up to 100MB/sec.

Drive Interfaces

There are two popular interfaces for hard drives: IDE (pronounced *I-D-E*) and SCSI (pronounced *skuzzy*). Each has its own advantages and drawbacks, as you'll see in the following sections.

IDE

Integrated Drive Electronics (IDE) is the "normal" interface for hard drives, and by far the most common. Most motherboards have two built-in 40-pin IDE connectors:

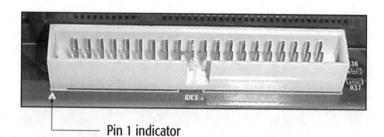

Pin 1 indicator

Each of those connectors can support up to two drives (on the same ribbon cable), for a total of four. You can also add expansion cards that have additional IDE connectors on them.

IDE is actually a generic term referring to any drive with a built-in controller. Back in the earliest days of hard drive technology, the hard drive and its controller were two separate pieces. With an IDE drive, however, the drive controller is part of the package. You have probably noticed that a hard drive has a little circuit board strapped to the bottom of a hard drive; that's the integrated drive controller. When the controller goes bad, the drive is toast as well. IDE was a real revolution in PC technology when it first came out, because it meant that drive makers did not have to make their drives compatible with a particular controller standard, so they could develop higher-performance drive/controller combinations that spoke their own proprietary language between them.

AT Attachment (ATA)

All IDE drives today (and for the last 10 years or more) are compatible with the AT Attachment (**ATA**) standard, and they are more or less compatible with one another. That means you can take an old hard drive and put it in a new system and the new system will be able to use it.

IDE
Integrated Drive Electronics. A drive with a built-in controller.

ATA
AT Attachment. A standard for IDE drives in PCs that makes it possible for PCs to share IDE devices without compatibility problems.

WARNING

You can put a new hard drive in an old system, but you might not be able to use its full capacity due to BIOS and operating system limitations. Some older BIOSes don't support drives of more than 8GB; if you have a drive bigger than that, you must get a BIOS update or be resigned to use a larger drive at the supported size. MS-DOS and Windows versions earlier than Windows 98 do not have large disk support. That means they don't support the FAT32 file system (32-bit File Allocation Table), so the drive size is limited to 2GB per logical drive. You can have multiple logical drives on a single physical drive, however, so the space isn't wasted (as with BIOS limitations); it's just chopped up.

Several additions have been made to the ATA standard over the years. Each one adds some new features or a new way of increasing the drive's speed. You don't need to know the details of each of the additions; just know that they are numbered, ATA-1 through ATA-6 (the 2000 revision).

NOTE

You may occasionally hear IDE referred to as EIDE. The extra E stands for "enhanced." EIDE originally meant any IDE device that supported ATA-2 or higher, but because all IDE devices nowadays do that, EIDE has come to be almost as generic a term as IDE itself.

Starting with ATA-4, a new means of improving data transfer speed was introduced called Ultra**DMA** (also called UltraATA). Originally it allowed for data transfer rates of up to 33MB/sec, but ATA-5 increased that to 66MB/sec, and ATA-6 further increased it to 100MB/sec.

UltraDMA comes with a couple of "gotchas," however. One is that the 66MB/sec and 100MB/sec versions require a special ribbon cable that has 80 wires instead of the usual 40. It still has only 40 pins/holes, though; the extra wires are spacers that help eliminate EMI between the wires so they can transfer data more reliably. The other issue is that when two drives share the same ribbon cable, they're limited to the maximum transfer rate that they can both support. So, for example, a 33MB/sec drive and a 100MB/sec drive would both act like 33MB/sec drives when on the same cable.

The motherboard and the drive must both be able to support a certain transfer rate to make UltraDMA speeds possible. An older motherboard may have been manufactured before some of the higher ATA standards were invented, so putting a brand-new, high-speed drive in such a system would be a waste.

Master/Slave Status

Because each IDE ribbon cable can support two drives, it needs a way of distinguishing between them, so data coming through the cable ends up at the correct drive. This is handled through the drive's master/slave status.

Each drive is designated either the **master** or the **slave**. All data comes through the master drive's controller, and then anything addressed to the slave drive passes through to it. The slave drive sees only its own traffic, but the master drive sees it all.

Jumpers on the drive determine its master/slave status. There may be up to four different jumper positions on an IDE drive:

Master   This drive functions as the master. There may or may not be a slave drive.

Slave   This drive functions as the slave. There must be a master drive on the same cable.

Cable select   The drive's master/slave status is determined by which ribbon cable connector is plugged into it. It requires a special cable and doesn't work with all drives.

Single   If present, it is used when there is only one drive on the cable. If Single is available, it must be used rather than Master in a single-drive situation.

To set a jumper, carefully remove the black cap that covers the pins and move it to another set of pins.

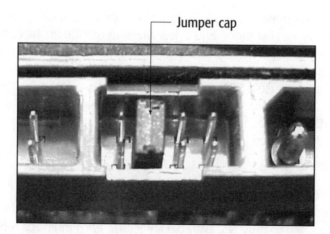

Jumper cap

Sometimes you might see a jumper hanging off a single pin. This is a storage position; having a jumper over one pin is the same as not having the jumper at all.

To determine the correct setting for the jumper, look for a chart on the drive's label. The following chart goes with the jumper just shown. It's a little confusing because it's rotated 90 degrees, but get used to it—you'll find this kind of confusion

Master
The drive designated to handle all the data traffic on the IDE cable.

Slave
The drive that receives all its data through the drive designated as master.

Jumper
A metal and plastic cap that fits over two pins on a circuit board, completing an electrical circuit between them and changing the flow of electricity through the board.

all over the place in PC hardware instructions. Notice in this particular chart that the settings for a single drive and for master are the same.

Current setting

JUMPER SETTING

SCSI

Small Computer Systems Interface (**SCSI**) is the other important type of hard drive connector you need to know about. SCSI used to be very popular in high-end systems because of the problems and limitations with IDE. However, IDE has improved over the years to the point where it's almost as good as SCSI in every way, so there is less reason to seek out SCSI equipment.

> **NOTE**
>
> SCSI is a parallel interface, like an LPT port or an IDE interface. FireWire (IEEE 1394) is a serial variant of SCSI. Other serial variants of SCSI, including Serial Storage Architecture (SSA) and Fibre Channel, are not very popular.

SCSI has always been less popular than IDE for three reasons. One is that the drives themselves cost more, and price-sensitive consumers have been unwilling to spend the extra money for them. The second is that most motherboards do not natively support SCSI, so you must add a SCSI controller card to your system in order to use a SCSI drive. Finally, SCSI device manufacturers have not done a very good job of educating the buying public about the advantages of SCSI over IDE. Even many computer professionals are not sure exactly why SCSI is better, although they've heard that it is.

So why is it better?

◇ SCSI has a higher overall throughput rate than IDE in some cases.

◇ You can chain more drives onto a single interface (at least seven, as opposed to only two with IDE). Because each interface requires system resources (such as IRQs), using SCSI drives can be an advantage if you are worried about running out of IRQs.

◇ Multiple drives on the same bus share bandwidth more gracefully than with IDE. If two or more devices on the same SCSI chain need to be used at once there is less likelihood of a bottleneck than with IDE.

Are these reasons significant enough to warrant the extra cost and hassle? That's a question to answer on a case-by-case basis.

Types of SCSI

SCSI has been around a long time and, like ATA, has gone through several changes. Here are the three main types of SCSI:

SCSI-1   The original. It used an 8-bit expansion card, and its bus operated at 5MHz. It could support up to seven devices on a chain. The standard was very loose, and as a result, proprietary SCSI devices sprang up like weeds, each with its own proprietary expansion card. It is now obsolete.

SCSI-2   Introduced in 1990 as a way to standardize SCSI so that devices could use common interfaces. SCSI-2 came in two speeds—standard (5MHz) and fast (10MHz). It also came in three bit widths: 8-bit (standard or narrow), 16-bit (wide), and the less-common 32-bit (also called wide).

SCSI-3   Improved SCSI standards operating at higher speeds. Also called Ultra SCSI. There are three speeds: 20MHz, 40MHz, and 80MHz, and two widths: 8-bit (narrow) and 16-bit (wide).

There are many descriptors out there for SCSI specifications, but they can all be grouped into one of the three types. For example, if you see "Fast Wide SCSI," you can assume that they're talking about a 10MHz, 16-bit SCSI-2. If you see "Ultra-20 wide SCSI," you can assume it's a 16-bit, 20MHz SCSI-3.

One of the main advantages of SCSI is that you can chain together multiple devices off a single expansion card. Most SCSI variants will work compatibly with other variants on the same chain. If you have a SCSI-3 expansion card, you can use it to run SCSI-2 and SCSI-1 devices as well. However, these older-standard devices are limited, and they will slow down the data access to any devices that follow them in the chain.

SCSI Interface Cards

A SCSI interface card adds the needed port(s) to the computer to support SCSI drives. Drives are not the only type of SCSI device—there are also SCSI scanners, CD-ROM drives, and so on. A single SCSI interface card can support up to seven different SCSI devices.

SCSI devices can be either internal or external. Internal devices are those that connect to the SCSI interface from inside the PC. This would include any drives, including hard or CD-ROM. External devices are those that sit outside the PC and plug into it via an external cable. A scanner would be one example; an external backup tape drive would be another. Many SCSI interface cards have both internal and external connectors, so you can use both types of devices.

You might find two types of internal SCSI connectors on SCSI interface cards. One is the SCSI A cable; it looks just like an IDE ribbon cable except it has 50 wires instead of 40. It's used for 8-bit SCSI-1 and SCSI-2. The other type is the SCSI P cable; it has 68 wires and a D-shaped connector (but there are the same number of pins in both rows, unlike on a traditional D-sub connector).

The external connector type depends on the SCSI type. SCSI-1 always has a 50-pin Centronics external connector (like on a parallel printer), and SCSI-3 always has a 68-pin female D-sub connector. However, a SCSI-2 card could have a 25, 50, or 68-pin female D-sub, depending on the model.

SCSI ID and Termination

Up to seven SCSI devices can be chained together so they run off the same interface. Internal SCSI devices usually run off the same ribbon cable; external SCSI devices usually have both an "In" and an "Out" port, so you can run one cable into the device and another cable out of it.

Because all the devices share an interface, there needs to be a way to keep the traffic for each device separate. In IDE, this is the master/slave setup; in SCSI it's an ID number assigned to each device. When a message comes from the operating system to the expansion card, it's accompanied by an identifier that tells which device number should have the message delivered to it. Each device listens only for its own ID number and ignores everything else. Therefore, it's important that you set each device to a unique ID number. Some devices are set with jumpers; others have a thumbwheel or a counter that increments when you press a button on it.

On devices that use jumpers to set the ID, the jumper settings are not nearly as obvious as on an IDE device. You might see three pairs of jumper pins, like this.

In this example, the 1 and 4 pins are "jumped," which adds up to a SCSI ID of 5.

The expansion card usually takes the SCSI ID 0 for itself, leaving IDs 1 through 7 for attached devices. If you are going to boot from a SCSI hard drive, you should set its ID to 1, so it is the first device on the chain. Other than that, the ID numbers are up for grabs.

Regardless of the number of connectors on the drive, the last device in the chain must be **terminated**—that is, it must be capped or blocked, either with a physical plug or with jumpers, to indicate that there are no more devices after it. On most hard drives, there is an extra jumper block for termination. When the jumper covers the pins, it's terminated; when it doesn't, it's not. Almost all problems that users experience with SCSI devices are due either to improper ID assignment or improper termination.

Terminate
To close the SCSI chain at the end, letting the system know that there are no other SCSI devices in the chain.

Measures of Hard Drive Performance

When shopping for a hard drive, you'll be bombarded with lots of specifications. Which are important? Which are not? The following sections help sort it out.

Maximum Data Transfer Rate

Here's an important specification: how quickly the drive can input and output data. On an ATA drive, this is tied in with the ATA specification to which the drive conforms. An UltraDMA/66 drive can transfer at up to 66MB/sec, for example.

Not all drives that conform to a particular standard are necessarily capable of achieving that transfer rate, though, especially on a sustained basis. Therefore, this specification is more of a theoretical measurement, a means for comparing two drives' "on-paper" capabilities, rather than an actual measurement of a particular drive.

In addition, the same drive might not always be capable of its theoretical maximum because of external factors. For example, if the motherboard's IDE interface does not support UltraDMA, the maximum transfer rate would be bottlenecked by the motherboard. A drive that would normally support 66MB/sec might be limited to only 16MB/sec or even less by an old motherboard. And as mentioned earlier, an IDE drive is limited to the maximum data transfer rate that it can agree upon with the other IDE drive on the same cable.

Read and Write Seek Times

These measurements tell how quickly, on the average, the drive can locate a particular piece of data to be read (read seek time) or locate a particular spot on the drive to write to (write seek time). These measurements are expressed in milliseconds (ms). An average read seek time might be 9ms, and an average write seek time might be 12ms. Lower is better.

Latency

The drive's average latency is the amount of time between when a command is issued to it and when it kicks in and executes it. It's measured in milliseconds too; an average amount is 5ms. Lower is better.

Rotational Speed

Some drives are advertised according to their rotational speed—that is, the speed at which the drive spins its disks or platters, in revolutions per minute (RPM). Generally speaking, a higher RPM means higher drive performance. An RPM of 5600 is typical of an UDMA/33 drive, while an RPM of 7200 is commonly found on UltraDMA/66 drives.

Rotational speed in and of itself is not that important. We don't care how fast the drive spins; we only care how fast it retrieves and stores data. However, faster RPM is typical of better performing drives, so the two factors are indirectly connected.

Installing Hard Drives

Installing a hard disk is not difficult, but there are several steps involved, and it's easy to forget a step and then have to spend time backtracking. For example, if you forget to set the jumpers before you mount the drive in the bay, you must completely remove it in order to set them (unless you have really tiny hands that can grab that jumper from an awkward angle).

Here's the big picture of how to install a hard drive; I'll describe each of these steps in more detail in the following sections.

1. Set the jumpers.
2 Put the drive in a bay.
3 Connect it to the motherboard via ribbon cable.
4 Connect it to the power supply.
5 Set up the BIOS.

That's just the physical part; after you install a drive, you must partition and format it, which I'll describe later in the chapter.

Step 1: Set the Jumpers

First, determine what type of drive it is and what other devices will share an interface with it.

If it's an IDE drive, and you're going to put it on the same ribbon cable as an existing IDE drive, check the existing drive's settings first. It will either be set to Single or Master, depending on whether the drive has a single setting. Set it to Master if needed. Then set the jumper on the new drive to Slave.

If it's a SCSI drive, check the SCSI ID settings for the existing SCSI devices, if any, and set the new drive's jumpers to an ID number that isn't taken. If this is to be the only SCSI device, terminate it. If not, you can either keep the existing terminated device and slip the new drive into the middle of the chain, or you can remove termination from the currently terminated device and then terminate the new drive.

Step 2: Put the Drive in a Bay

Hard drives are internal, so you don't need one of the externally accessible drive bays for it. Look for a bracket inside where the existing hard drive is mounted; there is probably room for another hard drive above or below it. Secure the new drive in the bracket with screws.

NOTE

Some cases don't use screws to hold drives in place; instead they use mounting rails that fasten to the sides of the drive and then snap the drive into place.

Step 3: Connect It to the Motherboard

There are two types of IDE ribbon cables: the 40-wire kind and the 80-wire kind. The 80-wire kind looks like it has more and thinner wires, but its overall dimensions are the same. If the drive came with an 80-wire cable, you should use it rather than an existing 40-wire cable in the PC. Otherwise you can use the IDE cable that is already there for the original hard drive.

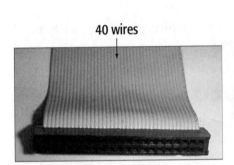
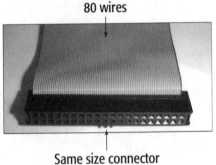

40 wires

80 wires

Same size connector

TIP

If the second IDE connector on the motherboard is unused, you might want to attach the new drive to it rather than hooking it into an existing IDE ribbon cable. That's because you might get slightly better performance if the two drives don't have to share.

If you need to install a new cable on the motherboard, here's how to do it. Notice on the cable that there are three connectors: one at each end and one slightly offset in the middle. Find the end that is farthest away from the middle connector; that's the end that connects to the motherboard.

Find the red stripe on the side of the cable; the side with that stripe needs to align with Pin 1 on the connector. Pin 1 is identified with a small "1" stamped on the motherboard or with an arrow pointing to it (as shown here).

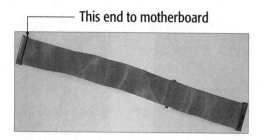

This end to motherboard

Push the connector firmly down onto the pins on the motherboard.

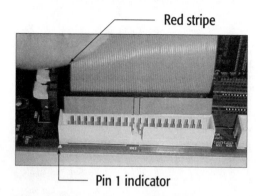

Red stripe

Pin 1 indicator

Now do the same thing to the drive. You can use either of the remaining connectors on the ribbon cable to hook into the drive. Make sure the red stripe aligns with Pin 1. Pin 1 on the drive is almost always the end that's closest to the power supply connector.

Step 4: Connect It to the Power Supply

Find a free connector from the power supply and plug it into the drive. The top edge of the connector is rounded so it can only fit one way.

Step 5: Set Up the BIOS

On almost all PCs today, the BIOS setup program can automatically detect a new drive without any intervention on your part. You just turn on the PC and a message scrolls by during normal startup about the BIOS setup having been updated.

However, if you want to check to confirm that the drive has been identified in the BIOS setup, enter your BIOS program (refer back to Chapter 3, "A Closer Look at the Motherboard," if needed) and find the list of installed IDE devices. If the new hard drive does not appear on the correct IDE bus (Primary Master, Primary Slave, Secondary Master, or Secondary Slave), the BIOS has not detected it.

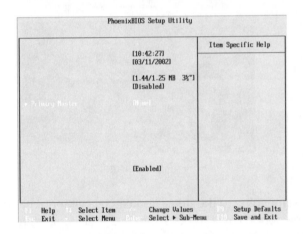

If the BIOS doesn't detect the drive, one of the following is going on:

- ✧ The drive is physically bad.
- ✧ The ribbon cable is bad.
- ✧ The ribbon cable is connected with the red stripe pointing the wrong direction at one or both ends.
- ✧ The ribbon cable isn't firmly seated at one or both ends.
- ✧ The power supply connector is not firmly seated.
- ✧ The BIOS program has been manually set to None for that IDE position, and it needs to be set to Auto so it can detect the drive.

All of these are physical problems except the last one. If the BIOS setup reports None for the IDE position where the drive is installed, look for a Detect IDE feature in the BIOS, or try setting the drive type for that position to Auto.

Then reboot. If you don't see anything on the screen about the new drive being detected, return to BIOS setup and check it out. When BIOS setup sees the new drive, it's physically installed correctly and ready to be prepared for use.

Preparing a Hard drive for Use

A brand-new hard drive has already been low-level formatted at the factory; all that remains is for you to partition and format it. You already know about partitioning and formatting from the discussion in Chapter 7, "Introduction to Disk Drives," so let's dive right in.

Starting the PC

If you are adding a second drive and have kept your first one, you can boot to Windows normally and then do the partitioning and formatting from within Windows. If not, you'll need to start the PC from a boot disk.

Windows 9x

Windows 9x (including Windows Me) enables you to create an emergency startup disk that contains utilities you'll need to prepare a hard drive such as FDISK and FORMAT. To create a boot disk, go to the Control Panel, choose Add/Remove Programs, and then click the Startup Disk tab and follow the instructions there.

Then start the PC using the startup disk you created, and when prompted to start the PC with or without CD-ROM support, choose Without. A command prompt will appear, and you'll be ready to start partitioning and formatting.

You can also access the partitioning utility, FDISK, from a command prompt window within Windows itself, but I prefer to do it from a "clean" boot from a startup disk, just for added safety. (I'm always a little afraid of running disk utilities from a command prompt in Windows because of the way disk utilities take command of the system at a low level.) Formatting can be done either from the command prompt or from within Windows; it's safe either way.

Windows 2000 or XP

Windows 2000 and Windows XP do not have the emergency startup disk feature because they are not based on MS-DOS. If you have a new drive to prepare in one of these Windows versions, you can do it through the Windows setup program or from within Windows itself.

To start the PC with the Windows 2000 or XP setup CD-ROM, set up your PC to boot from CD. To do so, go into the BIOS setup program and change the boot order for the system so that the CD-ROM drive comes first.

Then during the Setup program, you'll be asked about partitioning and formatting. Use the built-in utilities there to do that work instead of what's in the following sections.

Partitioning

You already know what partitioning is; here's how to actually do it.

Windows 9x

In Windows 9x/Me, get to a command prompt. You can do this by booting from your emergency startup disk or by choosing Start ➢ Programs ➢ Accessories ➢ MS-DOS Prompt from within Windows. (In some versions, it may just be Start ➢ Programs ➢ MS-DOS Prompt.)

From the command prompt, type **FDISK** and press Enter. In Windows 98 and Me, you'll see a message about enabling large drive support. If you choose Y, the partitions you create will be FAT32 partitions and won't be accessible from MS-DOS, Windows 95, or Windows NT. If you choose N, however, you will be limited to 2GB per logical drive.

From there, the main FDISK Options screen appears.

Changing to the New Drive

By default the primary hard drive's data is displayed in FDISK. If you have added a new hard drive and left the old one in place, you will need to turn FDISK's attention to the new drive. To do so:

1. Type **5,** and press Enter to choose Change Current Fixed Disk Drive. This option does not appear if you have only one physical hard drive.

2. Type the number for the drive you want to change to, and press Enter.

Creating a New Partition

Let's assume for now that you're working with a brand-new drive with no existing partitions. You will, therefore, need to create a primary partition. Let's also assume that you want the entire physical drive to be one big primary partition. Here's how to do it from the main FDISK menu:

1. Type **1,** and press Enter to choose Create DOS Partition or Logical DOS Drive.

2. Type **1** to choose Create Primary DOS Partition.

```
              Create DOS Partition or Logical DOS Drive

   Current fixed disk drive: 2

   Choose one of the following:

   1. Create Primary DOS Partition
   2. Create Extended DOS Partition
   3. Create Logical DOS Drive(s) in the Extended DOS Partition



   Enter choice: [1]




   Press Esc to return to FDISK Options
```

3. A message appears asking whether you want to use the maximum available size for the primary DOS partition. Press Enter to accept the default of Yes.

4. A message appears telling you to restart your system. Press Esc to exit FDISK.

5. If you are working from a command prompt within Windows, type Exit to return to Windows and then use Start ➢ Shut Down to restart the PC. If you are working from an emergency startup disk, just press Ctrl+Alt+Delete to restart your PC. Do not remove the startup floppy disk if you are using one; you will need it to restart.

After you have restarted, your new partition is ready to be formatted.

Windows 2000 or XP

In Windows 2000 or XP, you partition a new drive as part of the Windows setup program—provided that you want to install Windows on that drive. If you don't, and you already have a drive with Windows 2000 or XP installed on it, you can use the Disk Management utility to do the partitioning (and the formatting too).

To run Disk Management, choose Start ➢ Settings (in Windows 2000 only) ➢ Control Panel ➢ Administrative Tools ➢ Computer Management. Then click Disk Management to enter the Disk Management utility.

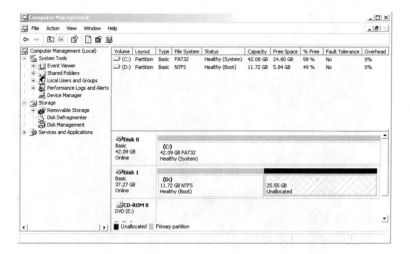

The new drive will show up with unallocated space on it. (The preceding figure shows the drive with an NTFS partition already on it, but yours will be all unallocated.) Do the following to create the new partition:

1. Right-click that unallocated space, and choose New Partition. The New Partition Wizard runs.

2. Click Next to continue.

3. Choose Primary Partition, and click Next.

4. Enter the amount of space to use for the partition, or leave it set to the default (the maximum). Then click Next.

5. If you want to assign a drive letter to the partition, choose it from the list; then click Next.

6. If you want to format the partition now, choose Format This Partition with the Following Settings. Then choose the settings you want. The default file system is NTFS for Windows 2000 and XP. Then click Next.

7. Click Finish. If you chose to format the partition as well as create it, you can then skip the Disk Formatting section that follows.

Disk Formatting

If you partitioned from FDISK, you must restart your PC afterwards before you format. If you partitioned from within Windows 2000/XP, you don't have to restart.

Disk Formatting from a Command Prompt

If you are working from a command prompt, type **FORMAT** *{drive letter}***:** and press Enter to start the formatting. For example, to format the C: drive, type **FORMAT C:**. A warning appears about formatting fixed disks; type **Y** and press Enter to move past it. Then just wait for the formatting to finish.

Disk Formatting from My Computer in Windows

After you have created a partition, it shows up in My Computer, even if it is not formatted. You can format it by right-clicking it and choosing Format. This opens the Format dialog box; choose a file system and other settings and click OK to format it.

Disk Formatting from Disk Management in Windows 2000/XP

As you saw earlier, you can format a drive at the same time as partitioning it through the New Partition Wizard. If for some reason you chose not to format it, you can format it later through Disk Management as well. Just right-click it and choose Format. Then follow the prompts. This opens a Format dialog box; make your selections of formatting options and click OK to format.

Common Hard Drive Problems

Here are some tips for troubleshooting problems with hard drives.

BIOS Doesn't See the Drive

This is almost always a physical or installation problem with the drive, and not the BIOS's fault. Check all the connections, and check the jumper settings. If you have two masters and no slave on a cable, or two slaves and no master, the BIOS won't see them. Try the drive in a different computer if possible.

No Drive Letter at Command Prompt or in My Computer

This usually means the drive hasn't been partitioned yet. It can also mean the drive has been partitioned using a system that the current operating system doesn't recognize. For example, Windows 2000 and XP have an option called Dynamic Disk that offers disk management improvements, but if you use that feature none of the drive's partitions can be seen in earlier Windows versions.

Can't See Files on Drive

If you can see the drive letter but can't get a file listing on it, the drive has probably not been formatted yet, or it's formatted with a file system that the current operating system doesn't recognize. For example, Windows NT doesn't recognize FAT32, and Windows 95, 98, and Me don't recognize NTFS.

Data Error or Problems with a Specific File

If you get an error message that says something about a data error, or if one particular file can't be read, there is probably a bad spot physically on the disk. Run the Scandisk utility (in MS-DOS or Windows 9*x*) or the Check Disk utility in Windows 2000 or XP and specify that you want a surface scan. This takes a long time (up to a few hours), but it will identify and isolate bad spots on the disk.

Focus on Hard Drives

To run Scandisk in Windows 9*x*, choose Start ➤ Programs ➤ Accessories ➤ System Tools ➤ Scandisk. In Windows 2000 or XP, right-click the drive in My Computer and choose Properties, and then on the Tools tab, click Check Now. You'll see this utility again in Chapter 18, "Troubleshooting Windows Problems," when we talk about Windows system problems.

Review Questions

1. Which type of interface allows up to seven devices to be chained off a single motherboard connection?

   _____

2. True or False: For 66MB/sec data transfer (UltraDMA/66), you need a 40-wire ribbon cable.

   _____

3. Suppose you put a new 30GB drive in an old PC, and the BIOS detects the drive as an 8GB drive. What do you need to do to make the PC recognize the full 30GB of space?

   _____

4. Suppose that you have a hard drive partitioned into three 2GB logical drives. How could you convert it to a single 6GB logical drive?

   _____

5. Suppose that you currently have a hard drive as Primary Master and a CD-ROM drive as Secondary Master. You want to add another hard drive and make it the Secondary Master. What jumper settings must change?

   _____

6. You want to add a SCSI hard drive to a system that does not have any SCSI devices. What do you need to do?

   _____

7. Latency, velocity, or seek time: which is *not* a measurement associated with hard disk performance?

   _____

8. When a new hard drive is being installed, what cables need to be plugged into the drive itself?

_____

9. What is probably the reason a BIOS cannot see a new drive?

_____

10. What utility can correct problems reading a specific file from the disk?

_____

Chapter

9

Focus on Removable Disk Drives

Removable disk drives are much simpler than hard drives, and there's a lot less technical detail to worry about with them. In this chapter, I'll run through some of the basic Dos and Don'ts for working with removables. This chapter covers:

 Installing removable drives

 Selecting and caring for disks

 Formatting and write-protecting floppies

 Common problems with removable drives

Installing Removable Disk Drives

If you read the material in the last chapter about installing hard drives, you probably won't need much help to install a removable drive. Here are the big-picture steps:

1. Select and prepare a drive bay.
2. Install the drive in the bay.
3. Connect the motherboard and power supply to the drive.
4. Connect any additional cables required.
5. Set up the BIOS.

Step 1: Select and Prepare a Drive Bay

A removable drive must go in an external bay because it needs an opening to the outside. As you saw way back in Chapter 2, "A Look Inside a PC," external bays come in two sizes: one for small drives like floppies and the other for large drives like CD-ROMs. Here's a system with two large bays (both full) and two small bays (both empty).

The extra slot below the small bays is for a proprietary style of floppy drive; not all PCs have that. Most PCs have a standard floppy drive in one of the small bays. If you run out of the small bays but still have some small drives to install, you can buy mounting brackets and a face plate that will convert a large bay into a small one.

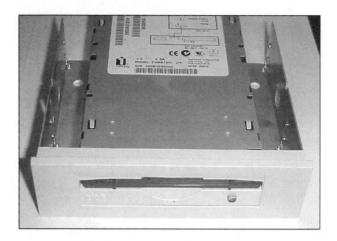

To prepare a bay, pop the plastic cover off it. It's usually easier to do this from behind—if "behind" is reachable without too much trouble. You can also stick the flat blade of a screwdriver into a crevice from the front to pop it out.

If you find a metal panel behind the plastic, don't freak out—it's removable. If there's a faceplate on the front of the PC, you might want to remove it first. Then pop out the metal piece with a screwdriver. You may need to wiggle it a bit first.

Step 2: Install the Drive in the Bay

Then just slide the drive into the bay. It should slide in freely. Push it in far enough that the front of the drive is even with the fronts of the existing drives.

You can fasten the drive in place with screws now, or you can wait to confirm that it works before you fasten it. You might find it easier to put the screws in later, after you've attached the cables.

Step 3: Connect the Motherboard and Power Supply to the Drive

Next, run the cables from the motherboard and power supply to the drive. An IDE or SCSI removable drive (such as a CD-ROM) is identical to a hard drive in the ribbon cabling, so turn back to Chapter 8, "Focus on Hard Drives," if you need to review that.

A floppy connects in the same way too, except it uses different cables. A floppy drive ribbon cable is smaller (34 pin), and it has a twist in some of the wires near one end. This twisted end must connect to the floppy drive that is to be drive A: (the primary floppy drive). The connector that goes to the motherboard is the one on the other end from that. Of course, the red stripe on the cable must go to pin 1 at both ends.

On the motherboard, the red stripes for floppy and IDE cables usually point the same way, so if you aren't sure how to orient the floppy ribbon cable, look at how the IDE cables are oriented. On the drive end of the floppy ribbon cable, the red stripe almost always goes toward the power supply connector.

The power supply connector for a floppy drive (called a Mini) is smaller than the regular Molex connector for the larger drives.

Step 4: Connect Any Additional Cables Required

Depending on the drive type, you might need to run other cables. For example, if it's a DVD drive, you might need an extra cable that connects the drive to an

MPEG decoder card or to the video card if the video card does MPEG decoding. The directions that came with the drive should tell what is necessary.

If it's a CD-ROM drive, and you want to play audio CDs on it through your computer's sound card and speakers, you must run an **audio cable** from the drive to the sound card (or to the motherboard if it's got built-in sound support). This is a three-wire cable, and it can be shielded or have bare wires, depending on the model. On one end is a flat, black four-hole connector; on the other end may be an identical connector or a smaller white four-hole connector, depending on the model. Most sound cards have several different connectors, so a variety of different audio cables will work with them.

Audio cable
A cable that runs from a CD-ROM drive to a sound card and enables the CD-ROM drive to play audio CDs through the sound card and its attached speakers.

Step 5: Set Up the BIOS

Most BIOSes detect IDE devices automatically, so you shouldn't have to worry about doing this when installing a CD-ROM drive. If yours doesn't, go back to Chapter 8 and go through the section on setting up the BIOS for a hard drive, but instead of setting the IDE position to Auto, set it to CD-ROM or ATAPI Device.

If you are replacing one floppy drive with another, you should not need to make changes to the BIOS setup unless the new floppy drive is of a different type. BIOS setup programs do not usually detect floppy drives automatically, so you will need to make changes there if you add an extra floppy drive or change to one with a different capacity.

Depending on the BIOS program, the floppy drive might go by different names. The disk referenced in the following figure is a Legacy Diskette. Notice that the A: drive is turned on and set for a 3.5-inch high-density (1.44MB) drive. Drive B: is currently disabled, but a menu has appeared to set a different setting for it.

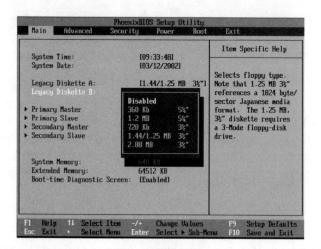

Considerations for Specific Drive Types

Is that all there is to setting up a removable drive? Usually, yes. But there are a few special cases where some more info or configuration would be helpful. Let's look at those now.

LS-120 Drive

An **LS-120** drive, also called a "super drive," is a floppy drive that runs on the IDE interface rather than the normal floppy interface. It reads and writes normal 1.44MB floppies, but it also reads and writes special 120MB "super disks."

You install and set one of these up just like a hard disk, CD-ROM, or any other IDE device. The BIOS will probably detect it automatically. If it doesn't, you might poke around in the BIOS setup to see whether there is a specific IDE Removable setting you can use for that IDE position.

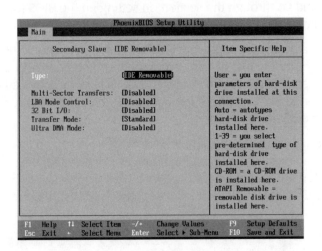

CD-RW Drive

A CD-R or CD-RW drive installs and sets up the same as a regular CD-ROM drive as far as the BIOS is concerned. It will operate just fine in any version of Windows right out of the box, but it won't have any writing capabilities until you install a CD writing application. The necessary software probably came with the drive, and you can also buy higher-end applications separately such as Adaptec's Easy CD Creator Platinum.

A CD-RW drive can write either to CD-R discs or to CD-RW ones. The CD-R blanks are write-once, and to write to them you use a CD burning application. The CD-RW discs are treated like ordinary floppy or hard disks, complete with drag-and-drop capability, thanks to a feature called **packet-writing**. You must install packet-writing software in order to enable this feature. Most drives come with a packet-writing program; one such program is Adaptec's DirectCD. Once installed, it loads automatically when Windows starts up.

TIP

When referring to a CD-ROM, the spelling is *disc* rather than *disk*. To keep it straight, think round versus square. Any disk that is square is a disk with a *K* (hard disks and floppy disks). Any disk that is round is a disc with a *C* (CD-ROM, DVD, and so on).

Packet writing
A feature that enables a CD-RW disc to be treated as a regular disk, and to be written and rewritten multiple times.

DVD Drive

A DVD drive looks and works just like a regular CD-ROM drive most of the time, but it can also read DVD data discs as well. It needs no special utilities, applications, or support to do this.

However, if you want to play DVD movies on your PC using a DVD drive, you must have MPEG decoding capabilities. MPEG compression is used to store the sound and picture for movies. A PC and its normal components don't have enough firepower to handle that amount of data all by themselves. An MPEG decoder takes on that burden and does all the decompressing needed for displaying the movie.

Early DVD drives required a separate expansion board to function as the MPEG decoder. Later on, some video cards were introduced that handled this function as a piggyback to their regular video card duties. Lately, software MPEG decompression has become popular, as programmers have figured out ways to make software do a good job of decoding without unduly burdening the rest of the PC. However, a separate expansion board for MPEG decoding still results in the best quality movie playback with the least disruption to the PC's other operations.

If you do have a separate MPEG decoder board, or decoding on the video card, a cable must be installed that runs from the DVD drive to that circuit board.

Working with Floppy Disks

Entire shelves at the local office supply store are devoted to blank disks of every type, size, and specification. The following sections help make sense of the choices and explain how to care for the disks you buy.

Quick format

A faster than normal way of reformatting an already-formatted disk that just wipes out the FAT contents rather than physically reformatting the data area.

Selecting Floppies

Floppy disks are simple to select because there's only one kind left on the market today: 3.5-inch high-density 1.44MB capacity ones. All the other standards and sizes have been obsolete for many years. You might run across some LS-120 (super disk) floppies for sale, but they'll be much more expensive (around $1 per disk).

The only decision to make when selecting floppies is whether to buy the ones that are preformatted for IBM-compatible PCs. The preformatted ones are more expensive, but they can save you some time in formatting. The unformatted ones must be formatted before you can use them (just like a hard disk must be), and it takes about 1–2 minutes to do so.

Formatting a Floppy

As I mentioned earlier, you can buy preformatted floppies or you can buy unformatted ones and do it yourself. The latter is a little cheaper.

When you format a floppy, you perform both a low-level and high-level format on it with a single operation. After a floppy has been formatted once, you can do a **quick format** on it if you ever want to reformat it. A quick format is quick because it's just a high-level format that just erases the FAT, rather than doing anything to the data area of the disk.

To format a floppy from a command prompt:

1. Type **FORMAT A:** and press Enter. That's assuming, of course, that your floppy drive is drive A:.

> **NOTE**
>
> There are lots of parameters you can add to the basic command, but you shouldn't need most of them. If you're interested, type **FORMAT /?** and press Enter to see the full list. One you might try is /Q for Quick format on a disk that has already been formatted once. The full command would look like this: FORMAT A: /Q.

2. Make sure the correct floppy is in the drive, and press Enter to format it.

3. When prompted for a **volume label**, type one and press Enter, or just press Enter to skip it.

4. When asked if you want to format another, type **N** and press Enter.

To format a floppy from Windows, do the following:

1. Right-click the drive icon in My Computer, and choose Format. The Format dialog box opens.

2. Change any of the settings if needed. (The defaults are almost always the best way to go, and most of the settings don't even have any other choices here.)

3. (Optional) If you are reformatting, save some time by marking the Quick Format check box.

WARNING

Quick Format doesn't touch the data area of the disk, so it doesn't detect and isolate any physically damaged areas. If you suspect some damage to the disk and are reformatting to correct it, don't use Quick Format.

4. Click Start. A warning box appears; click OK to move past it.

5. A Format Complete box appears; click OK.

6. Click Close to close the Format dialog box.

Volume label
An internal identifier for a formatted disk. It appears under the drive icon in My Computer in Windows and at the top of a file listing from a command prompt. It has no relationship to any physical label on the outside of the disk.

Write-Protecting a Floppy

To **write-protect** a floppy disk, slide the little black tab up so that the hole in the corner of the disk is open.

Old 5.25-inch disks had a tab in the side of the disk casing, and you had to cover that tab with a little sticker to write-protect the disk. This was the opposite of the deal with modern disks, where you *expose* a hole rather than closing it up.

Common Problems with Removable Drives

We'll round out this chapter by looking at some of the problems users encounter with removable drives and some possible solutions.

BIOS Won't See Drive   The drive may be physically defective, or it may not be hooked up correctly. Check the ribbon cable at both ends to make sure the red stripe is with pin 1. On an IDE or SCSI drive, check the jumpers (and termination for SCSI). On all drives, check the power supply connector.

In the BIOS setup program, try setting the drive type to Auto, CD-ROM, or ATAPI for an IDE CD-ROM. For a floppy drive, you will need to tell the BIOS setup exactly what size and capacity of drive it is.

Floppy Drive Light Stays On   If the floppy drive won't work and its light stays on all the time, the ribbon cable is plugged in wrong at one end or the other.

No Drive Light   If the drive doesn't work and its activity light never comes on, it is not receiving power. Try a different power supply connector.

Windows Can't Read Disk   Try a different disk to determine whether the problem is the disk or the drive. If it's the drive, the drive may have misaligned heads. (There's not much you can do about that other than replace the drive.) If it's the disk, the disk may have a scratch on it or be going bad. Try running Scandisk (or Check Disk in Windows 2000/XP) as described at the end of Chapter 8 to correct problems with a disk.

Can't Write to a Floppy   The floppy may be write-protected. Slide the tab so the hole is closed to remove write-protection. It's also possible that the disk is full.

Can't Write to CD-R   CD-R discs can be written to only once (in most cases) and require a special CD-writing application. Something may already have been written to the disc.

Can't Read from a CD-RW Disc   CD-RW requires packet-writing software to be installed in order to read or write it. If you take the CD-RW disc to another computer and you can't read it there, install the packet-writing software on that PC.

Review Questions

Terms to Know
- ❏ Audio cable
- ❏ LS-120
- ❏ Packet-writing
- ❏ Quick format
- ❏ Volume label
- ❏ Write-protect
- ❏ Safe Mode

1. What drive types can be installed in a large external drive bay?

2. What are the differences between a floppy ribbon cable and an IDE ribbon cable?

3. What do you need to install if you want to listen to audio CDs on your computer's CD-ROM drive?

4. What setting in the BIOS should you use for the modern type of floppy drive found in most PCs today?

5. What is the purpose of an MPEG decoder?

6. True or false: An IDE CD-ROM drive uses the same type of power connector as an IDE hard disk.

7. Under what circumstances would you want to buy unformatted floppy disks?

8. When a floppy disk is write-protected, what is the positioning of the sliding tab in its corner?

9. What is wrong if the floppy drive light stays on all the time?

_____

10. Why is a Quick Format quicker than a normal format?

_____

Chapter

10

A Look at Some Expansion Boards

By now you know that a motherboard doesn't stand alone—all sorts of devices attach to it. You also know that one of the ways this happens is with expansion boards. In this chapter, we'll take a look at some of these expansion boards, including the two most popular types: modems and sound cards.

This chapter covers the following topics:

 Installing an expansion board

 Selecting and configuring a modem

 Selecting and configuring a sound card

Installing an Expansion Board

No matter what type of expansion board you're installing—modem, sound card, network card, or whatever—you install it on the motherboard the same way physically. All expansion boards fit into expansion slots in a motherboard (or on a riser card in a slimline system). You learned about the various bus types in Chapter 3, "A Closer Look at the Motherboard," so you already know that there are ISA, PCI, and AGP expansion slots in the average motherboard and that you can buy expansion boards that fit into those various slots.

Backplate
A plate at the back of an expansion slot to keep the dust out of the PC case when that slot is not being used. You remove the backplate before you install an expansion card in that slot. Can also refer to the metal plate attached to the expansion card itself that fits into the same spot that the blank backplate occupied.

Here's how to install one:

1. Make sure you have a free slot of the correct type.
2. Check the expansion board to make sure there are no jumpers that need to be set on it.

TIP

Check the documentation for the board if you see jumpers. Some boards have jumpers that you don't need to set if you've got a Plug and Play PC and operating system.

3. If there's a blank **backplate** behind the slot you want to use, remove it. It might be held in place with a screw. If this is a new case, there may still be a piece of metal over the hole from the manufacturing process. If so, pop it out with a flat screwdriver. The following figure shows the backplate removed for an ISA slot.

4. Push the expansion board down into the slot. Use a see-sawing motion from front to back if needed, and don't be afraid to press hard—but press only on the edge of the board. Do not touch the circuitry. Here's an ISA sound card completely inserted into an ISA slot.

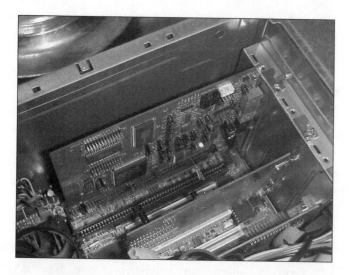

5. When the board is fully seated in the slot, its backplate's lip will rest on the case and the screw holes will line up. Secure the board with a screw.

After you install an expansion card, Windows may recognize it automatically with Plug and Play. If so, great. If not, try running the software that came with the device or (gasp!) read the instructions that came with it. If you're still having trouble, stick around for Chapter 17, "Working with Devices in Windows," which covers installing device drivers in Windows.

That's the generic picture. Now let's look at some specific examples.

Selecting and Configuring a Modem

Modem is short for *mo*dulator-*dem*odulator; it converts digital data to analog sound and then back again so digital data can be transmitted over analog telephone lines. Even though **broadband** Internet access is becoming more common with cable, DSL, and satellite service, the modem is still the tool of choice for most people for connecting to the Internet.

PC technicians need to know a lot about modems because modems are responsible for more than their fair share of problems with PCs. Some models can be quirky to install and have lots of confusing settings to adjust, and almost all modems are very susceptible to power spike and lightning strike damage. The following sections provide some essential information about modems for the would-be PC technician.

TIP

When you're troubleshooting modem problems, the problem is not always the modem itself; sometimes it is the Internet connectivity. A user might think that the problem is the modem, but it might actually be Windows' dial-up networking. Chapter 19, "Setting Up Internet Connections," covers dial-up networking connections.

Types and Features

Modems come in both internal and external models. An external modem is a separate box with its own power cord; it connects to the PC via a built-in COM port. An internal modem is an expansion board that fits into a motherboard slot.

An external modem is best if any of these conditions apply:

◇ The person who will be installing it does not feel comfortable working inside the PC case.

◇ It's a very old PC (pre-Pentium).

◇ There are no open PCI slots.

◇ The PC is running MS-DOS and Windows 3.*x*.

Otherwise, an internal modem would be better. External modems are more expensive, they take up desk space, and they consume more electricity. They also must be plugged in, further clogging up what is probably an already-full power strip under your desk.

Here's a picture of an internal modem.

Hardware modem
A modem that contains everything it needs to operate within its own hardware, so it can work with any operating system.

Software modem (Winmodem)
A modem that relies on a Windows application to team with its hardware in order to work. Software modems work only with a specific operating system (usually Windows).

This one happens to be for an ISA slot. Notice that it has its own speaker; it lets the user hear it dialing and connecting. Notice also that it has two phone jacks: one for incoming (from the wall) and one for outgoing (for a phone).

Your next choice to make is whether to use a **hardware modem** versus a **software modem**. Another name for a software modem is a **Winmodem**; it's a modem that is designed to work only under some version of Microsoft Windows. It's cheaper than a hardware modem because it doesn't have to be as smart—it offloads some of its processing duties to the PC's own CPU through its Windows driver.

I encourage my clients to buy hardware modems. Even with today's better versions of Windows, a Winmodem can be more difficult to install and configure, and it can use more device resources than a hardware modem. On top of that, sometimes a hardware modem is required for a task, and a software modem simply won't do. For example, when I recently installed DirecWay two-way satellite Internet access on my home PC, the setup procedure required a hardware modem to connect to the DirecWay server to download the configuration data for the setup. The instructions specifically stated that a Winmodem would not work.

Unfortunately, hardware modems are becoming more difficult to find these days. A recent trip to the local Best Buy revealed no hardware modems at all. This may be because modems are becoming less popular in general due to broadband Internet access, so stores are carrying fewer models. Or it may, as I suspect, be a reflection of the cheapskate nature of most computer users—they're unwilling to spend an extra $20 to have a decent hardware modem made by a reputable manufacturer. 3COM/U.S. Robotics still makes a hardware modem (they call it a Performance Modem), so look for that one while you're shopping.

The last shopping criterion to consider is the bus interface. As you probably know by this point in the book, PCI is better than ISA, so if the PC has a free PCI slot, that's definitely the way to go.

Installing a Modem

Modems come with detailed, idiot-proof instructions, so anyone can install one just by reading the manual that comes with a new modem. But in case you're not one for reading the instructions for things, here's a brief once-over.

To install an external modem:

1. Plug the modem's power cord into the modem and into the wall outlet.

2. Run a serial cable from the modem to one of the COM ports. You might need to buy a cable, or one might come with the modem.

WARNING

In Chapter 17, you'll learn how to disable a COM port in BIOS setup to free up IRQs for other purposes. Make sure the COM port you pick in Step 2 hasn't been disabled. If in doubt, try it. If it doesn't work, skip to Chapter 17 to troubleshoot.

That's it; that's all there is to installing an external modem. (Now you see why I recommended an external model for people who are scared of working on their PCs.)

To install an internal modem, go through the process outlined earlier in the chapter for installing an expansion board. The instructions that came with the modem might dictate some special procedure, such as running a setup program first, then installing the hardware, and then finishing up with another setup program. Usually you can skip all that and just do it as described earlier. However, if the modem doesn't work after you install it, you might go back and check out those instructions and give the prescribed procedure a try.

Whether you have an internal or external modem, the next step is to connect the telephone line to the Line port on the modem. This is the line that comes from the telephone jack on your wall. You can then attach a telephone to the

Phone port on the modem. Whenever the modem isn't using the phone line, the phone signal will pass harmlessly through the modem to the phone so you can continue to use the phone normally. Here's a close-up of the labeling on an internal modem. The label that looks like a drawing of a phone jack indicates the Line; the one that looks like a telephone receiver indicates the Phone.

WARNING

Make sure you don't get the Line and Phone jacks mixed up on the modem! They should be labeled. Some modems will work even if you get them switched, but other modems either won't work at all or will work very poorly.

Common Modem Problems

As I mentioned earlier, a good 25 percent of the service calls I make involve problems with modems and Internet access. Beginners seem more likely to use a modem for Internet connection than advanced PC users, so perhaps that's why modem users seem to require more help. Here are some of the common problems I've found with modems and some possible solutions.

Windows Doesn't See Modem

Check to make sure there aren't any jumpers set on the modem that are conflicting with the Plug and Play settings that Windows may be trying to use. Then look in Device Manager to see whether Windows recognizes that the modem exists, and if so, whether it thinks there is a problem with it. See Chapter 17 for help.

You can also try running modem diagnostics from the Windows Control Panel. To do so, open the Modems applet in the Control Panel (it may be called Phone and Modem Options in some versions of Windows). Double-click the modem to display its properties, and then look for a Query Modem or More Info button to click. Windows will send some test strings of AT commands to the modem. If the results come back with at least some of the lines reporting OK, the modem is installed correctly in Windows.

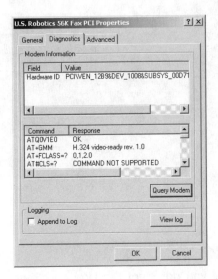

AOL Doesn't See Modem

Sometimes Windows may see the modem just fine, but America Online software won't. I've seen this happen when a client changed modems, for example, and AOL was still set up to use the old one. Try deleting all the modem drivers except the current one from the Modems applet in the Control Panel or from Device Manager. Then rerun the AOL setup software. Also in AOL's Modem Setup make sure it has the correct COM port identified for the modem.

No Dial Tone

This could mean that there is no phone line attached to the modem, that it's off the hook, that it's plugged into the wrong jack on the modem (one is for Line, or incoming, and the other is for Phone, or outgoing), or that there's a problem with the modem's driver (see Chapter 17).

Noisy, Staticky Connection

This can be caused by a poor-quality phone line, by a telephone cable that is very long, or by the phone line being plugged into the wrong jack on the modem.

Won't Stay Connected

If the modem dials okay but will not stay connected, it could just be the ISP being flaky. It happens. Give it a few hours and try again. But if you've never been able to stay connected (that is, it's not just a sporadic problem), check to make sure dial-up networking and TCP/IP are installed in the networking components. (See Chapter 19 for help with that.)

Selecting and Configuring a Sound Card

Sound card
An expansion board that functions as a converter between analog sound and digital data, enabling the computer to generate and receive audio output and input.

A **sound card**, like a modem, is also an analog-to-digital (and digital-to-analog) converter. It takes digital sounds from the operating system and its applications and converts them into sounds that play through the speakers, and it takes input from a microphone and converts it into binary data that can be stored in a file.

To hear the sounds from a sound card, you must plug a speaker (or a set of speakers) into it. These speakers are usually designed specifically to work with computers, and they are EMI shielded in a way that normal speakers (i.e., the kind for a regular stereo system) are not.

Waveform
A sound that originates in the real world, rather than being originated by a computer.

Waveform and MIDI Sounds

A sound card can play and receive two types of sounds: waveform and MIDI. **Waveform** sounds originate in the "real world." For example, suppose you take a microphone and plug it into your sound card, and then you use it to record a musician playing a song, a bird singing, or a friend telling a joke. You have made a waveform recording.

MIDI
Musical Instrument Digital Interface. An interface and method for creating sound and music files entirely digitally, with no analog origin.

In contrast, **MIDI** sounds originate in the computer. Suppose, for example, you buy an electric musical keyboard and hook it up to your PC's sound card. When you press a key, the keyboard sends digital signals to the sound card, which converts it to audio sound and plays it through the speakers. The entire process is digital—there is no conversion of analog audio to digital format.

It's important to note that waveform versus MIDI refers to the original source of the sound, not its current status. For example, if you buy the latest audio CD by your favorite diva, the music on the CD is digital. When you play it back on your PC or stereo, it continues to be digital up until it's channeled through the speakers into the air. That doesn't make the CD a MIDI recording. It is still waveform because there was a real-life singer with real-life instruments who sat in a studio and made music into the air as the origin of the recording.

FM synthesis
A method of computer simulating the sounds of various musical instruments. Results in artificial-sounding MIDI music.

Now, why am I telling you all this? Because different sound cards handle different types of audio files with varying degrees of finesse. Waveform audio is easy to play back, but MIDI audio is more challenging, and a higher-quality sound card will make for much more natural-sounding MIDI playback than a cheaper one. See the following section for more shopping tips for sound cards.

Types and Features

Throughout the history of sound cards, they have all been internal models, either on expansion boards or built into the motherboard. However, Creative Labs recently came out with an external sound card (actually it's not a card at all, more like a box) that connects to the PC via USB port. Because it's external, it isn't subject to the constraints of the PCI or ISA bus and will work on any PC with USB support—even a notebook PC. It's pretty cool—but also pretty high-end and overkill for most people.

Assuming you go with an internal model, you'll probably want a PCI bus version. ISA versions are still available (although becoming less common), but they are inferior for all the reasons I've outlined in earlier chapters concerning the differences in the buses.

It is not uncommon for an ISA sound card to take two DMA channels, one or two IRQs, and a large range of I/O addresses.

Next, there's **FM synthesis** versus wave table synthesis. This has to do with the way MIDI music is played and recorded. Originally all sound cards were FM synthesis. FM synthesis simulates musical instrument sounds when a MIDI program is creating or playing music. For example, suppose you have some MIDI software for your electric keyboard that can make it sound like an oboe. With an FM synthesis sound card, the computer calculates what an oboe sounds like and sends that approximation through the speakers. It doesn't sound exactly like a real oboe.

Wave table synthesis cards became popular several years ago, and nowadays almost all sound cards use wave table synthesis. These sound cards store waveform audio clips of various instruments playing various notes in their own Read Only Memory (ROM), and when a MIDI program calls for a particular instrument to play a particular note, the sound card plays the recording from its database. This results in MIDI music that sounds almost exactly like real waveform music.

Even though almost all sound cards support wave table synthesis to some extent, they vary in how many different instruments they have stored in them. Most cards have at least 128 instruments these days; some also have several different drums too. Cards also vary in how many voices they can support. A **voice** is a single instrument playing a single note. The more voices, the more notes and instruments can be heard simultaneously. Sixty-four-voice support is not uncommon in today's sound cards.

There are many other shopping specs for high-end sound cards, but they're not important to know for the A+ exam. You may want to look into them on your own if you're in the market for a sound card. Some of them include EAX Technology support, multi-speaker support (that is, support for multiple sets of stereo speakers), Surround Sound support, advanced encoders for creating MP3 files, and a digital signal processor.

Wave table synthesis

A method of storing waveform clips of various musical instruments in the sound card's memory and then playing them back when playing MIDI music. Results in much more natural sounding MIDI music.

Voice

A channel in the sound card that plays a single note by a single instrument. A typical sound card might have 64 voices, so 64 different sounds could be played at once.

Installing a Sound Card

Installing the actual sound card in an expansion slot is the same old thing that you learned at the beginning of the chapter. Prepare a slot, insert the card, and away you go.

After installing the card, however, you have some cables to run that connect to it, and this can get tricky.

First, hook up the speakers. The sound card has only one speaker jack (usually), so only one of the speakers can connect to it. The other speaker connects to the first speaker, rather than directly to the sound card. Some speakers run on batteries, but most of them run on AC power, so a power cord must plug into one or both of them. The port on the sound card for the speaker may be labeled as such, or it may be labeled SPK or Output. (Some cards have a separate Output port besides the speaker output; most don't.) On a sound card with color-coded ports, the speaker is the black one.

Next, if you have a microphone, hook it up to the MIC port on the sound card. It may be labeled as MIC or may have some cryptic little picture next to it that is supposed to represent a microphone. If there is color-coding, the microphone port is the red one.

The sound card will probably also have a Line Out port. This would be for an external recording device or an alternative set of speakers. This port is green on a color-coded card.

Depending on the model, there may be a fourth round port, Line In. This is for an external input source. For example, if you want to make a CD of your favorite LP, you could hook up your stereo receiver to the sound card through the Line In port. If there is color coding, this port is blue.

Finally, there will be a 15-pin female plug (two rows of pins, rather than the three on a video connector) for a MIDI instrument or joystick.

Common Sound Card Problems

Here are some problems people experience with sound cards and some ideas for fixing them.

Windows Doesn't See Sound Card

Look for the sound card in Device Manager (see Chapter 17). If it's not there at all, the card may be physically defective or not installed correctly (for example, not completely seated in the expansion slot). If it's there but there's an exclamation point next to it, or it's in the Other Devices category (or there's an unknown device in the Other Devices category), Windows has detected that it's a new device but it doesn't have the needed information about it. Run the setup program that came with the sound card to install the drivers for it, or install a driver manually as explained in Chapter 17.

No Speaker Icon in Notification Area of Windows

The lack of a speaker icon in the notification area (a.k.a. the System Tray) in Windows, down by the clock, can indicate that Windows doesn't see the sound card (see above). But it can also mean just that someone has turned off the display of that icon.

To turn the speaker icon display back on again:

1. From the Control Panel, double-click Multimedia (or Sounds and Multimedia in Windows 2000).
2. Select the Show volume control on the Taskbar check box.
3. Click OK.

No Sound At All

Check the easy fix first: check that the speakers are plugged into the correct port on the sound card, are turned on, are turned up, and are receiving power from whatever source they use (AC or battery).

Still no sound? Check in Device Manager to make sure Windows sees the sound card. (See Chapter 17.) Also make sure the sound has not been muted in Windows. To check this, double-click the speaker icon in the notification area to open the Volume properties box. Clear any Mute check boxes that are marked, and drag the volume slider up to increase the volume.

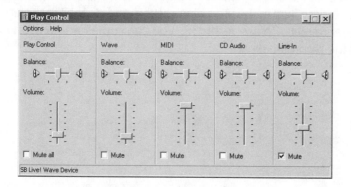

No Microphone Input

If sound goes out of the sound card but it doesn't come in, check that the microphone is plugged into the MIC jack on the sound card. Also check whether the microphone has an On/Off switch that might be off and that the Mic has not been muted in the Volume properties.

Notice in the figure shown in the preceding section that the Volume properties title bar reads Play Control. The sliders shown are for playback only. The Mic control doesn't appear there because microphones do not play back. If you want to check the input controls, such as the Microphone, choose Options ➤ Properties, click Recording, and click OK. This changes to the Record Control settings, which include Microphone. Notice also that instead of a Mute check box, there's a Select check box. The check box must be marked for the device(s) you want to record from.

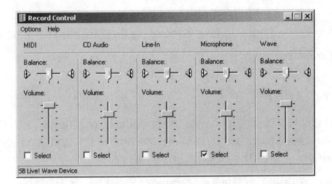

Crackling Noises

A persistent crackling from the speakers usually means that a recording device has been enabled and is picking up ambient static. Display the Record Control settings, as described in the preceding section, and clear all the Select checkboxes. If you ever need to do any recording, you can come back here and reselect the one for the recording device.

Review Questions

1. What physical feature distinguishes a non–Plug and Play expansion board from one that is Plug and Play compatible?

   _____

2. How does a modem make data transfer via phone lines possible?

   _____

3. What type of modem would you buy for a system with no available PCI slots?

   _____

4. What operating system do you need in order to use a hardware modem?

   _____

5. What line should be plugged into the Line jack on a modem?

   _____

6. What would jumpers on a sound card labeled with various IRQ numbers indicate?

   _____

7. If a No Dial Tone message appears when you try to dial up an Internet provider, what would you check?

   _____

8. What's an example of a waveform sound file?

   _____

9. What does an FM synthesis sound card lack that a wave table synthesis sound card has?

   _____

10. Suppose that a sound card has no labels on the plugs, but the plugs are color coded: red, green, black, and blue. What should you plug into the black one?

    _____

Terms to Know
- ❏ Backplate
- ❏ Modem
- ❏ Broadband
- ❏ Hardware modem
- ❏ Software modem
- ❏ Winmodem
- ❏ AT commands
- ❏ Sound card
- ❏ Waveform
- ❏ MIDI
- ❏ FM synthesis
- ❏ Wave table synthesis
- ❏ Voice

Chapter

11

A Few Other Essential Components

This chapter rounds out the coverage of the basic computer parts by addressing some of the essential but less-glamorous components such as the keyboard, mouse, case, and power supply. These components act up just as frequently as the higher-tech parts you've already learned about (well, except for the case—not much can go wrong with a metal frame), so if you become an A+ certified PC technician, you'll be dealing with them on a regular basis. This chapter covers:

 Keyboards

 Mouse

 Cases

 Electricity basics

 Power supplies

Keyboards

You know what a keyboard is already, right? It's that thing you type on. But what you might not know is that a keyboard is basically a collection of broken circuits called a **key matrix**. Electricity flows through the circuit board, but the circuit for each letter is not complete so nothing happens. Then when you press a key, it lowers a contact that completes the circuit, like with a jumper. The keyboard contains a processor that monitors the key matrix and determines at what spot a circuit is completed, and then uses that data to send a byte representing that character to the PC.

Data is sent serially to the PC, either through the keyboard interface or through a USB interface. Data comes from the keyboard in 11-bit packets. Each packet contains eight data bits (the 1-byte unique code for the character that was typed); the other three bits are for administrative use and contain info that aids the transfer.

Adjusting Keyboard Operation

Most keyboards have a 16-byte buffer that can continue to accept input when the computer stops accepting it. You might have noticed at some point when the computer stops responding, you can continue to keep typing for about 16 characters; then you start hearing error beeps. That's the buffer filling up.

When you hold down a key, after a brief delay it becomes **typematic**—that is, the character starts repeating rather quickly on the screen. Windows calls this feature *character repeat*. You can control the amount of delay before a key starts typematic behavior, and you can control the speed at which typematic repetition occurs. One way is with the MODE command at a command prompt, but a much easier way is to set the Keyboard properties in Windows through the Control Panel.

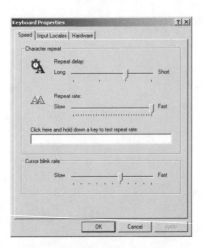

Key matrix
The grid of keys on a keyboard.

Typematic
The quick repetition of a typed character, such as holding down the period key to make a row of dots. Also called character repeat.

Keyboard Types and Features

Until the last few years, all keyboards used the keyboard interface built into the motherboard. However, many keyboards use the USB interface these days, and in future systems, there might not even be a motherboard keyboard connector. There are also wireless keyboards that use an infrared system for connecting to the PC.

There have been many different keyboard layouts over the years, with newer models adding more keys. For example, the original IBM PC keyboard did not have a separate set of arrow keys; the arrow keys were built into the numeric keypad. In addition, the original keyboard had function keys along the side of the normal keys, but in later versions they were moved to a row across the top. Knowing the different keyboard layouts and their differences is not important— just know that not all keyboards have the same keys.

Many keyboards made in the last several years are Windows keyboards. This basically means that they have a couple of extra keys that perform special functions in Microsoft Windows:

◇ The Windows key opens the Start menu (the same as if you had clicked the Start button). There are two of these, next to the two Alt keys.

◇ The Menu key opens a shortcut menu (the same as if you had right-clicked).

Some keyboards have a split design to help users avoid wrist strain. Such keyboards typically have a wrist rest (a sloping platform in front of the keyboard) built into them as well. They are called **ergonomic keyboards**.

And finally, some keyboards have buttons across the top that users can press as shortcuts to issuing commands. For example, my keyboard has a Mute button

Ergonomic keyboard
A keyboard designed to minimize the stress placed on the users' hands and wrists.

that can be used to mute the sound coming out of the sound card, which can be very useful when the telephone rings and I'm in the middle of listening to some heavy metal audio CD!

Keyboard Troubleshooting

Most keyboard problems result either from a defective cable or a stuck key. If the keyboard is not working in general, or if the wrong characters appear onscreen for the keys you pressed, the cable is probably bad. It's easier and usually more cost-effective to buy a new keyboard than to try to disassemble the keyboard to replace the existing cable.

A stuck key at startup could possibly generate an error message. More often the key is not actually stuck but has something leaning on it. For example, if you have books and papers stacked all over your desk, you might have the corner of a book sitting on a key without realizing it. If a key is truly stuck, you can try prying it up gently; if that doesn't work, you can give up and buy a new keyboard or futz around with it for awhile if you've got some time on your hands.

TIP

If the stuck key is a result of spilling sticky liquid inside the keyboard, try washing the keyboard in your dishwasher (top rack, no heated dry). Then let it sit for several days to dry before you try to use it.

Mouse

You already know what a mouse is too, right? The thing that makes the pointer move onscreen. A basic mouse consists of four parts:

- ◇ The body—that is, the part you hold with your hand.
- ◇ A ball that moves as you move the body, or sensors that notice how much you have moved the body.
- ◇ Buttons (usually two or three) that you press to make selections.
- ◇ A cord or wireless interface for transmitting the data to the PC.

The mouse works by converting physical movement to a digital code. The PC then takes that digital code and converts it to pointer movement. It's a type of analog-to-digital converter similar to a sound card or modem, but in this case the analog part is movement rather than sound. (Remember, analog means something that is continuously variable, rather than digitally defined.)

Types and Features

Several interfaces are available for mice. The original mouse interface was a COM (serial) port, because all PCs had them. Then PS/2 style mouse ports became popular. Finally, in the last several years USB mice have begun to be popular. Many mice for sale today come with adapters so you can use them in any of these ports. Because those ports are all serial, the data transfer is the same—bit by bit. The only difference is the connector and the speed at which the data is transmitted. Because a mouse's operation is very low-bandwidth, the speed of the interface is not a big factor.

The basic mouse has a roller ball on its underside and a "tail" cord that connects to the PC. Several variations are available that do away with one or both of those signature features, however. An **optical mouse** uses light sensors instead of a roller ball; the advantage here is that the inside stays clean because there's no ball to convey dirt inside. (See Chapter 1, "Safety and Preventive Maintenance," for mouse cleaning info.) A cordless mouse uses infrared signals to transmit data to the PC rather than a cord.

Instead of a mouse, some users prefer a **trackball**. Take a mouse and hold it on its back, and then roll the ball with your finger. That's the principle behind a trackball. The body sits still and you roll the ball manually. Trackballs are handy

---

Optical mouse
A mouse that uses light sensors instead of a ball to record movement.

Trackball
A mouse alternative in which the body stays stationary and the user rolls the ball manually.

in environments where there is not a lot of space to move a mouse, and for people who have trouble moving a mouse precisely.

Providing a mouse to a notebook PC has been a continual challenge since portable PCs were first invented. Notebook PC users don't want to carry around an external mouse, nor do they have the space to operate one. Early notebook PCs used a pointing stick, which was like a pencil eraser sticking up in the middle of the keyboard. Users could move the pointer onscreen by bending the stick, and then click by pressing buttons below the keyboard. This was awkward at best. Nowadays almost all notebook PCs have a touchpad—a rectangular touch-sensitive pad that you glide your finger across to move the mouse pointer. There are buttons below the touchpad for clicking, but you can also tap the pad to click.

Loading Mouse Drivers

Windows recognizes a mouse automatically (at least in a generic way), so you probably will not need to load a mouse driver in order to use Windows. If you have a mouse or trackball with special features (such as buttons on it that perform special tasks), however, you might need to install the software that came with it in order to enable them.

In MS-DOS, you must load a **real-mode** mouse driver in order for the mouse to work in DOS-based programs. Most mice come with a driver disk containing the needed file. The mouse file usually comes in two versions: MOUSE.COM (which can be loaded from Autoexec.bat or just by typing **MOUSE** at a command prompt) and MOUSE.SYS (which must be loaded from Config.sys).

You do not need to load a real-mode mouse driver when using a DOS-based program from within Windows because Windows takes care of it automatically. Therefore, you will probably never need to load a real-mode mouse driver (unless you spend time working with DOS-only PCs).

Real mode
MS-DOS mode, in which only a single task can be performed at once. MS-DOS operates in Real mode; Windows does not.

Double-click speed
The speed at which one click must follow another in order for the PC to perceive it as a double-click rather than two single clicks.

Adjusting Mouse Operation

Windows' Mouse controls in the Control Panel enable you to adjust several aspects of mouse operation, including the pointer movement, pointer appearance, **double-click speed**, and so on. I won't get into all those here, but you might want to check them out on your own.

Slowing down the double-click speed can be useful when training a novice to use a mouse. Beginners seem to have trouble double-clicking fast enough. They also tend to move the mouse between the clicks.

Mouse Troubleshooting

Here are some ideas for troubleshooting mouse problems.

Windows Doesn't See Mouse

If Windows can't detect a mouse at startup, a message appears to that effect. Check that a mouse is firmly plugged into the PC. Try that mouse with a different PC if there is any doubt as to its working order.

Mouse Pointer Freezes Up

If the mouse pointer works at first in Windows and then stops responding, the problem is likely a device resource conflict. In other words, the mouse wants to use a certain system resource, such as an IRQ, that some other device wants as well. See Chapter 17, "Working with Devices in Windows," to troubleshoot device conflicts.

A problem with an application or with Windows itself could also cause the mouse to freeze up and the entire system to stop responding, but this is not the mouse's fault. The mouse pointer being nonoperational is a side effect of the main problem, which is a program error. See Chapter 18, "Troubleshooting Windows Problems," to troubleshoot system problems.

TIP

To tell whether the mouse is the problem or the whole system is locked up, try using a keyboard alternative for an operation. For example, try closing the active window by pressing Alt+F4, or try opening the Start menu with the Windows key. If you seem to be able to navigate okay with the keyboard, the mouse itself is the problem.

Mouse Pointer Jumps Around

This is almost always the result of a dirty mouse. Clean it, as described in Chapter 1. If it still doesn't work afterward, one of its contacts or rollers inside is probably damaged or worn out—time for a new mouse.

Pointer Won't Move in One Direction

This indicates that one of the directional rollers inside the mouse is either so caked with dirt that it doesn't work anymore or has physically worn out. Clean the mouse; if the problem persists, buy a new one.

Cases

Once you've selected a case for the PC, you can pretty much forget about it. The case doesn't have any electronics of its own (except maybe a couple of lights), or any moving parts for that matter unless you count the power switch.

However, if you do need to select a case (for example, if you're building a PC from scratch), you need to a few things know about them to make the right choice.

Form Factors

Cases have form factors, just like motherboards. You must match up an AT case with an AT motherboard, ATX to ATX, and so on. This is not only so the motherboard will physically fit in there, but also so the connectors to the motherboard will be appropriate. Look back at Chapter 3, "A Closer Look at the Motherboard," for a reminder of the differences between AT and ATX. They include the type of power switch connection, the placement of the ports, and the power supply connector.

Cases also can have one of two orientations: **desktop** or **tower**. A desktop case sits with its largest side flat on the desk, and the monitor usually sits on top of it. A tower case stands up on end. Tower cases usually (but not always) have more drive bays.

Bays

Cases vary in the number of drive bays they have. Different case manufacturers have different names for their sizes of cases, but for exampe, a mini-tower case might have two large and two small external drive bays, while a mid-tower might have three large ones. A full-tower case typically has at least four large and two small external drive bays.

WARNING

When buying a case with a lot of drive bays, make sure you get a high-wattage power supply to go with it (300-watt would be good). All those drives will require a lot of power! See the section on power supplies later in the chapter.

Desktop case
A PC case designed to sit with its largest side flat on a desk.

Tower case
A PC case designed to stand upright.

Electricity Basics

Most PC technicians don't need to work with electricity—at least not much. Nevertheless, the A+ exam has several questions about electricity, so if you want to ace the test you have to study electrical concepts. With that in mind, the following is an extremely abbreviated tutorial in electrical concepts and measurements.

Volts
The measurement of the strength of a positive or negative electrical charge.

Positive and Negative Charge

When you plug in an electrical device to a wall outlet, two prongs must insert into that outlet (some plugs have an optional third prong for grounding). One prong is positive; the other is negative. Electricity flows into the negative prong, through the device, and then back out the positive prong into the socket.

Positives and negatives are very attracted to one another, and they are always looking for any opportunity to get together. (Think Romeo and Juliet—or the neighbor's male cat and your female cat.) Positives are repelled by other positives, and negatives are repelled by other negatives. We start out with a whole bunch of negatives together in one prong of an electrical outlet. They don't want to be there together—they want to go out and find positives. So when an electrical cord is connected to the outlet, the negatives immediately travel down the path provided for them. They travel through the outgoing wire in the cable, up into the electrical device, and the flow of the negatives through the device is like water current that turns a waterwheel. Then they travel down a second wire that leads back toward the outlet, and this second wire points directly into the positive side of the socket.

Volts

The greater the difference in charge between the positives and the negatives, the greater the drive for them to get together and the more power each positive/negative pair supplies on their way to meet one another. This drive is measured in **volts** (v). Ordinary household electricity is 110v in the United States; in some other countries, it is different (such as 220v in most of Europe). It's important that the entire country has a standard agreed-upon voltage because electrical devices are designed to work only with a specific voltage. Too much voltage and a device will fry; too little and it won't work.

The devices in a PC (drives, etc.) each have different voltage requirements. For example, the CPU might need +3.3v and a drive might need +12v, +5v, or both. One of the jobs of the power supply is to step down the 110-volt power to the voltage required by each component.

Amps

There is not just one pair of positives/negatives; there are billions upon billions of them, just like there are billions of water molecules in a rushing river. A single water molecule can't turn a waterwheel; but when billions of them work together, they can make the wheel spin really fast. The volume of electricity is the **current**, just like with water flow. Current is measured in amperes, or **amps** for short.

Watts

Wattage is the overall amount of power a device actually uses. It's determined by multiplying volts by amps. So, for example, a 75-watt light bulb uses 0.68 amps of 110v power (because 110 times 0.68 is approximately 75).

A light bulb is a good example because different wattages of bulbs will work in the same light socket. For example, suppose someone replaces a 75-watt bulb with a 100-watt bulb; the device would still use 110v, but it would draw about 0.91 amps.

This illustrates an important point: the amperage is controlled by the device receiving the power. The device "draws" the amps it needs out of the outlet; the outlet doesn't push the amps onto the device proactively. When several different devices connect to the same extension cord, each one uses the same voltage but different amps, resulting in different wattages.

Resistance

The positives and negatives always seek each other through the shortest, easiest path they can find; this is the path of least resistance. That's not just an old cliché. **Resistance** is an electrical term that measures the amount of obstacle placed in the electricity's path, and it's measured in **ohms**. The Greek omega symbol (Ω) represents ohms as a unit of measure.

Resistance measurements are used to describe the path(s) that electricity can take. Given the choice, the electricity will always prefer the lower resistance. Electricity needs a resistance of less than 20 ohms in order to be able to connect negative and positive. Infinite ohms (abbreviated with the "infinity" symbol ∞) means there is total resistance—that is, no possible path.

Resistance does not have anything to do with any of the other factors discussed so far—it's a measure of the device itself. So resistance is always tested when the device is removed from any power source. Why? Because a device will always

Current
The volume of electricity flowing through a circuit. Measured in amps.

Amps
Short for amperes. A measurement of electrical current or rate of flow.

Wattage
The amount of electricity a device uses, determined by multiplying volts by amps.

Resistance
The amount of obstacle in an electrical path.

Ohms
The unit of measurement for resistance.

have the same resistance—that is, the same capacity for impeding electricity from passing through it freely—no matter what electricity is available to it.

Grounding

Just as water is always seeking sea level, and will flow downward until it gets there, electricity is always seeking the ground. When people get struck by lightning, the electricity takes a path to the ground through their bodies. When birds sit on an electrical line, they don't get electrocuted because they are not touching the ground. The electricity has no reason to pass through the bird's bodies because the birds do not offer a path to the ground. If a bird (okay, a *really big* bird) were to put one foot on the wire and the other foot on the ground, the bird would get fried, as would a human.

Remember back in Chapter 1 when we talked about the importance of grounding with static electricity? That same principle is in effect for the power coming from the wall outlet to the PC as well. The third prong on a connector—the round one—is a ground line, and it plays no role in the normal in-and-out electrical flow through the socket. Instead, it's there to provide a path of very little resistance to the ground should it be needed (for example, if a short-circuit occurs that dumps a lot of electricity into the system at once). It's a safety feature—nothing more.

AC versus DC

Earlier I explained how the negatives travel from one of the holes in the wall outlet to the other, looking for positives. That was an oversimplification. In fact, the holes alternate between being positive and negative many times per second. The speed at which they alternate is measured in cycles per second, or hertz (Hz). Ordinary household electricity alternates at 60Hz. This type of electrical delivery is called *alternating current* (AC). AC is a more efficient way of sending power over wires, especially over long distances. When devices run on battery power, however, they use *direct current* (DC). With direct current, power always flows the same direction all the time—from negative to positive. Batteries use DC because they have no need to be far away from the devices they power and because it requires lower overhead (which is desirable for a simple, battery-operated system).

PC components require DC power, but the wall outlet supplies AC, so one of the jobs of the power supply is to convert AC to DC. We'll look at this further in the next section.

Power Supplies

Now that you know about electricity, this discussion of power supplies will probably make a lot more sense to you than it otherwise might.

The power supply in a PC takes in 110-volt AC current from the wall outlet and converts it into DC current. It also steps down the voltage and sends different voltages to the various components via the different colored wires. For example, the red wires are for +5v and the black wires are for grounding.

Power supplies come in two styles: AT and ATX. The power supply must match up with the case and motherboard type because the power supply connector on the motherboard is different for each. Besides that, the main differentiation of one power supply from another is in its wattage, which is discussed next.

Wattage Ratings

A power supply has a maximum wattage, such as 200 or 300 watts. The more devices you connect to the PC, the higher wattage power supply you need. That's why cases with more drive bays usually come with higher wattage power supplies than smaller cases—because there is the potential for hooking up more drives that each need wattage.

Remember, wattage is voltage times amps, and each device draws amps as needed. To determine what wattage power supply a system needs, you multiply the volts by the amps for each device and then add the answers together.

Many devices indicate on their label the amount of amps they draw, like this CD-RW drive, for example:

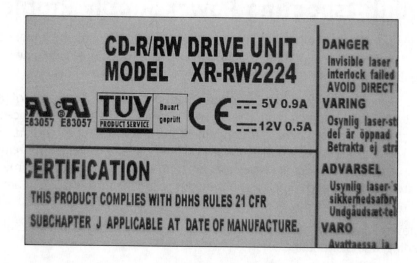

This drive uses 0.9 amps of +5v power and 0.5 amps of +12v. That's (0.9× 5) + (0.5×12), or 10.5 watts.

Not all devices say so clearly how much they draw, so use this list as a rough, conservative estimate:

- A motherboard: 20 to 30 watts
- CPU: 30 watts for Pentium II or III; 65 watts for Pentium 4, 70 watts for Athlon
- An AGP video card: 20 to 50 watts
- An average PCI circuit board (including video card): 5 watts
- An average ISA circuit board: 10 watts
- Floppy drive: 5 watts
- CD-ROM drive: 10 to 25 watts
- RAM: 8 watts for every 128MB
- IDE hard drive: 5 to 15 watts
- SCSI hard drive: 10 to 40 watts

Name-brand PCs usually come with power supplies with adequate wattage, so the main occasion for worrying about wattage would be if you were assembling a PC from scratch and needed to select the power supply appropriate to the components you were going to put into it. The A+ exam doesn't go into too much depth about wattages—you don't need to know the specifics for any particular device type, for example. The main thing to remember is the formula:

$$\text{volts} \times \text{amps} = \text{watts}$$

Troubleshooting Power Supply Problems

A dead power supply is just that: dead. The fan won't spin; the PC won't start up. If you've got one of these, swapping out the power supply with a new one is the first thing to try.

A partially failing power supply, on the other hand, can cause all sorts of problems that do not appear to be directly related, leading the less experienced technician on a wild goose chase through memory, processor, motherboard, and hard disk errors. When troubleshooting an intermittent problem that seems to jump around—for example, a memory problem that reports a different memory address as faulty each time, or spontaneous rebooting after a random amount of time—suspect the power supply.

A power supply can cause a problem for three reasons: physical failure, overloading, and overheating.

In a physically failing power supply, the power supply is not generating its rated amount of power, or it is providing the wrong voltages on some wires. The PC generally will not start at all if such a condition exists. See the next section, "Testing a Power Supply," for help determining whether a power supply is working correctly. Replacing a faulty power supply is the best solution; repairing power supplies can be dangerous for inexperienced technicians, and it is seldom cost-effective.

On an overloaded power supply, there is not enough wattage to support all the devices plugged into it. On a system with an overloaded power supply, problems will often occur at startup, when all the drives are spinning up, or when accessing a drive. See the preceding section to calculate how much wattage the system needs. Then replace the power supply with a higher-wattage model if needed.

Overheating happens when the power supply fan (or in some cases the processor cooling fan) is not doing its job adequately, or when the system case's airflow is obstructed. Most computer cases are designed to pull fresh air through the case, across the major heat-producing components. The air flowing through the restricted space is very important. Removing the case cover, or leaving empty-slot backplates off, prevents the air from flowing as designed, and overheating can result. If the system starts up okay but then starts having problems after several minutes of operation, inadequate cooling is almost always the problem. Make sure the airflow path is unobstructed, that the processor heat sink or cooling fan is in place and operational, and that the power supply fan is working quietly and correctly.

Power_Good Wire
Also called Power_OK wire. The wire from the power supply to the motherboard that tests the power supply's performance before the rest of the system starts up.

Testing a Power Supply

When the PC starts up, the power supply sends a signal to the motherboard via the **Power_Good wire** (one of the wires that leads from the power supply to the motherboard). The motherboard looks for a voltage of between +3v and +6v on this wire. When it receives it, it knows the power is "good" and it allows the system to start up. If it doesn't receive it, or if it receives some other voltage, it suspects the power supply is bad and it continually resets itself, refusing to start up. This is a protection system built into every motherboard to prevent damage from a faulty power supply.

Therefore, when you suspect that a power supply is at fault, the first thing to test is that Power Good pin. On an AT power supply, it's the orange wire, the first pin on the P8 connector. On an ATX power supply, it's the gray wire. If those test okay, you can test the rest of the wires too. See the following sections to learn more about it.

Multimeter Basics

Computer technicians use a device called a **multimeter** when taking electrical measurements. The "multi" part of the word refers to the fact that it is actually several meters in one: a voltmeter to measure volts, an ammeter to measure amps, and an ohmmeter to measure ohms. The meter has a dial or switch that can change between the different measurements.

There are two types of multimeters: analog and digital. Remember that analog refers to continuously variable devices. An analog multimeter has a gauge with a needle, and the needle moves to show the measurement. It is continuously variable, meaning that there is no fixed division between one measurement and the next. A digital multimeter, in contrast, has an LED screen that shows the measurement as a number, and the division between one value and another value is mathematically quantifiable.

Analog multimeters are fine for some jobs, but digital ones are much better for working on computer equipment. There are three reasons for this. One is that the digital readout is easier to read accurately. Another is that an analog meter does not show negative voltages; to test something with negative voltage, the probes must be reversed. The final, most important reason is that when a multimeter measures resistance, it sends a small pulse of electricity through the device being tested to see how much it impedes that pulse's progress. Analog multimeters must send a much stronger pulse because they need more electricity to move the needle. This stronger pulse of electricity can damage some sensitive electronic components. A digital multimeter, on the other hand, can use a much weaker pulse that won't hurt anything.

Multimeter

A meter that is capable of taking several electrical measurements, including voltage, amperage, and resistance.

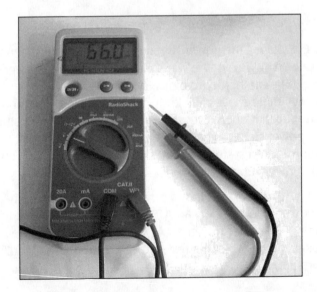

The multimeter has two long skinny probes: one red and one black. The red probe goes on the live wire and the black one on a ground wire, and the gauge reports the measurement. There are typically at least two dials or range selectors: one to switch between the various functionalities (ohms, amps, or volts) and one to switch between ranges. Some newer multimeters adjust the range automatically, so there is no manual selector for it.

Measuring Voltage

Voltage must be tested with the computer on. Because a connector must not be unplugged while the PC is running, you must stick the probe down into the back of the connector, where the wire comes into it. This is called **back probing**. To test a wire, set the multimeter to volts. Then place the red probe as far down as possible inside the connector where the wire in question enters the plug, and place the black probe down inside where a black wire (a ground wire) enters the same plug. So, for example, on an ATX power supply, you would test the Power_Good wire (gray wire) by sticking the red probe down inside the gray wire's hole and the black probe down inside one of the black wires' holes.

Back probing
Testing electricity while the device is on by sticking the multimeter probes down the back of the connector.

![NOTE icon]

NOTE

Electrical testing is one of the few reasons for working on the inside of a PC while it is running. But you're not really "working on" it in terms of adding or removing anything—you're just running a test. Besides, if you suspect voltage problems, the computer will probably not start up at all, so the fact that the power is on does not mean that the computer is necessarily operating.

If the Power_Good pin tests out okay in the power supply, try testing the other pins. Tables 11.1 and 11.2 list the wires in the two types of power supply connectors and what their voltages should be.

Table 11.1: Voltages for AT Power Supply Wires

Wire Color	Correct Voltage
Orange	Between +3v and +6v
Red	+5v
White	−5v
Yellow	+12v
Blue	−12v
Black	0v (need not be tested)

Table 11.2: Voltages for ATX Power Supply Wires

Wire Color	Correct Voltage
Orange	+3.3v
Red	+5v
Gray	Between +3v and +6v
Purple	+5v
Yellow	+12v
Blue	−12v
White	−5v
Black	0v (need not be tested)

Review Questions

1. A customer is having problems with wrist strain when typing on his PC. What could you recommend that might help?

   _____

2. Where in Windows can you adjust the typematic rate for a keyboard?

   _____

3. True or False: An optical mouse is cordless.

   _____

4. If you have an ATX motherboard, what type of case do you need?

   _____

5. Why do larger cases have higher wattage power supplies?

   _____

6. What is the unit of measure for resistance?

   _____

7. What is the unit of measure for current?

   _____

8. If a device draws 0.7 amps of +5v and 0.5 amps of +12v, how many watts does it use?

   _____

9. What color are the +5v wires on an AT-style power supply connector?

   _____

Terms to Know

- ❏ Key matrix
- ❏ Typematic
- ❏ Ergonomic keyboards
- ❏ Optical mouse
- ❏ Trackball
- ❏ Real mode
- ❏ Double-click speed
- ❏ Desktop
- ❏ Tower
- ❏ Volts
- ❏ Current
- ❏ Amps
- ❏ Wattage
- ❏ Resistance
- ❏ Ohms
- ❏ Power_Good wire
- ❏ Multimeter
- ❏ Back probing

Chapter

12

Printing Basics

Now that you've mastered the hardware basics for PCs themselves, let's look at the printer, the other "big gray box" on your desk. Data goes in; printouts come out. But how? In this chapter, you'll find out. This chapter explains the basic components of a printer, like memory and fonts, and then looks briefly at what differentiates one type of printer from another and what can go wrong with a printer. The topics covered include:

 Common printer features

 Measurements of printer performance

 Types of printers

 How a printer communicates with a PC

 Cleaning a printer

 Printer troubleshooting

Common Printer Features

No matter what type of printer you have, it works basically the same way conceptually. So before we get into the differences, let's first look at the similarities.

Line printer
A printer that prints one line of a page at a time.

Page printer
A printer that waits until it has a whole page of data in its memory and then prints the entire page at once.

Sheet fed
A paper feed system that uses individual pre-cut sheets of paper.

Tractor fed
A paper feed system that uses continuous paper (where one sheet is attached to the next at top and bottom) and pulls the paper through the paper path with gears that grab onto perforated holes on the sides of the pages.

Electronic Control Unit

The Electronic Control Unit (ECU) is a circuit board or a series of boards that handles all the "brain" functions of the printer. The incoming data goes to the ECU, and the ECU gives commands based on it. The ECU tells all the mechanical parts when and how to operate—when the paper should feed, how much ink should be dispensed, what image should be created on the paper, and so on.

Memory (RAM)

A printer has some RAM, just like a PC does. A printer's RAM holds any fonts that the operating system has downloaded to it, plus it acts as a holding tank and funnel for the incoming print data.

The amount of memory a printer has depends partly on the type of printer. Printers can be broken down into two categories: line printers and page printers. Line printers require much less memory.

A **line printer** accepts data from the PC and prints it out one line at a time; examples include inkjet and dot matrix printers. The paper feeds through gradually as the printer continues to accept data for that page from the PC. Because it does not need to hold the entire page of data in its memory before it begins printing, a line printer needs only a few kilobytes of memory—enough to hold a single line. If it has more memory than that, the extra memory functions as a buffer to hold incoming data until the printer is ready for it. With line printers, the amount of memory is not an important issue.

A **page printer**, in contrast, accepts data from the PC and holds it in its memory until it gets a full page; then it prints it all at once to the page. A laser printer is the most common type of page printer. Because it must compose the entire page in memory, a page printer requires quite a bit of memory. Very old laser printers came with only 512KB of memory, but this was not enough for a full-page graphic and, therefore, out-of-memory error messages were common with those printers. Today's laser printers all come with at least 2MB of memory—usually more.

Paper Transport System

The paper transport system is a series of gears, rollers, grabbers, etc. that feeds the paper through the printer. Depending on the type of printer, it could be a set of rollers that pull in single sheets at a time, or it could be a set of tractor-feed gears that pull through a continuous stream of paper.

All printers have a means of feeding paper in and out. Most printers today are **sheet fed**, which means they use individual pre-cut sheets of paper. The exception is dot matrix printers (which are uncommon these days but do still exist); these are **tractor fed**. They use continuous paper and employ a system of gears to pull the paper through by means of perforated holes on the sides.

Printing System

All printers have a way of making marks on the page—the printing system. The printing system varies depending on the type of printer. In an inkjet printer, it's the ink delivery system; in a laser printer, it's the system that writes to the drum, applies the toner, and fuses it to the paper. Later in the chapter, I'll discuss the types of printers in more detail.

ROM and Fonts

Just like a PC, a printer has some Read Only Memory (ROM) that contains its startup instructions (for self-testing, etc.) and any built-in **fonts**. All printers have at least one **resident font**, which is used to print test pages. A resident font is one that's built into the printer itself—that is, the printer is not dependent on the PC to provide it. Most printers have at least two or three.

When you install a printer driver in Windows, the driver knows what resident fonts the printer has, and it makes them available in your applications. If you want to print using a font that the printer does not have, you must download a **soft font** (that is, a software version of the font) to the printer. Windows does this automatically when you send a document to the printer that requires a font the printer does not natively have. Windows comes with several **TrueType** soft fonts, which are scaleable to any size and work with any printer and any Windows program.

Viewing Installed Fonts in Windows

To see what soft fonts are installed, open the Fonts utility in the Windows Control Panel. Notice the different icons for the fonts. The O icons are for OpenType

---

Font
Strictly defined, a particular typeface at a particular size. However, *font* has lately come to be synonymous with *typeface*.

Resident font
A font that is stored in the printer's ROM and is available at all times, regardless of what PC is connected to it.

Software font
A font provided to the printer via software stored on the PC.

TrueType font
A software-based outline font that works with any Windows-supported printer and application. TrueType fonts are also used on Macintosh computers.

fonts, an improved version of TrueType that comes with Microsoft Office XP and Microsoft Windows XP. The TT icons are for TrueType fonts. The A icons are for fonts that are neither OpenType nor TrueType. You can see a sample of a font by double-clicking it.

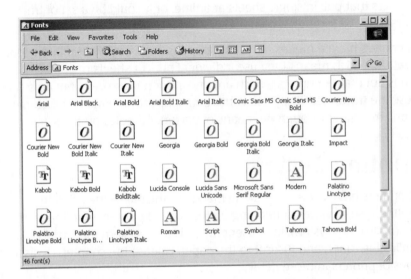

The Fonts folder is a real folder on your hard disk, in the Windows folder. But instead of just copying font files into that folder, you should properly install them to make sure they are registered in the Windows Registry. Here's how:

1. Open the Fonts folder from the Control Panel in Windows.
2. Choose File ➢ Install New Font.
3. Navigate to the drive and folder containing the font(s) to install.
4. Select the font(s) to install. Then click OK to install the fonts.

Measurements of Printer Performance

Choosing a printer is a complex matter—you must think about the printer's technology, the paper tray size, the resident fonts, and many other factors. However, when it comes right down to it, the two most important factors are

- ◇ The quality of the output
- ◇ The speed at which the output occurs

Print Quality

One of the most critical factors in a printer's output quality is the resolution at which it prints. **Print resolution** refers to the fineness of the individual dots that make up the printout. On modern printers, print resolution is measured in dots per inch, or **dpi**.

Page printers typically have only one dpi measurement that refers to the dot spacing both vertically and horizontally. That is, a 300dpi printer will print 300 dots per vertical inch and 300 dots per horizontal inch, for a total of 9,000 possible dots per square inch. Some line printers, however, will have two separate measurements for vertical and horizontal, such as 720×1440. The first number is the horizontal; the second is the vertical.

Most printers enable you to use them in any of several different resolutions; the lower the resolution you choose, the faster the printing speed. Look for a resolution setting in the printer driver's Properties box—see "Printer Drivers" later in this chapter for help.

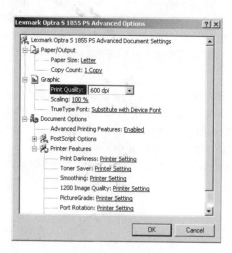

Print resolution
The number of individual dots that make up a printed image, measured in dpi.

Dpi
Dots per inch, a measurement of printer output quality.

Ppm
Pages per minute, a measurement of printer output speed.

Color is also an issue if the printer is capable of color output. The original printers were black ink only; color printers are a relatively recent innovation. Some printer technologies, such as inkjet, translate naturally and easily into color. Color inkjets are now the norm; you'd be hard-pressed to find a black-only inkjet on the market today. Other technologies, such as laser, are very difficult to convert to color output, so color models of these printers are very expensive and high-end.

Some printers produce much more accurate color output than others. There is no industry-wide rating system for evaluating color quality on a printout; you have to see a sample from a printer and evaluate it subjectively. Various schemes for improving the color accuracy of a printout may be available through the printer driver's Properties; experimentation with these is the best way to figure out which are valuable for your situation.

Print Speed

On very old printers, speed was rated in characters per second (cps). Printer speed on most printers today is expressed in pages per minute (**ppm**). An average speed these days is about 8ppm (higher for laser printers and black-and-white printouts, lower for inkjet printers and color printouts).

A printer's rated speed is its physical maximum—that is, the amount of time it takes for the paper to physically feed through the paper path. If there is any delay while the printer processes data or lays down ink for a complex printout, extra time is required. Therefore, you can't expect to achieve the rated speed in real-life usage. The rated speeds are useful primarily for comparing one printer to another.

As I mentioned in the last section, one way to improve a printer's actual speed is to turn down the resolution. Depending on the printer, there might also be some sort of Draft setting in the Properties that can improve print speed at the expense of print quality. For a color printer, you might also be able to temporarily set it to black-and-white mode to improve the quality of a draft print.

Printer Types

Printer types can be broken into two big categories: impact and nonimpact. This has to do with the way the image is placed on the page.

An impact printer is one that uses physical force to place an image on a page. If any of you still remember typewriters, you'll recall that a typewriter was an impact device. A typewriter used little hammers with pictures of the various letters on them; when you struck a key, the hammer jumped up and hit an inked ribbon, which left ink on the paper behind it. Nonimpact printers squirt or fuse colored material (liquid ink or dry toner) onto a page instead.

The following sections explain briefly how several different printer types work and why you might—or might not—want one of them.

Dot Matrix

Dot matrix printers are impact printers; they strike an inked ribbon with an array of metal pins, forming an image on the paper behind the ribbon.

The dot matrix print head consists of a grid of pins that can pop in or out depending on instructions from the ECU. The pattern of popped-out pins form each character. The original models had only 9 pins, but later models had 24 pins, resulting in much easier-to-read letters.

> **NOTE**
>
> How can only nine pins form a character? Simple—they can't. Dot matrix printers do not print an entire line of text at once; they make two or more passes per line of text. So the pins arrange themselves to print just the top half of a letter in one pass, then the bottom half of it in the next pass.

A dot matrix printer can—in theory—generate any typeface at any size because it's not really printing the letters but only the images of them. However, most dot matrix printers have only two or three resident fonts, so you need an application with software fonts or an operating system that supports TrueType fonts in order to get much font flexibility.

The paper feeds past the print head vertically, and the print head moves horizontally. Sprockets in the sides of the printer pull continuous-feed paper through by grabbing onto the holes along the sides of the paper. After the printing, the rows of holes can be removed by tearing off the perforated edges.

Dot matrix printers are mostly obsolete now, but some businesses still use them for multipart forms that need an impact strike to make several carbon copies at once. Dot matrix printers are also very economical to operate because they use low-cost ribbons rather than the more expensive ink or toner cartridges of other types of printer.

Laser

The main problem most people had with dot matrix printers was the print quality. It just didn't look as good as output from a typewriter, even at the highest quality printing modes. Laser printers solved this problem by producing extremely high quality output (300dpi on the early models) that looked even better than a typewriter's. Laser printers remain the workhorses of business today because they continue to produce beautiful text output—nowadays in resolutions of up to 1200dpi.

Laser printers are page printers—they form the entire page's image in memory and then transfer it all at once to the page. Therefore, the amount of memory a laser printer has is significant, as is the speed and power of the printer's ECU.

If you are old enough to remember mimeograph machines, they provide an excellent analogy to the way a laser printer works. Recall that a mimeograph machine took a typed sheet of paper and wrapped it around a metal cylinder. As that cylinder rotated past ink and then paper, it created copies of the page clinging to the drum. That's what a laser printer does except electrical charges cling to the drum and pick up toner. The drum has a very powerful negative electrical charge, and a laser neutralizes the charge in certain spots. When the drum passes by a reservoir of toner, the toner jumps out and clings to the neutralized spots. Then when it passes by some paper, it jumps off onto the paper, and a heater fuses it there.

If you take the A+ exam, you will need to memorize the sequence of events involved in laser printing. Here are the events, which you can study now or just file away for future reference:

Cleaning   All remnants of the previous print job are scraped off the drum with a cleaning blade, and any residual electrical charges are removed.

Conditioning   The **primary corona wire** applies a uniform negative charge of −600v to the drum's surface.

Writing   The laser sweeps across the drum's surface, turning itself on and off at precise moments. Wherever the laser was on, the drum surface charge is reduced to about −100v. The image of the entire page is written to the drum this way.

Primary corona wire
A negatively charged wire in a laser printer that applies a uniform −600v charge to the drum in preparation for writing a page image to it.

Developing   The drum rotates past toner on a developing cylinder, which has the same 600v charge as the un-lasered portions of the drum. The areas of lesser negative charge on the drum attract the metallic toner, which jumps onto the drum and sticks to it at those spots, but the toner and the drum ignore one another in the spots where the charge is the same. Now the image of the page exists on the drum in toner.

Transferring   The **transfer corona wire** applies a +600v charge to the incoming paper. When the paper passes by the drum, the −100v toner particles on the drum jump off onto the paper because its positive charge, at 600v, is greater than the drum's negative charge at 100v. Then the paper runs past a static charge eliminator, a row of metal teeth with a negative charge that neutralizes the paper's high positive charge.

Fusing   At this point, toner is held on the paper by gravity and weak electrostatic forces. The fuser applies pressure and heat to the paper, melting the plastic resin particles in the toner so that they stick to the paper. The paper then ejects from the printer.

Color laser printers are typically much m̶o̶r̶e̶ than regular ones because the laser printing technology does̶ ̶ ̶ ̶ ̶ ̶ readily to multicolor printing. To print in color, a laser p̶r̶ across the same page, laying down a different co̶l̶ llow, and black). The need for cheap color printin̶g̶ jet printers, which are discussed next.

Inkjet

Inkjet printers are the most popular printers for personal or home use these days because they provide a cheap way for the average person to get color printouts.

Inkjet printers blow jets of ink onto paper. They utilize a nonimpact print technology; the print heads do not touch the paper at all. There are somewhere between 21 and 256 nozzles for each of the four colors (cyan, yellow, magenta, and black) in the print head, and the ECU tells the jets to squirt ink in different combinations and proportions to form whatever colors are needed.

Two technologies are used to force the ink out of the nozzles: thermal and piezoelectric.

A **thermal inkjet printer** heats the ink to about 400 degrees Fahrenheit, which creates vapor bubbles that force the ink out. This creates a vacuum inside the cartridge, which in turn draws ore ink into the nozzles. This technology is also called bubble jet. Most inkjet printers made by Hewlett Packard and Canon use

Transfer corona wire
A wire in a laser printer that applies a positive charge to the paper on which the image will be printed.

Thermal inkjet printer
An inkjet printer that heats the ink to create vapor bubbles that force the ink out.

this technology. Because the heat tends to degrade the print heads over time, ink replacement cartridges for these models often include replacement print heads as well. (That's one reason why you should avoid home-refilling inkjet kits—because when you simply refill the ink, you don't get a new print head.)

A **piezoelectric inkjet printer** moves the ink with electricity instead of heat. The nozzles contain piezoelectric crystals, which change their shape when electricity is applied to them and force the ink out. Piezo technology is newer and is used in most of the inkjet printers sold today by Epson and Lexmark. It's easier on the printer because the printer doesn't need to contain a heating element, and it's better for the output because the ink used is less prone to smearing.

The main gripe people have with inkjets is the cost of operation. The ink cartridges are rather expensive, and they don't last very long, making the cost per page (cpp) very high for inkjet printers compared to laser or dot matrix printers.

Piezoelectric inkjet printer

An inkjet printer that moves the ink through the print nozzles by applying electrical charges to piezoelectric crystals.

How a Printer Communicates with a PC

Now that you know something about how printers work, let's look at how they work with the PC. You need to consider two factors: the physical connection between the pieces of hardware and the printer driver software in Windows.

Physical Connection

The most common way to connect a printer to a PC is through the parallel port. Nearly all printers sold today have a parallel connector.

At the PC end of a parallel printer cable is a 25-pin male connector, which fits into the 25-pin parallel port on the PC. The maximum length for a parallel printer cable is 10 feet; any longer than that and you begin to have problems with the signal breaking up. At the printer end of a parallel printer cable is a 36-pin male Centronics connector. It fits into a 36-pin female connector on the printer, and it is secured in place by wire loops:

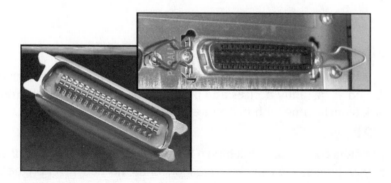

Many years ago, serial printers were common alternatives to parallel ones. Having a serial printer meant that you could have two separate printers on the same PC—one parallel and one serial. Back then, PCs had only one parallel port and it was not as easy to add a second one via an expansion card as it is today. However, serial printers suffered from speed problems. Because a serial cable can send only one bit at a time, rather than a full byte as with a parallel cable, serial printing was extremely slow.

USB is fast becoming a popular way of connecting all kinds of devices to a PC, and it works for printers too. Most printers sold today include a USB connector option, along with parallel. As with other USB devices, the advantages include more foolproof Plug and Play, the ability to connect/disconnect while the PC is on, and higher speed transfers.

Printer driver

A piece of software that acts as a translator and traffic director between a printer and the operating system.

Print spooler

A program that holds print jobs in a queue while they are waiting to be printed. The spooler takes the pressure off the operating system, freeing it to work on other tasks.

> **NOTE**
>
> Printers can also connect to PCs via network interface. There are two ways to use a printer on a network. One is to connect it to a PC, which is then in turn connected to the network; the other is to use a network interface built into the printer to connect it directly into the network, independent of any one PC. You'll learn more about networking in Chapter 13, "Introduction to Networking."

Printer Drivers

The printer and the operating system speak different languages. For them to work together, they need a translator. This translator is the **printer driver**, a file or group of files that take instructions from the operating system and relay them to the printer.

Installing a Printer Driver in Windows

Some printers (particular USB ones) are truly Plug and Play. You connect them, and Windows instantly notices and prompts you for a driver disk. You insert that disk (which came with the printer), click OK, and seconds later you're ready to print.

Other printers come with a full-blown Setup program on a CD-ROM. If Windows detects your printer, you can allow it to look for the needed driver on the CD-ROM, or you can click Cancel and then run the Setup program. Inkjet printers often work better if you run the full Setup program for them because they often have their own **print spooler** software.

If there is no Setup program for the printer, and Windows doesn't detect it automatically, the next-preferable way is to use the Add Printer (or Add New Printer) utility in the Printers folder (Control Panel). This wizard walks you through the process of installing a driver. You'll need to do this if you want to install more than one driver for the same printer, or if you want to set up Windows to use a printer that's not physically connected to your own PC (that is, a network printer).

Changing Printer Driver Settings

Once a printer driver has been installed, an icon for it appears in the Printers folder. To change a printer's properties, right-click that icon and choose Properties. This opens a Properties box with many tabs. Explore these tabs to learn about the settings available for that printer.

The settings are different for different types of printers—that is, inkjets versus lasers, PostScript versus non-PostScript, and so on. However, here are a few settings that they all have in common:

◊ The General tab provides text boxes for naming the printer driver and providing comments and location information. This can be useful if the printer is network-shared and other people might need to know where they can pick up their printouts. The General tab also has a Print Test Page button, which prints a test page (of course!) and a Printing Preferences button that opens a dialog box in which you can set defaults for page orientation, number of copies, and so on.

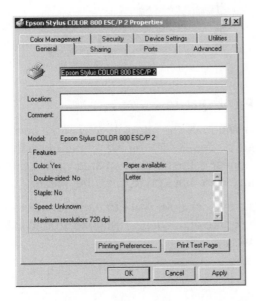

The Sharing tab enables you to share the printer with other computer users on a local area network. See Chapter 13 for more information about sharing a printer.

◊ The Ports tab enables you to select the port to which the printer is attached. This can be useful if you move a printer to a different port and don't want to have to reinstall its driver.

◆ The Device Settings tab is present for all printers, but the options on it are different depending on the printer driver. Some printers have a lot of options here, as shown below; other printers might have only one or two options.

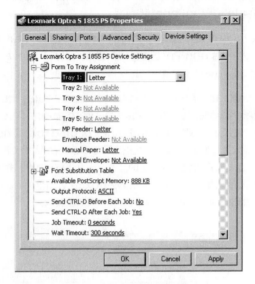

Managing a Print Queue

When you print in Windows, the print job goes into a queue for that printer. You can view the queue by double-clicking the printer's icon in the Printers folder. A printer icon may appear in the notification area while a printer's queue is active. If so, you can double-click that icon to open the queue.

From the printer's queue window, you can pause or delete individual jobs or pause or purge the entire print queue. Just poke around in the menu system to see what's available.

Cleaning a Printer

All printers tend to accumulate paper particles and dust inside, and they must periodically be cleaned to remove it. The best tool for this job is a soft cloth; don't use a vacuum because the toner particles can get through the vacuum filter and circulate in the air, where people could breathe them in and get sick. You will probably want to wipe down the outside of the printer casing as well occasionally, if only for cosmetic reasons, and make sure no dust balls are accumulating near the vents.

Some printers have specific cleaning routines or features. For example, some Hewlett Packard laser printers have a cleaning procedure that involves running a sheet of paper through the printer so that a uniform layer of black toner is printed on it, and then running the same sheet back through again. This removes excess paper and toner particles on the fusing assembly.

Some laser printers have a removable felt pad on a plastic mounting that you must change every time you change the toner cartridge. (For such printers the felt pad comes with the new toner, so you don't have to buy the pad separately.)

Inkjet printers periodically must have their inkjets cleaned to ensure smooth operation. In the printer's manual, you should be able to find instructions for running this cleaning utility by pressing certain buttons on the printer in a certain order. You can also initiate the cleaning from Windows through the properties for the printer driver.

Print quality problems such as white or black streaks on the page of a laser printer's output are often caused by dirty corona wires. As you learned earlier in the lesson, the primary corona applies the negative charge to the drum and the transfer corona applies the positive charge to the paper. The primary corona is usually inside the toner cartridge; the transfer corona is somewhere near where the paper enters. One, both, or neither may be accessible, depending on the model. (In some newer models, the functions of the corona wires have been taken over by other technology, so they don't exist. Check your manual.) If a corona wire is accessible, you can clean it either with a special cleaning tool or with an alcohol-dipped cotton swab. Be very careful, though; too much pressure and the wire will break.

Common Printer Problems

Here are some ideas for troubleshooting problems with printers.

Paper Jams

With laser printers, because they run at faster speeds than other printers, most errors occur due to paper jams. Other printer types can also have jams too.

A lot of paper jam problems can be avoided simply by using the right type of paper. Any paper that is extra-heavy (more than 24 pounds) or extra-light (less than 16 pounds), or is torn, curled, or wrinkled is likely to cause a jam—so is paper that is heavily textured or embossed. Paper jams can also be the result of paper and toner particles inside the printer, so clean the printer thoroughly as a first step. See the printer's manual for instructions.

Sometimes when the humidity is high, the paper can stick together in the paper tray, feeding multiple sheets at once and causing jams that way. To avoid this, take the paper out and fan it.

If you're still having jam-ups, check to see whether the printer has some sort of control that specifies the thickness of the paper it is using. If this adjustment does not match the actual paper in use, jams can result.

If none of these solves the problem, and the printer is old, perhaps the paper feed rollers are getting worn and too smooth. Try roughening them up slightly with a kitchen pot-scrubber or fine-grain sandpaper. This helps the paper advance through the feed mechanism.

Laser Quality Problems

Here are some common problems with laser output:

Printout faint in some spots   This can happen when the toner in the cartridge starts running low. Take out the toner cartridge and shake it from side to side several times (never up-and-down, or it could spill). Then put it back in and it should be good for another 100 pages or so.

Faint printing can also be the result of the drum reaching the end of its useful life. On printers where the drum and toner are separate, the drum has a longer life but must eventually be changed. Such printers usually have a print density control that adjusts the amount of toner used for each page. When the drum is new, this setting should be on Low, but as the drum ages, you might need to turn it up gradually to compensate for the drum's growing ineffectiveness.

Faint printing can also indicate a dirty transfer corona. Remember, the transfer corona charges the paper so that the toner on the drum will be attracted to it. If the transfer corona is dirty, the paper doesn't receive the full charge and the toner isn't as attracted.

Loose or smeared toner   A tiny bit of loose toner now and then might simply mean the printer is dirty inside and needs to be cleaned. However, if the toner is consistently loose and the image suffers, the fuser is probably not heating well enough to melt the plastic resin in the toner.

Vertical white streaks   This can indicate dirty corona wires. Clean them if possible.

Gray mist   If the whole page looks like it has been airbrush-painted with a fine mist of toner, the corona wires probably need to be cleaned. If could also be the result of the print density control being turned up too high or of the drum not holding a strong enough charge.

Horizontal black lines   This is usually a dirty or damaged roller problem. You can measure the distance between the black lines to determine which roller is the problem, but the rollers on different models are different sizes so you must consult the printer manufacturer for help.

Regularly spaced splotches   Probably a scratched or dirty drum.

All-white page   Broken transfer corona, or the printer is out of toner.

All-black page   Broken primary corona. If the drum is not charged enough, the toner will jump off indiscriminately onto the drum, resulting in a full page of toner.

Inkjet Quality Problems

Quality problems with inkjets are usually the result of empty or dried-up ink cartridges or clogged print heads. This could manifest itself as one color being entirely missing, as odd discolorations, or as colored stripes on the printout.

If your printer has a self-test, run it, and see which color(s) are missing, either entirely or in spots. Then check the ink to make sure you have plenty of ink of that color in the printer.

If lack of ink is not the problem, try running the head-cleaning utility, and then run the self-test again. If you see a little improvement after the cleaning, clean again. Keep cleaning until you are not seeing any more improvement or until print quality is acceptable.

Platen
The roller bar behind the ribbon on an impact printer that absorbs the impact and keeps the paper in place.

Review Questions

1. Why does a laser printer require so much more RAM in it than an inkjet printer?

2. What type of printer is commonly associated with tractor-fed paper?

3. What are some advantages of TrueType fonts?

4. How do you install a new font in Windows?

5. What is the unit of measure commonly used to express printer resolution?

6. An inkjet printer advertises a maximum print resolution of 720×1440. What is its horizontal resolution?

7. Which type of printer would you want to buy if you needed to print on multipart carbon copy forms?

8. At what step during the laser printing process does the toner jump off onto the drum and cling to the areas of lesser negative charge?

9. Name at least two interfaces a printer might use to connect to a PC.

_____

10. What needs to be done if an inkjet printer's output has colored stripes on it?

_____

Terms to Know

- ❑ Dpi
- ❑ Ppm
- ❑ Primary corona wire
- ❑ Transfer corona wire
- ❑ Thermal inkjet printer
- ❑ Piezoelectric inkjet printer
- ❑ Printer driver
- ❑ Print spooler
- ❑ Platen

Chapter

13

Introduction to Networking

When I began studying computer hardware, networking was the hardest thing for me to master because I had the least opportunity for practice with it. Consequently, it intimidated the heck out of me for longer than I care to admit. Don't let that happen to you! Networking is really not all that complex or mysterious, and you can set up a simple network for practice with as few as two computers.

This chapter covers the following topics:

 Basic network concepts

 Hardware required for networking

 Connecting a simple peer-to-peer network

 Sharing files and printers

 Accessing shared resources

Basic Network Concepts

In the next several pages, I'll run through some networking vocabulary words that you might hear thrown about, and I'll break down networking in several different ways so you can see how an average network fits together. You'll need to know this stuff if you decide to take the A+ exams.

A **network** is a group of computers connected together so they can share resources such as hard disks and printers. A network can also serve as a conduit to other resources. For example, you can share an Internet connection over a network, so that all the PCs in the network can take advantage of the same single high-speed connection. The Internet is really just a big file-sharing system, after all—a way of linking up millions of networks to one another.

A **Local Area Network (LAN)** is a network in which the computers are located near one another. "Near" is rather subjective here; some people consider a network a LAN if all the PCs are located in the same building, for example, while other people would say a LAN exists if the computers are in adjacent buildings as well. A **Wide Area Network (WAN)** is a network where the computers are not near each other. The Internet is the biggest example of that.

Peer-to-Peer versus Client/Server

There are two basic network architectures: client/server and peer-to-peer.

A **server** is a computer that exists only to serve the needs of the other computers in the network. It manages the network traffic between the **client** PCs (that is, the PCs that are in everyday use by end users) and serves as a central storage repository for files that users want to make available to other users. A **client/ server network** is a network that includes one or more servers and one or more clients. Almost all business networks are client/server. The advantage is that the server(s) handle the network overhead, so the client PCs' performance does not suffer. The disadvantages are that you must have at least one PC set aside to be the server and it must have a special server version of the operating system.

Network
Two or more computers connected together to share resources.

Local Area Network
A network in which all the resources are located near one another.

Wide Area Network
A network in which resources are separated physically from one another (not in the same building).

Server
A computer that serves data to other PCs and provides access to network resources.

Client
A computer that uses network resources as an end user.

Client/server network
A network that includes both client and server PCs.

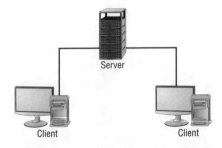

230

NOTE

A network can have more than one server. Big corporate networks often have lots of servers, each with a specific function such as file server, print server, Internet hosting server, and so on.

Peer-to-peer network
A network that consists only of clients, with no central server.

Network topology
The physical layout of a network.

A **peer-to-peer network** has no central server; each of the client PCs takes on a portion of the burden of maintaining the network. For example, instead of a server managing the traffic, all the PCs in the network listen for traffic and grab any messages that are addressed to them. Instead of a server storing shared files, the shared files remain on the client hard disks. Whenever someone wants to access them, the client hard disk reads the file and the OS sends it down the network pipeline. Small networks (under five computers or so) work very well in peer-to-peer formation, but when the number of computers grows beyond that, peer-to-peer traffic begins to become too much of a strain on the participating PCs.

Network Topology

The physical way in which a network is laid out with cabling or wireless connections is called the **network topology**. The topology has nothing to do with whether the network has a server or not. In the following pictures, I've made them all clients, but any of them could just as easily have been a server; the server does not need to occupy any particular physical spot on the network.

If you decide to take the A+ exams, you will need to study the various network topologies. Briefly, the ones to know include:

Bus   PCs are arranged in a single line, running from PC to PC in a daisy-chain fashion. Messages travel back and forth along the line.

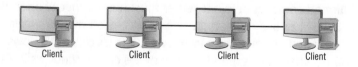

Ring   PCs are connected in a circle. Messages travel around the circle to reach the intended recipient.

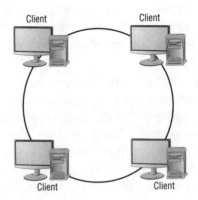

Star   PCs all connect to a central gathering point in the center, such as a hub. The hub then manages the traffic among them.

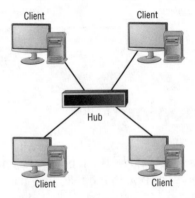

You'll need to know a lot more about these topologies if you get serious about networking, but since we're just doing the once-over-lightly treatment here, let's leave it at that.

Network Operating Systems

As I mentioned earlier, a network server must have a special operating system version; it can't just use ordinary Windows. Microsoft makes special versions of Windows designed for servers; for Windows 2000, it's called Windows 2000 Server. (Catchy name, eh?) The high-end version of it is called Windows 2000 Advanced Server. A peer-to-peer network doesn't have a dedicated server, so it doesn't need a special operating system; all the PCs in it can use their regular client versions of Windows.

Windows Server is not the only **Network Operating System (NOS)**, however. Novell NetWare is another popular NOS. A NetWare server runs NetWare as its operating system, but client PCs can run any ordinary operating system that includes NetWare drivers in it. (All versions of Windows do, for example.)

Types of Networks

One of the reasons that people get so stressed out about "learning networking" is that there are so many ways of breaking a network down. So far we've looked at client/server versus peer-to-peer, network topology, and network operating system, but there is one other way to differentiate networks: the network type.

Ethernet is the most popular type of network by far, but there are several alternatives to it including Token Ring and Fiber Distributed Data Interface (FDDI). The network type has no direct relationship to the NOS or the topology, but not all topologies and NOSes will work with all network types. For example, an Ethernet network can use either Novell NetWare or Windows Server as the NOS, and it can use either the bus or the star topology.

How a Network Moves Data

From a user perspective, network communications are pretty simple. You hook up some PCs and the cables send the data from place to place, just like the buses do on a circuit board. But there are some rather complex standards and rules for the way data is sent, received, and interpreted. I won't get too deep into that here, but I want you to at least get a feel for the basics of it.

Data Packets

Data is transmitted over a network as bits and bytes translated into electronic signals. In preparation for the transmission, the data is divided into segments, each having a header and trailer attached (like an envelope for mailing). The entire unit is called a **packet**. The data packets are sent as independent units over the network. The packet size varies depending on the NOS. When the receiving PC gets the data, it strips off the header and trailer and reads the data, just like you would open and discard an envelope and read the letter inside.

Network Protocols

Remember how we talked about each piece of hardware speaking its own language and needing a driver to translate for it? Well, networking is the same way. Networks require **protocols** for communication. The protocol determines

---

Network Operating System (NOS)
An operating system designed to help a server PC provide access to files, printers, and other network resources to client PCs.

Packet
A piece of data packaged for network transit, including the data itself plus addressing information. Also called a frame.

Protocol
A language or set of rules for transmitting data between devices.

the type of error checking method; a data compression method, if any; how the sending device indicates that it has finished sending a message; and how the receiving device indicates that it has received a message.

When you install a network card in Windows, you also install one or more protocols to work with it. The most common protocol in Windows-based networking is **TCP/IP**. It's also the dominant protocol on the Internet. However, there are many other protocols as well. For example, IPX/SPX is the standard protocol on Novell networks. NetBEUI is an older, very efficient protocol (that is, small packet size due to smaller headers and trailers) that works well on small networks but is not suitable for large-scale network use.

When you work with the Internet, you encounter other protocols. These are still protocols in the sense that they are languages for exchanging data over a network, but they do not work directly with your network hardware and do not require drivers to be installed for them. They include FTP, HTTP, PPP, POP, IMAP, and SMTP. For more information about them see Chapter 19, "Setting Up Internet Connections."

TCP/IP
Stands for Transmission Control Protocol/Internet Protocol. A communications protocol used on the Internet and in many LANs.

Networking Hardware

Now that your head is probably swimming with all the networking terminology and concepts you've just learned, let's turn to the practical side of things: the hardware you need to buy and install in order to create a network.

Network Interface Card

Each computer in the network needs a network interface card (NIC). This can be a circuit board inserted in a motherboard slot, an external USB device, or a PC Card in a notebook PC.

The NIC type must be matched to the network type. So, for example, if you are creating an Ethernet network, you need an Ethernet NIC. There are several sub-types of Ethernet, each with a different top speed, so when buying a NIC you must make sure you get the right type. The most popular by far is 100BaseT, which can transmit data at up to 100MB/sec. An earlier version of it was 10BaseT, which had a top rate of 10MB/sec. Most NICs for sale today advertise themselves as 10/100BaseT, which means they can work on either speed of Ethernet network. Both have the same type of cable connector on them—an RJ-45 jack, which looks like a wide telephone connector. Here's a picture of a 10/100BaseT NIC:

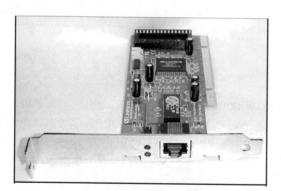

An older type of Ethernet was 10Base2. It transmitted data at a lower speed and used coaxial cable (similar to the kind used for cable TV).

NOTE

NICs can be wired or wireless. Wireless networking connects the networked PCs using radio waves rather than cables. If you have a wireless NIC, you must also have a wireless access point or wireless router for it to communicate. More about those later.

Hub

Most networks these days use a form of the star topology for connecting PCs in a LAN. Sometimes several small stars are connected together, either in a larger star or in a bus arrangement. Recall that a star topology has all the PCs connecting to a central point called a hub.

In my small peer-to-peer network in my home office, I have two PCs connected full-time plus a notebook PC that I connect occasionally. I have a small hub into which each of the PCs connects, and then they can all communicate with one another as if they were all individually connected to each other. Here's a picture of my hub. Large networks have much bigger ones, and even entire closets full of stacks of hubs and other expansion devices such as routers and gateways. (See the section "Expansion Devices" later in the chapter to learn more about those.)

Cables

Assuming you're working with a wired network rather than wireless, you will need some cables. As I mentioned earlier, most Ethernet adapters these days use cables with RJ-45 connectors on them.

This type of cable is called twisted-pair because inside the casing are pairs of wires twisted together. It can either be shielded (that is, protected from EMI) or unshielded. Unshielded is the most common type.

Unshielded twisted-pair (UTP) cabling can be further broken down into categories. You may have heard someone talk about "Cat-5 cabling"—that refers to Category 5 unshielded twisted-pair cabling. You don't need to know the specifics of each category; just know that as the category numbers go up, the speed at which the cable can transmit data increases. Standard telephone cable is Category 1; it can't be used for data. The other categories (2 through 6) are all made for data and transmit data at between 4Mbps and 155Mbps. A 10BaseT network can use category 3, 5, or 6; a 100BaseT network must use category 5 or 6.

Other types of cable are utilized in networking too, but not as often. For example, older Ethernet networks might use coaxial cable, and high-priced, high-speed networks might use fiber optic cable.

Router
A traffic director box on a network that allows data addressed to a PC on a network segment to pass through to that segment while blocking other traffic from entering.

Gateway
A network box that can translate and transfer data between two unlike network systems.

Expansion Devices

For a simple peer-to-peer network, all you need are the NICs, the hub, and the cable. If you start putting together more complex networks with lots of clients and servers located in various departments, you'll need expansion devices to manage things. A hundred computers can't connect to the same hub, for example, and you wouldn't want them to because the amount of traffic would be burdensome. Instead, you would probably break the network into small workgroups of less than a dozen PCs each and then connect the workgroup hubs together.

A hub sends all the traffic to all the PCs connected to it, but you can get better network performance by assigning each PC a specific address and keeping the traffic within that network segment separate from the outside traffic. **Routers** are hub-like devices that intelligently manage the traffic flow, so that only traffic addressed to a PC on a particular segment gets routed into it.

Networks can only connect with other networks of the same type by default. If you need to connect an Ethernet network to a Token Ring network, for example, or to a Macintosh computer network, you need a device that can translate between the two systems: a **gateway**.

Wireless Networking

The latest thing in local area networking is wireless Ethernet, a.k.a. IEEE 802.11b (another catchy name). It works just like regular Ethernet without the cables. Each PC has a wireless NIC, and somewhere within a few hundred feet of the PC is a wireless access point, which is like a hub or router. The PC and the access point exchange signals via a type of radio wave. The wireless access point typically has a connector for hooking into a regular network, so a network can use both wired and wireless technologies for different PCs.

237

Connecting a Peer-to-Peer Network

If you have never constructed a network before, now's your chance to give it a try. All you need are two PCs, two NICs, some cables, and a hub. Then do the following:

1. Install the NICs in each PC.

2. Connect each NIC to the hub via cable.

3. Connect the hub's power cable to the wall outlet.

That's it! You're done with the physical part. You then need to set up Windows networking on each of the PCs, as described in the following section.

Setting Up Windows Networking

The setup in Windows can be easy or difficult, depending on the version of Windows you have. Later versions are much better at automatically configuring networking, to the point where the latest version, Windows XP, can do everything automatically. Earlier versions, especially consumer versions like Windows 95/98, require a bit more manual configuration.

What Windows Needs

To communicate on the network, Windows (all versions) needs the following items to be loaded:

NIC driver   Just like any other piece of hardware, the NIC requires a driver to be installed for it. Most NICs are Plug and Play, so Windows recognizes them and installs the driver for them automatically the first time you start the PC after the physical installation.

Client driver   Windows needs a client driver installed to manage the interface. Usually, this is Client for Microsoft Networks, the default client program, but it could also be Client for NetWare Networks or some other client that came with a different NOS.

Protocol   Windows needs at least one protocol installed that's common to all the PCs in the network. This is usually TCP/IP, but for a NetWare network it might be IPX/SPX.

NOTE

All the Windows stuff in the rest of this chapter is actually pretty simple; it just seems complicated here because I'm trying to cover several versions of Windows. The A+ examinations cover multiple versions of Windows, so as you prepare for the exams, you should try things out in at least a couple of versions if possible. I suggest Windows 98 and Windows 2000. If you don't have two PCs to play with, set up dual-booting (see Chapter 14, "Operating System Basics") or use a utility that lets you run one operating system from within another, such as VMWare (www.vmware.com).

Seeing What's Already Installed

First, let's see what Windows already has installed for you. To do so in Windows 9x/Me, do the following:

1. Open the Control Panel, and double-click Network.

2. Look on the Configuration tab to see what's installed. For example, in the following figure the following items are installed:

   NIC   AMD PCNet Family Ethernet Adapter

   Client driver   Client for Microsoft Networks

   Protocol   TCP/IP

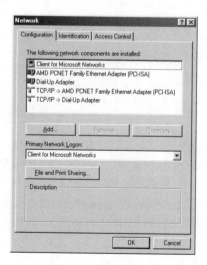

Notice also that a Dial-Up Adapter is installed. This is not a real NIC; it's an interface that enables you to connect to the Internet via a dial-up connection, independently of any network card. You'll learn more about that in Chapter 19.

In Windows 2000, the process is a little different. You install protocols and clients for specific connections rather than in general. This gives you more flexibility. If you already have a network connection configured, you can check out what it uses by doing the following:

1. From the Control Panel, double-click Network and Dial-Up Connections.
2. Right-click the icon for the connection, and choose Properties.
3. Check out the client(s) and protocol(s) installed. For example, in the following figure there are the following items:

   NIC   The NIC is pre-chosen and appears in a gray box at the top. It can't be changed; you must create a new connection to use a different NIC.

   Client driver   Client for Microsoft Networks

   Protocol   TCP/IP

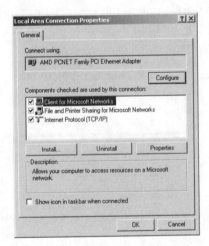

Notice that File and Printer Sharing for Microsoft Networks is also installed. This is a service, rather than a client or protocol. This makes it possible to share files and printers from this PC with others on the network. We'll discuss that more later.

If you don't already have a network connection configured, you can create one by double-clicking New Connection in the Network and Dial-Up Connections window.

Installing the NIC Driver

Installing a driver for a NIC is the same as installing a driver for any other piece of hardware. Run the setup program that came with the device, or use Add

New Hardware in the Control Panel. See Chapter 17, "Working with Devices in Windows," for help if needed.

Installing the Clients and Protocols

In some versions of Windows, a wizard walks you through the steps for setting up a network connection. This setup procedure installs the clients and protocols needed.

- ◇ In Windows 2000, run the Network Connection Wizard by double-clicking the New Connection icon in the Network and Dial-Up Connections window.

- ◇ In Windows XP, run the Network Setup Wizard by choosing Start ➢ All Programs ➢ Accessories ➢ Communications ➢ Network Setup Wizard.

In Windows 95 and 98, there is no wizard; you must install the needed clients and protocols manually if it was not done by Setup when you installed Windows. To do so:

1. Start at the Network window (from the Control Panel).

2. Click Add.

3. Click the category of item you want to install (Client or Protocol). Then click Add.

4. Click Microsoft on the list of manufacturers, and then click the item you want to install. Then click OK.

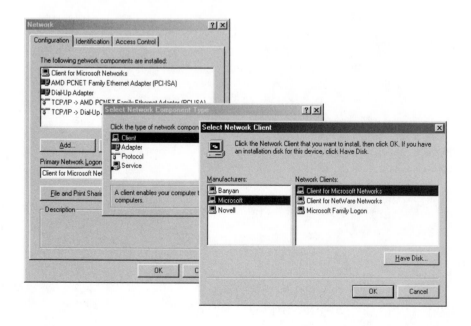

Once you get all the adapter drivers, clients, and protocols installed, reboot the computer and try out your new connection by double-clicking the Network Neighborhood (or My Network Places) icon on the Desktop and then browsing the network resources. (See "Accessing Shared Network Resources" later in the chapter.) If you're setting up your own network and you haven't configured any of the other PCs yet, don't bother—there won't be anything to see. See the following section to learn how to make resources available.

Sharing Files and Printers on a Network

You can share two categories of things on a network: files and printers. "Files" also includes entire folders and drives. By default, nothing is shared. You decide what you want to share with others.

The first step is to install the File and Printer Sharing for Microsoft Networks service if it is not already installed. To do so:

In Windows 95/98:

1. From the Control Panel, double-click Network and then click the File and Print Sharing button.

2. In the File and Print Sharing dialog box, mark both check boxes and click OK.

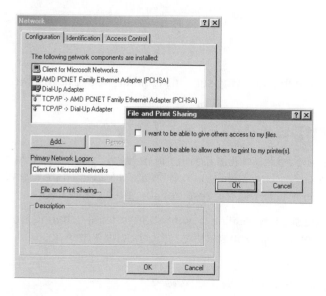

In Windows 2000/XP:

1. From the Control Panel, double-click Network and Dial-Up Connections.
2. Right-click the connection and choose Properties.
3. If File and Printer Sharing for Microsoft Networks does not already appear on the list, click Install.
4. Click Service, and then click Add.

5. Click File and Printer Sharing for Microsoft Networks, and then click OK.

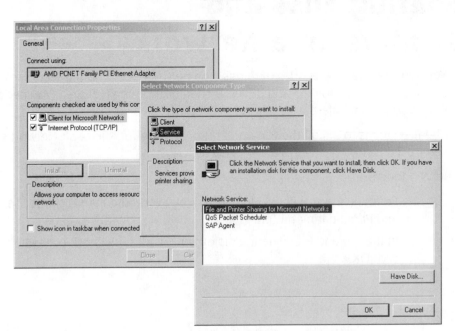

From there, see the following sections to share a specific resource.

Sharing a Folder or Drive

You can't share an individual file on the network; you can share only entire folders and drives. However, you can create a folder, share it, and then put a single file into it, with the end result of sharing a single file.

The following sections outline how to share a folder; sharing a drive is basically the same thing except you start by right-clicking a drive instead of a folder.

Sharing a Folder in Windows 9*x*

To share a folder, first make sure File and Printer Sharing is turned on, as in the preceding section. Then do the following:

1. Right-click the folder, and choose Sharing.
2. Click the Shared As button and then enter a share name in the Share Name box. This can be the same as the folder's real name or a pseudonym.
3. Mark the Read-Only, Full, or Depends on Password option button.

4. Enter passwords in the boxes in the Passwords section depending on your choice in Step 3.

5. Click OK.

Sharing a Folder in Windows 2000 or XP

To share a folder, first make sure File and Printer Sharing is turned on, as in the preceding section. Then do the following:

1. Right-click the folder, and choose Sharing (in Windows 2000) or Sharing and Security (in Windows XP). If you don't see such a choice on the menu, File and Printer Sharing is not turned on.

2. Click the Share This Folder button, and then enter a share name in the Share name text box. It can be the same as the folder's regular name or different—your choice.

3. If you want to establish permissions for the sharing so that not everybody has full access, click the Permissions button, set that up, and then click OK.

4. Click OK to accept the new sharing settings.

Sharing a Printer

Sharing a printer is a lot like sharing a folder except you start by right-clicking a printer's icon in the Printers folder.

1. Choose Start ➤ Settings ➤ Printers.

2. Right-click the printer to share and choose Sharing.

3. Click the Shared As button.

4. Enter a share name. Windows 9x has a separate Share Name box; Windows 2000/XP has a blank box next to the Shared As button.

5. In Windows 9x, enter a comment and/or a password if desired. In Windows 2000/XP, you set passwords and security for the sharing on the Security tab.

6. Click OK.

TIP

Sharing resources can be a lot more involved than what's described here, especially in Windows 2000 and XP. Experiment on your own with the settings on the Sharing and Security tabs for a printer or folder.

Accessing Shared Network Resources

Now let's look at the other side of the equation: accessing the resources that someone else has shared. The sharer will have already gone through the sharing procedures described in the preceding section, so all you need to do is tap into those resources.

Accessing Shared Folders

One way to access a shared folder is to browse the network until you find what you want. The Network Neighborhood (a.k.a. My Network Places) is just like My Computer, except it's for the network rather than your local PC. Just keep double-clicking icons in it to move to the workgroup, then computer, then drive, and then folder that you want to see. Here's a look at the available shared resources (both folders and printers) on a particular PC, for example:

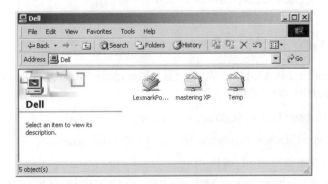

If there's a particular network location you use frequently, you can create a shortcut for it on your Desktop just as you would create a shortcut for any local file. Right-drag it to the Desktop, and choose Create Shortcut(s) Here from the menu that appears. You can also create network shortcuts with the Add Network Place Wizard in the My Network Places folder or the Network Neighborhood folder.

You can also create a shortcut from within an application. Most 32-bit Windows applications enable you to choose Network Neighborhood or My Network Places from their Look In and Save In drop-down lists in the Open and Save As dialog boxes, respectively. From there you can select a network location as easily as you can a local folder.

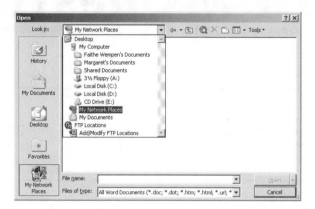

If you run into an application that doesn't let you browse the network as described, you can map a shared folder on the network to a drive letter. This is called mapping a network drive, and it makes a folder on the network show up as a separate drive in any application. To do that:

1. Open My Network Places or Network Neighborhood, and choose Tools ➢ Map Network Drive.
2. Choose a drive letter from the Drive drop-down list.
3. Click the Browse button, and select the folder you want to set up; then click OK to return.
4. Click Finish.

Using a Shared Printer

Setting up a shared printer is a bit more involved—you need to install it as a network printer on your PC and load a driver for it. To do so, run the Add Printer Wizard from the Printers folder and when asked whether it is a local or network printer, choose Network. Then browse the network to locate, and select the printer.

WARNING

If you are using a different Windows version than the PC that is sharing the printer, you might need to provide a disk containing the driver for that printer for your own operating system. Be prepared for that, and if you don't have such a disk, download the driver from the Internet before you start setting up the printer.

Once you've installed the printer, it appears in your Printers folder, the same as any other printer. You can select it from any application that allows you to choose which printer to use for its print jobs.

Review Questions

1. What's a WAN?

2. True or False: A client/server network must have at least one PC functioning as a server.

3. What are the three main topologies used for networking?

4. What is the most popular protocol used on the Internet?

5. What is the fewest number of NICs you can have in a network?

6. The subtypes 10BaseT, 100BaseT, and 10Base2 are all parts of what type of network?

7. What type of cabling would you need for a 100BaseT network connection from a NIC to a hub?

8. What networking hardware would you need to connect two different network types such as a Macintosh network to an Ethernet network?

9. What service must be installed in Windows networking in order to share your printer with others on the network?

_____

10. What must you run to set up your PC to use a printer that some other user on the network has shared?

_____

Terms to Know
- ❑ Network Operating System
- ❑ Packet
- ❑ Protocol
- ❑ TCP/IP
- ❑ Twisted-pair
- ❑ Routers
- ❑ Gateway

Chapter

14

Operating System Basics

The operating system is the software interface between the PC's hardware and the programs that users run to get their work (or play) done. As such, it must translate between the hardware, which likes everything to be in binary code, and the humans, who like friendly little pictures. That's no small task! In this chapter, you'll learn how operating systems do their jobs, focusing mostly on various versions of Microsoft Windows. You'll also learn how to install and upgrade an operating system. The topics we will cover include:

 What an operating system does

 How memory management fits in

 Understanding Windows version numbers

 Installing an operating system

 Upgrading an operating system

 Setting up dual-booting

What an Operating System Does

Operating system (OS)

The system program that runs on the PC all the time and makes it possible for other programs to execute and for the user to issue commands.

Graphical User Interface (GUI)

An operating system that provides a picture-based interface with which the user interacts.

Command line

A line onscreen where user-typed text appears.

The **operating system (OS)** has two functions: to start things up and to keep things running.

When you turn on the PC, it goes through some self-tests (described in Chapter 15, "Starting Up a PC") and then passes control to the OS. From that point on, the OS handles the tasks of loading the needed programs that will display the user interface, load the drivers for the hardware, and execute any programs that are set to load at startup.

As soon as everything is ready to roll, the OS starts its second job, as "site supervisor" of the entire operation. It accepts commands from the user and executes those commands, doing whatever it takes to get the job done—running a program, translating some code for the benefit of a driver, displaying a message, and so on.

Operating systems come in two basic classes:

♦ Command line based, like MS-DOS and some versions of Unix

♦ **Graphical User Interface (GUI)** based, like Microsoft Windows and the Macintosh OS

The difference has to do with the way the OS accepts commands from the user and displays the results of them.

Command Line Operating Systems

A **command line** operating system displays an onscreen command prompt, like this:

    C:\>

The user types on the keyboard, and the words being typed appear next to that command prompt. The user presses Enter to execute that line:

    C:\>COPY A:\MYFILE.DOC C:\BOOKS\MYFILE.DOC

A lot of typing (as well as a lot of command and syntax memorization) is required to use a command line operating system.

Command line OSes are mostly single-tasking systems (although there are some exceptions), which means they do only one thing at a time. They run one command, and then they accept another.

The primary advantage of a command line OS is efficiency. It requires very little in the way of processing power and memory, so even a very old PC can work well with a command line OS like MS-DOS.

GUI Operating Systems

A GUI operating system, such as Microsoft Windows, uses pictures and a pointing device as the primary user interface. Whereas a command line operating system is typing based, a GUI operating system is point-and-click based, making it less intimidating for beginners.

A GUI interface requires much less memorization because users select from menus of available commands rather than relying on memory to determine which command to use in a particular situation.

Users can also **multitask** more freely with a GUI operating system because multiple programs can run in different areas of the screen simultaneously.

The disadvantage to multitasking is its high overhead. Executing the programs required for creating and maintaining the pictures on the screen takes up a good deal of the CPU's time and the RAM's storage space, leaving less for running programs. Therefore, a PC running a GUI OS must have a much more powerful CPU and a lot more memory than a PC running a command line OS. Each successive version of Windows has required more of the CPU and RAM's attention, with the result that only fairly new PCs (a few years old or less) are capable of running the latest Windows versions.

It's All about Memory Management

Later in the chapter, you'll learn about the differences between various versions of MS-DOS and Microsoft Windows; however, for that information to make sense, you first need to know something about how an operating system uses memory.

Conventional and Upper Memory

Remember from earlier chapters that PCs based on the 8086 CPU had only 1MB of RAM. It was divided into two sections. The first 640KB was **conventional memory**, and the rest was **upper memory**. Only conventional memory could be used for running programs and loading the operating system files and drivers; upper memory was reserved for system use. One "system use" was for **ROM shadowing**; another was to serve as a staging area for copying data to and from the RAM on the video card. However, a good deal of the upper memory went unused and wasted.

The main problem with this conventional/upper memory split was that as programs got bigger, they began to require more than 640KB. Additional memory was available in upper memory, but it was reserved and programs couldn't utilize it. More non-reserved memory was needed.

Multitask
To execute more than one program at once.

Conventional memory
The first 640KB of a PC's RAM. Used for running programs.

Upper memory
The last 360KB of a PC's first megabyte of RAM. Reserved for system use.

ROM Shadowing
Copying the data from a ROM BIOS chip into RAM for quicker access to it.

253

Expanded Memory

The next generation of PCs, the 80286s, allowed the use of add-on memory boards with **expanded memory**. Expanded memory was divided into 16KB sections called pages, and a typical expanded memory board contained a couple of megabytes in total. The **page frame**, a 64KB area in the PC's upper memory, could hold four of these pages at a time. Data was swapped into and out of this upper memory area from the expanded memory, enabling the PC to access the full amount of the expanded memory (typically about 2MB, but up to 16MB was available).

A driver for the board was loaded at startup. Each brand of board required a different driver, and only programs written specifically for use with expanded memory could take advantage of it. The standard for expanded memory was called **EMS** (Expanded Memory Standard). Another name for EMS was LIM, which stood for Lotus-Intel-Microsoft (the three companies that jointly developed the standard).

Real and Protected Modes

At this point, Microsoft might have rewritten MS-DOS to allow programs to directly access multiple megabytes of RAM, scrapping the entire conventional/upper memory limitation. If MS-DOS had been rewritten, however, it would have lost all backward-compatibility with older programs, and Microsoft was afraid PC users wouldn't buy it. Their solution was to create two separate modes in which a PC could run. **Real mode** would run all the older programs, and it would be limited to 1MB; **Protected mode** could access up to 16MB of RAM. (Later versions of Protected mode would address even more RAM than that.)

Extended Memory

Soon motherboards began to be built to accept multiple megabytes of memory on them (**extended memory**). Utilizing these advanced motherboards was much easier than utilizing add-on memory boards, so expanded memory quickly became a thing of the past. Concurrently with this advance, programmers began writing applications to take advantage of extended memory using the eXtended Memory Specification (**XMS**).

In order for an application to be able to use XMS memory, a device driver called **HIMEM.SYS** needed to be loaded into memory. It was placed in the **CONFIG.SYS** startup file so that it loaded automatically at startup. A side benefit of HIMEM.SYS was that it enabled another command to be used in CONFIG.SYS (DOS=HIGH) that relocated parts of MS-DOS from conventional memory to the first 64KB of extended memory above the 1MB mark, freeing a few kilobytes of precious

---

Expanded memory
Additional memory over 1MB supplied via an expansion board for 80286 PCs.

Page frame
The 64KB area in upper memory used to swap data into and out of expanded memory.

EMS
Expanded Memory Standard. The industry standard specification for expanded memory usage.

Real mode
A PC operating mode compatible with 8086 CPU operation, addressing only 1MB of RAM.

Protected mode
A PC operating mode compatible with 80286 and higher CPUs, addressing multiple megabytes of RAM.

Extended memory
Additional memory above 1MB on a motherboard.

conventional memory for running programs. This 64KB area is known as **high memory** or the HMA (High Memory Area).

Back then, some applications required the memory to be available in the EMS standard, while other applications required the XMS standard. A utility called **EMM386.EXE,** also loaded in CONFIG.SYS, enabled the OS to take charge of the extended memory so it could emulate whatever type of memory was needed—either EMS or XMS.

On PCs with an 80386 chip or higher, EMM386.EXE also has a side benefit. Remember that as a side benefit HIMEM.SYS loads part of MS-DOS into high memory. EMM386.EXE (when used with the DOS=UMB command in CONFIG.SYS) takes any leftover portions of DOS that could not load into high memory and places them in upper memory, further freeing up conventional memory.

Windows 95 (and higher) handles all memory management automatically, so you do not need to know any of what you just learned in 99 percent of real-life PC technician work today. So why did I go to the trouble of telling you? For two reasons. One is that a familiarity with all these terms will make the next sections of the chapter much easier to understand. Another is that memory management is still part of the A+ exam, and you need to know this stuff to pass.

XMS
Stands for eXtended Memory Specification. A standard for using extended memory in applications.

HIMEM.SYS
A memory management driver loaded at startup that allows programs to use extended memory under the XMS specification.

CONFIG.SYS
A file that lists the drivers that should automatically be loaded each time the PC starts.

High memory
The first 64KB of RAM above the 1MB mark. Also called High Memory Area (HMA).

EMM386.EXE
A memory management utility that allows the operating system to use extended memory to supply either EMS or XMS support to an application as needed.

Windows Versions

It would be easy to say "Every PC should have the latest version of Windows" and leave it at that. But as I mentioned earlier, one of the problems with a GUI is high overhead, and the latest version of Windows will not run on every PC. Therefore, you need a passing familiarity with many older versions of Windows as well as the latest thing.

The following overviews of the various Windows versions are also helpful in understanding how the current version of Windows works, because many of the features that still exist today had their origins in these earlier versions. Rather than trying to absorb the whole picture at once, it's much easier to learn about one version and then build on that knowledge version-by-version until you get the complete story.

Windows 3.1

Windows 3.1 was a whole different "Windows" than the one we know today. To start with, it was not really an operating system, because it required MS-DOS (the "real" operating system) to be running behind it. It was more like an add-on to MS-DOS that enabled people to run Windows-based GUI programs.

Windows 3.1 was a 16-bit system, and it could run either 8-bit or 16-bit programs. At the time Windows 3.1 was popular, people ran a mix of MS-DOS and Windows programs on their PCs, so it was important to be able to leave Windows and get back to the bare DOS prompt to run some of the programs. Windows 3.1 allowed this. Some other features of Windows 3.1 included:

Virtual machines   Windows 3.1 could run either in Standard mode (on 80286s, which was like the old 286 Protected mode) or Enhanced mode (on 80386s and higher, which was a 386-optimized Protected mode). In Enhanced mode, it could run more than one program at once by creating **virtual machines**. A virtual machine is a simulated 8086 CPU operating in its own separate address space. An 8086 CPU can execute only one task at once, but multiple virtual machines running at once results in multiple programs being able to run at once.

Cooperative multitasking   Only one of those virtual machines can use the real CPU at once, but Windows 3.1 could detect when one of them was taking a break and sneak some processing in for one of the others. This gave the illusion that multiple programs were running at once. This is called **cooperative multitasking**. Each application is in charge of signaling to Windows that it is taking a break and releasing its grip on the CPU. This caused problems because not all applications were well-written enough to do this consistently without generating errors.

Virtual machine
A simulated separate CPU that runs programs independently of other activities occurring on the same physical system.

Cooperative multitasking
Multiple virtual machines taking turns using the main CPU one at a time, with each application being in charge of releasing the CPU when it is finished with it.

Data sharing   The Windows Clipboard used a technology called Dynamic Data Exchange (DDE) that enabled users to cut and paste data from one application to another. This was a really big deal at the time, and one of the primary benefits to Windows programs over MS-DOS ones.

Virtual memory   The hard disk could be used to simulate RAM, making it possible to load more programs into memory at once than the physical RAM would support. This was needed because of Windows' ability to run two or more programs at once and also because of its high overhead that ate into the available RAM with its own functions. You learned about how virtual memory works in Chapter 5, "Understanding Memory."

Windows 3.1 had three key components that stayed loaded in memory at all times while it operated: User, Kernel, and GDI. It stored all its system settings in a file called SYSTEM.INI and all its user and program settings in a file called WIN.INI.

Windows 95, 98, and Millennium Edition

Windows 95 was a combination of 16-bit and 32-bit operating system. It could run the 16-bit Windows programs designed for Windows 3.1, but it could also run a new breed of 32-bit Windows programs that worked only with it. For MS-DOS compatibility, Windows 95 allowed MS-DOS programs to run in a window inside Windows, but it also offered an MS-DOS Mode that enabled the system to reboot into a pure MS-DOS environment for running programs that did not work well from within Windows. Some of the benefits of Windows 95 included:

32-bit code   Windows 95 is mostly a 32-bit OS. It retains just enough 16-bit code for compatibility with older applications. It runs 32-bit programs and uses 32-bit device drivers. This is useful because 32-bit programs execute faster.

Preemptive multitasking   Windows 95 allows more than one program to timeshare the CPU, as with cooperative multitasking, but it allows the CPU itself to control the shares doled out to each program. This is **preemptive multitasking,** and it increases stability because the system does not have to rely on the individual programs being correctly written for multitasking.

Plug and Play   With **Plug and Play**, Windows 95 can "talk" to new hardware you install, determine its specifications, and install a driver for it automatically. The actual success rate of the feature has improved in later Windows versions.

Preemptive multitasking
Multiple applications taking turns using the main CPU with the CPU itself being in charge of how much time each application gets at once.

Plug and Play
A standard for devices to talk to operating systems to report their specifications and driver requirements so the operating system can set them up without user intervention.

Windows virtual machines   Windows 95 greatly improves on the virtual machine (VM) concept. Windows 3.1 segmented each running program in a separate VM, but Windows 95 runs multiple Windows programs in a single VM, so they can exchange data more easily.

Object Linking and Embedding (OLE)   Windows 95 greatly improved on the Clipboard in Windows 3.1 by adding **OLE** support. Not only can you move and copy data, but you can create dynamic links between them so that when data changes in one, it also changes in another.

Registry   Rather than storing settings in SYSTEM.INI and WIN.INI, Windows 95 stores all settings in a central location called the **Registry**. The Registry actually consists of two separate files: USER.DAT and SYSTEM.DAT. However, they are accessed as a single unit using the Registry Editor (REGEDIT.EXE).

Windows 98 is nearly the same as Windows 95 in all the important system-level ways. It offers a few improvements, such as support for the FAT32 file system, for USB devices, and for power management.

Windows Me (Millennium Edition) is a minor update to Windows 98. It offers some new utilities and home/small business user features, and it provides wizards that make it easier to perform some complex tasks like setting up a home network. It is not covered on the A+ examinations.

Windows NT and 2000

Windows NT is a whole different class of operating system, predating Windows 95. NT stands for New Technology. It was designed for business use, especially for servers and other mission-critical network PCs. Windows NT did not promise universal backward compatibility; instead it offered a true 32-bit environment, enhanced stability, and solid networking features.

The significant versions of Windows NT were 3.51, which resembled Windows 3.1 in its interface, and NT 4, which resembled Windows 95. We won't get into Windows NT 3.51 here, as it's just too old and hardly anybody uses it anymore.

Windows NT 4 was similar to Windows 95 in appearance, and in many facets of its operation. For example, it used 32-bit code, a Registry, preemptive multitasking, and OLE.

Some of the benefits of Windows NT include:

Server version   Windows NT came in two versions: Workstation and Server. It was the first Microsoft operating system to offer two separate versions,

OLE
Object Linking and Embedding. A standard for sharing information between applications that allows data to maintain a link with its data file and/ or application of origin.

Registry
A configuration file that specifies how Windows 95 and higher will look and act in relation to users, applications, and hardware.

recognizing the different needs of a network client PC versus one operating as a server.

Stability   In Windows 95, when one program crashed, all the other programs usually did too. Windows NT keeps each running program more separate in memory than Windows 95 does, so programs affect each other to a lesser extent.

Security   In Windows NT, you can set up complex systems of security permissions for various individual users and groups.

NTFS   Windows NT supports an alternative file system: New Technology File System (**NTFS**). When you use NTFS rather than FAT16, you gain additional file management features such as the ability to assign permissions to individual files. Windows NT 4's version of NTFS was called NTFS4.

Dual Boot   Windows NT offers the ability to dual-boot—that is, to have both Windows 95 and Windows NT installed on different partitions of the same PC. To set up dual booting, you simply install Windows 95 on the primary partition, and then run the Windows NT Setup program and install it on a separate partition.

WARNING

Windows 95 and 98 cannot read NTFS partitions, and Windows NT cannot read FAT32 partitions. The only common file system they share is FAT16, so if you dual-boot Windows 95/98 and Windows NT, all of the drives that are accessible to both must be FAT16.

One big drawback to Windows NT is that it doesn't support Plug and Play hardware installation. You must run a Setup program to install each device's driver, and you must have a driver disk that came with the device.

The most important thing to know about Windows NT is that it was a precursor to Windows 2000, and that Windows 2000 was built on the same basic technology as NT 4.

Windows 2000 is an upgraded version of Windows NT. It contains all the features and capabilities of Windows NT listed in the preceding section, plus it adds the major Windows 95 features that Windows NT lacked. It also has many new features of its own.

Windows 2000 is built on the Windows NT kernel. That means that Windows 2000's behind-the-scenes operation is much more similar to Windows NT 4 than it is to Windows 95. The way Windows 2000 runs programs is similar to Windows NT (each 32-bit application in its own separate space), and the way it deals with hardware is similar. That's why device drivers designed for Windows NT 4

NTFS
NT File System. The file storage system native to Windows NT, offering efficiency and feature improvements over FAT16.

will probably work in Windows 2000; device drivers designed for Windows 98 probably won't.

Some of the advantages that Windows 2000 offers over Windows NT 4 include:

Windows 95/98 feature integration Windows 2000 supports Plug and Play, FAT32, USB, and ACPI power management, all of which were present in Windows 98 but missing from Windows NT 4.

Different server versions Windows 2000 offers three different versions of the server software. Each is appropriate for a different size of network: Windows 2000 Server for small to medium-sized networks, Windows 2000 Advanced Server for large ones, and Windows 2000 Datacenter Server for extremely large ones.

Active Directory A networking feature that allows all network resources to be administered from a single point. Windows 2000 servers (all versions) provide Active Directory, and Windows 2000 Professional PCs can use the directory.

Dynamic disks An alternative to normal partitioning that stores the disk configuration in a disk management database in the last 1MB of storage on the drive. Dynamic disks offer many advantages over standard disks, such as the capability of being resized and combined with other partitions. However, they cannot be read by any earlier version of Windows or MS-DOS.

Windows XP

Windows XP is the latest version of Windows. It is not covered on the A+ examinations. The main thing to know about Windows XP is that it is the culmination of a 10-year project to merge the two Windows tracks: the consumer side with Windows 95/98/Me and the business side with Windows NT/2000. From an internal standpoint, it is based on Windows NT/2000, so it is very stable, but the user interface is chock-full of features designed to make the average end user feel at home. The end user (client) product comes in two versions: Professional and Home Edition. The Home Edition is the same as Professional except it lacks a few features and utilities and costs about $100 less. The server version is called .NET rather than XP, and it is scheduled for release in early 2003.

Selecting an Operating System

Now that you know the differences between some Windows versions, and the key concepts behind them, you can select the right operating system for a particular PC.

Each version of Windows requires a certain minimum hardware configuration. Table 14.1 lists the requirements. For the A+ exam, you should familiarize yourself with the requirements for Windows 98 and Windows 2000 especially.

Table 14.1: Windows System Requirements

Version	CPU	Memory	Hard Disk	Other
Windows 95	386DX (486 recommended)	34MB (8MB recommended)	50–55MB	VGA monitor, floppy drive, CD-ROM drive if installing from CD-ROM, mouse recommended
Windows 98	486DX 66 (Pentium recommended)	16MB (24MB recommended)	165-355MB	VGA monitor, floppy drive, CD-ROM drive, mouse
Windows NT 4 Workstation	Pentium	16MB (32MB recommended)	110MB	VGA, CD-ROM drive or network access, mouse
Windows 2000 Professional	133MHz Pentium	64MB (more improves performance)	2GB with at least 650MB free	VGA, CD-ROM drive or network access, mouse
Windows Me	Pentium 150	32MB	480MB-645MB	VGA, CD-ROM drive or network access, mouse
Windows XP	233MHz (300MHz recommended)	64MB (128MB recommended)	1.5GB	Super VGA (800×600), CD-ROM drive or network access, mouse

Product activation

An anticopying measure in Windows XP and some other Microsoft applications that makes it nearly impossible to install the software on additional PCs once it has been installed and activated on another PC.

A computer that does not exceed the requirements will likely run Windows very slowly; in all cases, a faster CPU and more memory will improve performance substantially.

Office supply and computer stores will gladly sell you a copy of the most recent Windows version. However, if you decide that an older OS is the right choice for a particular PC, you might need to pick up a used copy. Try eBay (www.ebay.com). If you do buy a used copy, make sure it comes with the installation key code, a 25-digit combination of numbers and letters (usually; original equipment manufacturer (OEM) copies may have different numbers) that you must enter when you install the product.

In addition, if you buy a used copy of Windows XP, make sure that copy has never been activated. **Product activation** locks the installation key code to the hardware on which it was originally installed, so you can't install it on another PC.

Windows Setup

Each version has a Setup program (SETUP.EXE) that guides you through the installation process. Once you get that program started, installation is fairly self-explanatory. There are several ways to run the Setup program:

From an earlier Windows version   If you are upgrading from an earlier version of Windows, insert the CD-ROM and a box should appear informing you that the CD-ROM contains a more recent version and offering to perform the upgrade. Click Yes. Then follow the onscreen instructions. If nothing appears automatically, open My Computer and double-click the icon for the CD-ROM drive, and then double-click SETUP.EXE. See the section "Upgrading from Earlier Windows Versions" later in this chapter for more details.

From a bootable CD-ROM   Most Windows versions come on bootable CD-ROM discs. In order to boot from the CD-ROM, you will probably need to change the boot drive order in the BIOS Setup program. Change it so that the CD-ROM is searched before the hard disk. Then restart the PC, and the Windows Setup program should load from the CD, without any special drivers needed. This is useful for installations on a new or empty hard disk. It works only on systems that have a BIOS that supports bootable CDs.

From CD-ROM at a command prompt   If you have a bootable floppy disk containing CD-ROM drivers, such as one created in Windows 98, you can select the CD-ROM drive (by typing its drive letter and pressing Enter) and then type Setup and press Enter. This is useful for installations on a new or empty hard disk when installing a version of Windows that does not come on a bootable CD. The downside is that you must have a bootable floppy, or you must have access to a Windows 98/Me PC on which you can make one.

From Setup files copied to the hard disk   Some people prefer to copy the Windows Setup files to the hard disk first, and then run the Setup program from the hard disk instead of from CD-ROM. This makes for a slightly faster Windows installation, and it also keeps the Windows Setup files close at hand so you don't have to reinsert the Windows CD-ROM later when you add or remove Windows components. A folder on the CD contains all the files you need; its name depends on the Windows version. For Windows 98, for example, it's called WIN98. You don't have to copy the entire CD's contents to the hard disk—just that one folder.

Network installation   You can install over a network just as you can from files copied to the hard disk. All you need is command-prompt network access, which you can get by booting from a startup disk containing MS-DOS network drivers. Once you have command prompt access to the network drive containing the Windows Setup files, you can either run SETUP.EXE directly from there, or you can create a folder on the hard disk and copy the Setup files there as in the preceding section.

The Setup Process

Each Setup program is a little different, tackling tasks in varying order, so exact step-by-step instructions would not be meaningful here. However, they all do these things sometime during the process:

- ◇ Check to make sure there is a valid partition on which to install.
- ◇ Format the partition if needed.
- ◇ Run a quick Scandisk check of all the drives on the PC.
- ◇ Copy installation files to the hard disk.
- ◇ Determine which hardware is installed and what hardware drivers are needed.
- ◇ Ask for an installation key (the string of numbers/letters on the back of the CD-ROM case).
- ◇ Ask for a username and business name.
- ◇ Confirm the current date/time.
- ◇ Set up networking components.
- ◇ Set up the PC to automatically start Windows at startup.

Because each Setup program prompts you at each step, you do not need to memorize which versions do the steps in which order; simply follow along.

Upgrading from Earlier Windows Versions

If you are upgrading from another Windows version, you will need less free hard disk space than for a full, new installation because some of your existing files will be overwritten or deleted during the upgrade process.

Some Windows releases come in Full and Upgrade versions. The Upgrade version is cheaper, but it requires that you have an earlier version of Windows from which to upgrade. Some Upgrade versions will accept any earlier version; others are picky and work only with a specific list. Check Microsoft's website for Windows (www.microsoft.com/windows) to find out the upgrade requirements for a certain version.

Depending on the Windows version you are installing, the upgrade steps might be slightly or substantially different from those for a fresh install. For example, the Setup program might ask for your installation key at a different point in the process, or it might detect your hardware at a different point. However, the full Setup and the upgrade Setup perform the same basic tasks and arrive at the same result.

When Setup runs on a PC that already contains Windows, you have the option of specifying that you don't want an upgrade, but would prefer a fresh installation in a different folder. However, you cannot use your old version of Windows anymore after the upgrade even if you do choose a different folder location. If you need to dual-boot (that is, have two different operating systems installed on the same PC and be able to switch between them), see the next section, which explains how that works.

Dual-boot
A system on which two (or more) operating systems are installed, each on a separate partition. At startup the user can choose which one should run.

Dual-Booting

Dual-booting consists of installing multiple operating systems on a single PC, each on a separate partition. Then when the computer starts up, a menu appears that enables you to select which of the operating systems you want.

Third-party software has been available that allowed dual-booting of all operating systems for some time. However, Windows NT, Windows 2000, and Windows XP can dual-boot with other operating systems without any add-on software if you set them up correctly.

To set up dual-booting between two operating systems where one of them does not support dual-booting directly (for example, Windows 95, 98, or Me), you must install the non-supported one first so that it is on the primary partition. Then when you install the operating system that is dual-boot capable, it will notice that another operating system is already installed and it will enable you to set up dual-booting.

For example, to dual-boot between Windows 98 and Windows 2000, here's what you would do:

1. Install two hard disks in the PC, or partition a single hard disk into multiple drive letters.

2. Install Windows 98 on the primary partition (the C: drive).

3. Boot from the Windows 2000 CD-ROM, and let the Setup program start running. When asked whether you want to upgrade or install a new copy, choose New Copy. Then choose one of the other partitions (the D: drive or higher).

4. Continue installing Windows 2000 normally.

When you're finished, a BOOT.INI file (a hidden file) will be in the root directory of the primary partition; this contains the menu that will appear each time you start the PC. By default, this menu will appear onscreen for 30 seconds at startup. If no action is taken during that time, it will automatically boot to the default OS.

Review Questions

1. What is a GUI operating system?

   _____

2. What is the difference between cooperative and preemptive multitasking?

   _____

3. What is the memory area between 640KB and 1MB called?

   _____

4. What standard governs extended memory usage?

   _____

5. What file loaded in CONFIG.SYS allows the operating system to work with extended memory?

   _____

6. What two files comprise the Windows Registry?

   _____

7. Which Windows versions support NTFS?

   _____

8. Which Windows version introduced Active Directory?

   _____

9. What are the CPU and memory requirements for Windows 2000 Professional?

   _____

10. When you are setting up a dual-boot system where one operating system directly supports dual-booting and the other does not, which should you install first?

    _____

Terms to Know

- ❑ Operating system (OS)
- ❑ Graphical User Interface (GUI)
- ❑ Command line
- ❑ Multitask
- ❑ Conventional memory
- ❑ Upper memory
- ❑ ROM Shadowing
- ❑ Expanded memory
- ❑ Page frame
- ❑ EMS
- ❑ Real mode
- ❑ Protected mode
- ❑ Extended memory
- ❑ XMS
- ❑ HIMEM.SYS
- ❑ CONFIG.SYS
- ❑ High memory
- ❑ EMM386.EXE
- ❑ Virtual machine
- ❑ Cooperative multitasking
- ❑ Preemptive multitasking
- ❑ Plug and Play
- ❑ OLE
- ❑ Registry
- ❑ NTFS
- ❑ Product activation
- ❑ Dual-boot

Chapter

15

Starting Up a PC

Most of the time, a PC simply starts up when you turn it on—no big deal. But for those times when it doesn't, it's useful to know the steps involved in a normal startup so you can figure out where the process is breaking down. You'll also benefit from knowing a few tricks for "back-door entry" into a PC that won't start normally and knowing how to diagnose startup problems.

In this chapter, we'll look at the following topics:

 What happens when a PC starts up

 How dual booting works

 Alternative startup modes

 Using a Windows 9x startup disk

 Using the Windows 2000/XP recovery console

What Happens When a PC Starts Up?

MS-DOS kernel

The portion of MS-DOS that gets loaded into memory at startup and remains resident there while the PC is running.

CONFIG.SYS

A file that lists the drivers that should automatically be loaded each time the PC starts.

AUTOEXEC.BAT

A file that lists the programs that should automatically be run at startup.

If you decide to take the A+ OS Technologies exam, you'll need to memorize the names of the files involved in the boot process for Windows 9x and Windows 2000, and the order in which they load. For now, though, just review the following sections as FYI stuff, and don't stress out trying to memorize it all.

The MS-DOS Boot Process

It's good to know something about MS-DOS because you'll find many remnants of it in Windows 9x (that is, Windows 95, 98, and Me). To really understand Windows 9x, you need to know what items are there for backward-compatibility and which are necessary for Windows 9x operation.

A disk requires three files on it in order to boot MS-DOS:

❖ IO.SYS: The controller for hardware interaction

❖ MSDOS.SYS: The controller for software interaction including the **MS-DOS kernel** itself

❖ COMMAND.COM: The command interpreter that interacts with the user

They load in that order. The functions of IO.SYS and MSDOS.SYS are actually a little more complicated than that, but let's keep it simple for now.

An MS-DOS bootable disk can have two startup configuration files: **CONFIG.SYS** and **AUTOEXEC.BAT**. Both are optional; MS-DOS can boot just fine without them. Both are plain text files that you can edit in a text editor such as EDIT (MS-DOS's own text editor program).

CONFIG.SYS contains instructions to load device drivers for various pieces of hardware and to set environment settings. You learned about HIMEM.SYS and EMM386.EXE in Chapter 14, "Operating System Basics." Both of these files are loaded through CONFIG.SYS. A driver for a CD-ROM drive would also be in CONFIG.SYS. CONFIG.SYS can run only at startup.

AUTOEXEC.BAT contains instructions to run any programs that you want to automatically execute at startup. It runs automatically at startup, but it can be rerun at any time by typing **AUTOEXEC** and pressing Enter. The .BAT extension stands for "batch file;" a batch file is a list of commands that should be run as a group, or batch. Examples of commands in AUTOEXEC.BAT might include MSCDEX.EXE (the DOS utility for controlling the CD-ROM driver), PROMPT (which specifies the appearance of the command prompt itself), and MOUSE.COM (which loads a mouse driver).

Here's an outline of the boot process for MS-DOS:

1. The BIOS performs a Power-On Self Test (**POST**).

2. The BIOS searches the drives for a Master Boot Record (**MBR**). The MBR contains data about the partitions, including which partition is active.

3. The MBR takes control and locates IO.SYS.

4. IO.SYS takes control. It identifies the installed hardware. It looks for CONFIG.SYS, and if it finds it, it executes its instructions.

5. MSDOS.SYS takes control. It loads MS-DOS (the operating system kernel) into memory, and looks for AUTOEXEC.BAT. If it finds it, it executes its instructions.

6. COMMAND.COM displays a command prompt, indicating it is ready to accept user commands.

NOTE

If the system being booted contains a CONFIG.SYS and/or AUTOEXEC.BAT file, you won't be prompted for the date and time at startup. Otherwise, the first thing you'll see after startup is an Enter Current Date: prompt.

Once you've started up MS-DOS, you type commands at the prompt. There are two kinds of commands: internal and external. Internal commands are built into the DOS kernel, so they're available at all times. Examples include COPY, DIR (brings up a directory listing of files), and DEL (deletes files). External commands are the names of programs stored on the disk that you can run. The files for the external commands are stored in the DOS directory (folder). Examples of these include FORMAT and FDISK.

The Windows 9*x* Boot Process

Windows 9*x* actually has two parts: a graphical user interface (GUI) and a DOS Protected-Mode Interface (**DPMI**). You can boot to either of them, and it's still Windows 9*x*. However, ordinary users almost never use the DPMI; they boot directly into the graphical interface that has become synonymous with Windows 9*x* itself.

Here's the sequence for Windows 9*x* booting:

1. The BIOS performs a POST.

2. The BIOS searches the drives for the MBR.

3. The MBR takes control and locates IO.SYS.

4. IO.SYS takes control. It looks for MSDOS.SYS and processes its instructions.

POST

Power-On Self Test. A set of low-level hardware diagnostics that confirm the basic operability of the motherboard, memory, CPU, and some other essential components.

MBR

Master Boot Record. Information stored on a drive about its partitions and boot capabilities.

DPMI

DOS Protected-Mode Interface. Like an MS-DOS command prompt interface except it's in Protected mode rather than Real mode.

NOTE

In Windows 9x, all the functions of the MS-DOS IO.SYS and MSDOS.SYS have been combined into IO.SYS. There is still an MSDOS.SYS file (see Step 4), but it has a totally different purpose. Rather than being in charge of anything itself, it's just a passive list of settings with which IO.SYS works.

Splash screen
The graphic that appears while Windows or some other program is loading. It usually lists the program name and version number.

5. IO.SYS looks for a LOGO.SYS file, which is a graphic file that contains the Windows **splash screen**, and displays it.

TIP

You can press Esc while the splash screen displays to clear it away so you can watch startup commands being executed at the command prompt.

6. IO.SYS looks for the Registry files, SYSTEM.DAT and USER.DAT, and checks them. Then it loads SYSTEM.DAT.

7. IO.SYS looks for CONFIG.SYS and AUTOEXEC.BAT and executes them if found. They are not integral to Windows 9x, but they might exist for backward compatibility.

8. IO.SYS loads HIMEM.SYS if it was not already loaded in CONFIG.SYS. (Remember from Chapter 14 that HIMEM.SYS enables the use of extended memory.)

9. IO.SYS loads WIN.COM, which is the main Windows program, and then it hands off control to it.

10. WIN.COM loads the virtual memory manager, VMM386.VXD.

11. VMM386.VXD loads the 32-bit device drivers into memory.

12. WIN.COM reads SYSTEM.INI if present and executes its instructions. SYSTEM.INI was the Windows 3.1 equivalent of SYSTEM.DAT.

13. WIN.COM loads the GUI by loading three files: KRNL32.DLL, GDI.EXE, and USER.EXE.

14. WIN.COM reads and executes any commands from WIN.INI if present. WIN.INI was the Windows 3.1 equivalent of USER.DAT.

15. WIN.COM checks the content of the StartUp folder on the Start menu, and executes any programs that have shortcuts there.

Knowing the functions of all these files can help greatly in troubleshooting Windows problems. For example, suppose you see an error message involving

VMM386.VXD. You know that this is the virtual memory manager, so you know there is likely a problem with the virtual memory paging file. Without knowing what VMM386.VXD is, you would have no idea where to start.

The Windows 2000 Boot Process

Windows 9x is based on MS-DOS, so all of the boot processes start out the same way and involve the same files: IO.SYS and MSDOS.SYS. Windows 2000 is a totally different animal. It's based on Windows NT, not MS-DOS, so it involves different files and processes.

Here's the Windows 2000 boot process.

1. The BIOS performs a POST.

2. The BIOS searches the drives for the MBR.

3. The MBR takes control and locates NTLDR (which stands for NT Loader). NTLDR is the Windows 2000 equivalent of IO.SYS.

4. NTLDR switches the CPU into 32-bit Protected mode.

5. NTLDR finds and reads BOOT.INI, the file that controls the menu for dual-booting. If there are multiple operating systems, it displays a menu for user choice. If the user chooses Windows 2000, or if there are no other operating systems, it continues the Windows 2000 boot process. Otherwise, the other chosen OS takes over.

6. NTLDR runs NTDETECT.COM, which detects the installed hardware and sends the information to the Registry.

7. NTLDR reads NTOSKRNL.EXE into memory. This is the equivalent of the DOS kernel loaded in MS-DOS by MSDOS.SYS.

8. NTLDR locates the drivers for the hardware that the Registry reports is installed (but does not install them yet).

9. NTLDR hands over control to NTOSKRNL.EXE.

10. NTOSKRNL.EXE loads the device drivers and the GUI.

How Dual Booting Works

You can buy add-on programs that enable PCs to dual-boot among multiple operating systems. If one of your operating systems is Windows 2000 or XP, however, all the needed software is built-in. As discussed in Chapter 14, install the other OS first and then Windows 2000 or XP (on a different partition). The Setup program creates the BOOT.INI file and configures it for your installed OSes.

As you saw in the preceding section, this BOOT.INI file is the key to dual-booting. When Windows 2000 (and XP) starts up, it looks for a BOOT.INI. BOOT.INI contains both the text for the menu system and the instructions for each menu option. You can open it in Notepad and take a look:

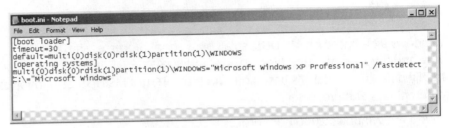

By default, the menu appears on the screen for 30 seconds. If no selection is made during that time, it boots to whichever OS is set as the default.

Although it is possible to edit BOOT.INI directly from Notepad, it is much safer and easier to control options for this menu from the System Properties. Right-click My Computer and choose Properties, click the Advanced tab, and click Startup and Recovery.

TIP

By default Windows 2000 is set up to hide protected operating system files, which means BOOT.INI will not appear in file listings. To change this, open a file management window and choose Tools ➢ Folder Options. Click the View tab, and deselect the Hide protected operating system files check box.

Alternative Windows Startup Modes

Now that you know what Windows startup is supposed to look like normally, let's take a look at some alternatives that might be useful in special circumstances.

Displaying the Startup Menu

In most Windows versions, you can press the F8 key at startup to see a Startup menu. Don't hold the F8 key down, or you'll get a Keyboard Stuck error. Instead, wait for the Starting Microsoft Windows message to appear and the beep to sound, and then press F8 immediately. If you see the Windows splash screen, you're too late. If you aren't fast enough on the draw, try continually pressing and releasing the F8 key in 1-second intervals as soon as you see any text on the screen at startup.

If you are using a dual-boot configuration, a menu appears at startup anyway, enabling you to choose the operating system. To get to the Startup menu for a particular operating system, highlight it on that list and then press the F8 key.

If you are troubleshooting a startup problem, the Startup menu might appear automatically. After an unsuccessful startup, the Startup menu appears by default the next time you restart with Safe mode selected as the default. (See the next section to learn more about Safe mode.)

This Startup menu is handy because it lets you choose among several operating modes. The following sections describe some of these operating modes. Different versions of Windows have different choices, and the wording may be a little different. For example, here's the one for Windows 98:

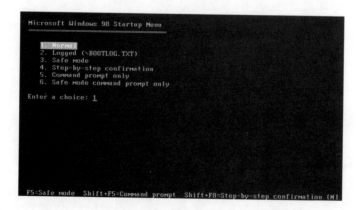

In Windows 2000, it's called the Advanced Options menu and it looks like this:

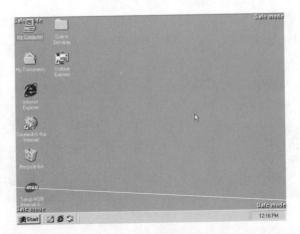

Safe Mode

Safe mode is a GUI operating mode in which the drivers for all nonessential hardware remain unloaded. This circumvents any startup problems that might be occurring due to device conflicts. For example, let's say you have just bought a new scanner and loaded the software for it, and now Windows won't start. It's a good bet that the driver for the scanner is causing the problem, so you could start the computer in Safe mode and then remove the scanner software. (That's a short-term solution, of course; in the long run, you would want to go to the scanner maker's website and find out why it isn't working with your Windows version and your PC. Maybe a downloadable fix is available.)

Safe mode also loads a generic **VGA display** rather than the specific driver for your video card. It does this just in case the problem is being caused by a corrupted video driver file. When you're in Safe mode, the words "Safe mode" appear on the Desktop in the corners so you won't forget. Depending on the Windows version, a troubleshooting Help window might also appear.

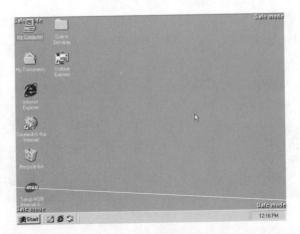

You should not operate the PC in Safe mode for your regular activities because there is only very limited access to the hardware. Your CD-ROM drives will probably not be available in Safe mode, for example.

Some Windows versions have different subtypes of Safe mode available, such as Safe Mode with Networking (same as regular Safe mode except that it loads the drivers needed for accessing network resources) and Safe Mode with Command Prompt (opens a command prompt screen).

Logged Mode

Logged mode is just like a regular startup, except that it takes copious notes about the startup process and saves them in a file called BOOTLOG.TXT. You can then open that file in a text editor such as Notepad and review the boot process to figure out what's wrong.

Step-by-Step Confirmation

This option loads all the regular startup drivers, but it does so one step at a time, and you have the opportunity to say "No" to any line item individually. This is available only for Windows 9x versions, not for NT 4, 2000, or XP.

I have found this mode useful for troubleshooting startup problems that are caused by a particular driver locking things up. I go step-by-step through the startup, answering "Y" to each line, until the PC locks up. Then I look on the screen to see what the last line was that I said Yes to, and that's the one that's causing the problem. Then to confirm, I restart and go through Step-by-Step again, but this time I choose "No" for that line. If Windows boots without locking up, I am then sure that that line had been the problem. Then I figure out what program or device that line is associated with and troubleshoot from there.

Command Prompt Only

This mode, available only for Windows 9x versions, displays a plain command prompt without loading any drivers or any portion of Windows. It's useful when you need to run an MS-DOS program or utility that is incompatible with Windows for troubleshooting purposes.

If you need to run an MS-DOS application that doesn't run well from within Windows, another way to do it is with MS-DOS mode (available only in Windows 95 and 98). To use it, choose Start ➤ Shut Down and then choose Restart in MS-DOS mode. Then when the PC restarts in DOS, run the program for a command line. You can also set the properties for an MS-DOS program's executable file to use MS-DOS mode.

Starting with a Windows 9x Startup Disk

Startup disk
A bootable floppy disk containing command line utility programs for troubleshooting.

RAM disk
A temporary virtual hard disk created out of RAM.

A **startup disk** is a bootable floppy disk containing command line utility programs that can be used to troubleshoot and correct serious system errors that prevent Windows from starting. You can create a startup disk in the 9x versions of Windows (95, 98, or Me) but not with any of the NT-based Windows versions (NT 4, 2000, or XP). It doesn't work with NT-based versions because they are not based on a command line operating system (like MS-DOS), so they have no native command line interface behind the GUI to fall back to. With NT versions of Windows, instead you have the Recovery Console, which is discussed later in this chapter.

Making a Startup Disk

The best time to think about a startup disk is before anything goes wrong. Make one now, so you'll have it later when you need it. To make a startup disk:

1. Insert a blank floppy disk (or one that contains nothing you want to keep) into your floppy drive.
2. Choose Start ≻ Settings ≻ Control Panel and double-click Add/Remove Programs.
3. Click the Startup Disk tab, and then click Create Disk.
4. Follow the prompts to create the startup disk.
5. Label it Startup Disk, along with the Windows version number, and store it somewhere safe.

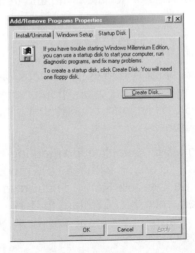

The resulting disk contains the files needed to boot to a command prompt, plus several essential external MS-DOS commands needed for preparing a hard disk for use, transferring files, and so on.

The startup disk needs to contain more files than a single 1.44MB floppy disk can hold, so it utilizes a compression scheme. It contains a few of the files on the floppy disk itself, ready to go, but most of them are contained in a compressed archive file. When a PC boots from the startup disk, it creates a **RAM disk** and then decompresses the rest of the files to that RAM disk. Therefore, when you boot from a startup disk, all your removable drive letters will be off by one. For example, if your hard disk is C: and your CD-ROM is normally D:, the RAM disk will be D: and the CD-ROM will be E:.

NOTE

Startup disks created in Windows 98 and Me contain real-mode CD-ROM drivers so that your CD-ROM drives will work from the command prompt, but Windows 95 startup disks do not. You must manually edit the CONFIG.SYS and AUTOEXEC.BAT files on a Windows 95 startup disk to add CD-ROM support. It's a good idea, therefore, to have a Windows 98 or Me startup disk in your troubleshooting toolkit. It can be used on Windows 95 systems.

Using a Startup Disk

A startup disk is useful in situations where the current Window installation is so badly damaged or corrupted that it is not salvageable, or when preparing a brand-new hard disk for use.

When you boot from a startup disk, it asks whether you want to start the PC with or without CD-ROM support (Windows 98/Me versions only). Then it extracts the compressed files to a RAM disk and presents you with a command prompt. Table 15.1 lists some of the internal MS-DOS commands you can use from a command prompt, and Table 15.2 lists some of the files on the startup disk you can use for troubleshooting and system reconstruction.

TIP

You don't just type the command and press Enter in most cases; you need to type some parameters along with it in a specific order and syntax. Type a command followed by /h to get instructions on a particular command.

Table 15.1: Internal MS-DOS Commands

Command	Purpose
Dir	Displays a listing of files and folders
Copy	Copies files and folders from one location to another
Del	Deletes files
CD	Changes to a different directory
MD	Creates a new directory
RD	Removes directories
Ren	Renames files and folders

Table 15.2: Windows 9x Startup Disk Commands

Command	Purpose
Extract	Extracts files from compressed archives, such as those that Windows setup files are stored in on the Windows CD-ROM.
Fdisk	Runs the Fixed Disk Management partitioning utility program, for creating and deleting disk partitions.
Attrib	Shows, sets, and changes attributes on files such as Read-Only, Hidden, and System.
Chkdsk	Performs a basic data integrity check on the file system. This is an older utility; Scandisk is the newer version.
Edit	Runs the MS-DOS Editor, a text editing program similar to Notepad but not Windows-based.
Format	Formats hard and floppy disks.
Scandisk	Performs data integrity and physical disk surface checks on disks.
Sys	Transfers the bootable system files from one disk to another.

The Windows Recovery Console

Using the **Recovery Console** in Windows 2000 and XP is somewhat like booting to a command prompt from a startup floppy disk in Windows 9x. It provides a command prompt at which you can type certain commands for recovering from problems that prevent the PC from starting.

Recovery Console
A command line interface for troubleshooting problems with a Windows 2000 or XP installation.

Entering the Recovery Console

By default, the Recovery Console exists only on the Windows CD-ROM. To use it from there, do the following:

1. Boot from the Windows CD. The Windows Setup program starts.
2. At the Welcome to Setup screen, type **R** to select Recovery Console.
3. Type **1** to select the first Windows installation on your system.
4. If prompted for the Administrator password, type it and press Enter.

You can also install the Recovery Console program on your hard disk, so you won't need the CD if you should ever require the Recovery Console. To do so:

1. While Windows is running normally, insert the Windows 2000 CD in the drive. If a window opens automatically for the CD, close it.
2. Choose Start ➢ Run. Type **x:\i386\winnt32 /cmdcons** (where *x* is the drive letter of the CD-ROM) and click OK.
3. A confirmation message appears. Click Yes.
4. After the installation, another confirmation appears. Click OK.

One of the side effects of installing the Recovery Console on the hard disk is that the dual-boot boot menu appears automatically from then on, each time you start Windows, as if you had multiple operating systems installed. You can choose the Recovery Console from there.

Using the Recovery Console

When you enter the Recovery Console, it asks which Windows installation you want to log onto. In most cases you'll only have one, so just type **1** and press Enter to choose it. Next, it asks you for the administrator password. Type it and press Enter. If there is no administrator password, press Enter without typing anything.

```
Microsoft Windows 2000(TM) Recovery Console.

The Recovery Console provides system repair and recovery functionality.

Type EXIT to quit the Recovery Console and restart the computer.

1: C:\WINNT

Which Windows 2000 installation would you like to log onto
<To cancel, press ENTER>? 1
Type the Administrator password: ******_
```

At this point, you'll end up at a command prompt like this:

```
C:\WINNT>
```

To see a list of the available commands you can use, type **HELP** and press Enter.

Some of the commands available are the same as with a Windows 9x startup disk. These include ATTRIB, CD, MD, COPY, DEL, CHKDSK, DIR, EXIT, EXPAND, FORMAT, MD, RD, and REN. Table 15.3 lists a few extra commands that are unique to the Windows Recovery Console.

Table 15.3: Windows Recovery Console Commands

Command	Purpose
Batch	Executes batch commands in a specified text file.
Disable	Disables a particular Windows 2000 service or driver.
Diskpart	Manages hard disk partitions; roughly equivalent to FDISK.
Enable	Enables a particular Windows 2000 service or driver.
Fixboot	Writes a new boot sector on the boot partition.
Fixmbr	Repairs the master boot record on the disk.
Listsyc	Lists all available drivers, services, and startup types.

Review Questions

1. What three files must be present to make a disk bootable under MS-DOS?

   _____

2. What two configuration files are executed automatically during MS-DOS startup, and in what order?

   _____

3. What two files comprise the Windows 9x Registry?

   _____

4. Which *two* of these files are involved in the Windows 2000 boot process—NTLDR, NTOSKRNL, and NTKRNL32—and in what order do they load?

   _____

5. What initialization file controls the dual-boot menu during Windows 2000 startup?

   _____

6. What key do you press as the PC is booting to display the Startup menu?

   _____

7. If you choose to create a log file from the Startup menu, what is the name of the log file?

   _____

8. Which Control Panel applet do you use to create a startup disk in Windows 9x?

   _____

9. What Windows 2000 feature enables you to boot to a command prompt for troubleshooting purposes?

   _____

10. Why would you not install new programs from CD when in Safe mode?

   _____

Terms to Know

- ❑ MS-DOS kernel
- ❑ CONFIG.SYS
- ❑ AUTOEXEC.BAT POST
- ❑ POST
- ❑ MBR
- ❑ DPMI
- ❑ Splash screen
- ❑ Safe mode
- ❑ VGA display
- ❑ Startup disk
- ❑ RAM disk
- ❑ Recovery Console

Chapter

16

Essential Windows Tools and Skills

Almost the entire A+ OS Technologies exam—one half of your total A+ testing experience—is devoted to Windows tools and skills. Fortunately, most people studying for A+ certification are already experienced Windows users, so they already know a lot of this stuff just from using it on a day-to-day basis.

There's an awful lot to know about Windows—it's a huge operating system! And the A+ exam covers several versions of Windows, so you've got two or three times the information to get through. So rather than trying to cram it all into a single chapter or two, break down the topics so you can figure out what you know already and what you need to go back and review on your own.

This chapter covers the following topics:

 Checklist of file management skills

 A tour of Windows tools and utilities

 Installing and removing programs

 Interacting with a command prompt in Windows

Checklist of File Management Skills

Let's start with the basics. Every Windows user—especially those who aspire to being PC technicians—needs a thorough understanding of file, folder, and disk structure and management.

Individual **files** are organized in **folders** (which were called directories under MS-DOS), and folders are stored on drives. Each drive has a drive letter. You can work with folders and files at a command prompt, in Windows Explorer (shown here), or in the My Computer window.

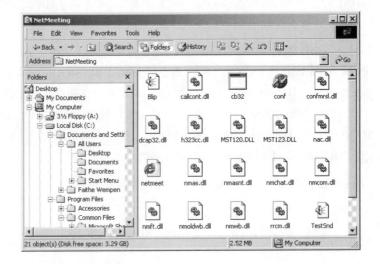

Here's a checklist of skills to practice:

Moving and copying files between folders and disks   There are several methods, including Cut/Copy and Paste, drag-and-drop, and Move and Copy menu commands. You need to master them all. Familiarize yourself both with the standard **Windows Clipboard** and the enhanced one in Microsoft Office. Brush up on the Clipboard Viewer utility in Windows as well.

Deleting files and folders   Again there are several methods, including the Delete key, the right-click shortcut menu, and the regular Windows Explorer menu system. Also review the **Recycle Bin**, and how to retrieve files from it, empty it, and set its properties.

Renaming files and folders   Make sure you know the various ways of making a name editable, including pressing F2, clicking inside it, and using the Rename command.

Creating new files and folders   The easiest way is to right-click and choose New, but master alternative methods as well, including menu commands and toolbar buttons. You should also know how to create new folders from within an Open or Save dialog box in Microsoft Office applications.

Finding files and folders   You'll need to know how to use the Find (or Search) feature in Windows to locate a file based on its name, contents, creation date, size, or any other search criterion. Different versions of Windows handle this a little differently, so make sure you study several of them.

Setting file management options   Make sure you know how to control the options for file management windows (hint: Tools ➢ Options, or in some versions of Windows it is View ➢ Options). This includes displaying or hiding **file extensions**, displaying or hiding hidden and system files, and choosing Classic versus Web view.

TIP

For more help with file management in Windows, check out some of the excellent Windows books published by Sybex at www.sybex.com. I won't recommend any specific book because you'll want different ones depending on the Windows versions you have, but the whole Mastering series is especially good. If you have Windows XP, you might like my book on the subject: *Windows XP Home Edition Simply Visual* (also published by Sybex).

File extension
A code (usually three characters) following a file's name that indicates the file type. For example, in MYFILE.DOC, the .doc extension indicates a document.

A Tour of Windows Tools and Utilities

A good PC technician also knows the ins and outs of the various tools and utilities that Windows provides for keeping a PC healthy and performing well. Here's a rundown of the major ones to know. Not all of these are installed by default, so if you don't see the one you want, use Add/Remove Programs in the Control Panel to install it. (That's covered later in this chapter.)

Scandisk or Check Disk   Scandisk (called Check Disk in Windows 2000 and XP) checks and corrects a disk for logical errors in the FAT and also for physical surface errors that affect data storage. Right-click the drive in My Computer and choose Properties, and then click the Tools tab and click Check Now. In Windows 95, 98, and Me, you can also access it with Start ➤ Programs ➤ Accessories ➤ System Tools ➤ ScanDisk.

Disk Defragmenter   Disk Defragmenter checks a drive for files stored in **noncontiguous** clusters and rearranges the data physically on the disk so that as few files as possible are fragmented. Choose Start ➤ Programs ➤ Accessories ➤ System Tools ➤ Disk Defragmenter.

DriveSpace   DriveSpace was a method of increasing the storage capacity of a hard disk, and it was popular during the era of expensive hard disks. Nowadays they are cheap so there is little reason to use it. Early versions of Windows (95 and 98) provide a Windows interface for managing DriveSpace volumes. To run it, choose Start ➤ Programs ➤ Accessories ➤ System Tools ➤ DriveSpace. Windows Me comes with a stripped down version of the utility that enables you to manage existing DriveSpace drives but not create new ones.

NOTE

Originally, DriveSpace was called DoubleSpace, and it was included with MS-DOS 6.2. Stacker, a company that made a competing product, sued Microsoft for infringement on their compression algorithm. Microsoft released MS-DOS 6.21, which did not contain it anymore. Then soon afterward Microsoft released MS-DOS 6.22, which contained DriveSpace instead. It does the same thing, but the math for doing it is different enough to pass legal muster.

FAT32 Converter   Windows 95 supported only FAT16; Windows 98 and higher supports FAT32. Ordinarily, the only way to change over to FAT32 is by repartitioning and reformatting, but Windows 98 came with a converter utility that performed the conversion without any data loss. To run it (Windows 98 only), choose Start ➢ Programs ➢ Accessories ➢ System Tools ➢ DriveSpace.

System Information   This utility provides detailed information about the hardware, memory usage, drivers, and other details involved in the behind-the-scenes housekeeping of the Windows program. To run it, choose Start ➢ Programs ➢ Accessories ➢ System Tools ➢ System Information.

System Restore   This utility, available in Windows Me and Windows XP only, is a "go back" type of program that enables you to revert to a previous Windows configuration if you install or remove something and Windows starts acting up. You run it once to take a snapshot of the system while it's working, and then run it again to restore to that snapshot when problems occur. To run it, choose Start ➢ Programs ➢ Accessories ➢ System Tools ➢ System Restore.

System Editor   System Editor, or SYSEDIT as it is more popularly known, is not available on any Windows menus. You must run it with the Start ➢ Run command. It opens several key configuration files in a multi-window Notepad-like editing program, so you can make changes to them from one convenient location. The included files are AUTOEXEC.BAT, CONFIG.SYS, WIN.INI, and SYSTEM.INI. Because all these files exist only for backward compatibility and have not been necessary in their own right since Windows 3.1, System Editor is not as useful in recent Windows releases.

System Configuration Utility   Here's an essential tool in the PC troubleshooter's toolkit, but like System Editor is it not available from the menu system. Choose Start ➢ Run and run MSCONFIG to open it. It lets you control the way Windows starts up, enabling you to exclude certain startup lines, turn off certain drivers, and more to identify and eliminate startup problems.

Registry Editor   Recall that the Registry is the repository for all Windows settings in Windows 95 and higher. The Registry Editor is an Explorer-like window that enables you to view and edit its settings. Beware when using this tool, though, because improper edits to the Registry can cripple or disable a PC to the point where Windows must be completely reinstalled. Choose Start ➢ Run and run REGEDIT to open it.

Backup   Microsoft Backup is used to transfer copies of files to removable media for backup purposes. It compresses the backed-up files so they take up less space, but they must be run through Backup again using the Restore feature to be uncompressed when needed. Not all versions of Windows come with Backup, and most that do don't install it by default.

Installing and Removing Windows Programs

Windows components
Programs, utilities, and add-ons that come with Windows itself rather than being purchased separately.

As you probably already know, installing a Windows program is more than just copying files to your hard drive. You must run a Setup utility for that program to make the required changes in the Windows Registry. Similarly, removing a Windows program involves more than just deleting the program's files from the hard disk. You must either use the program's Uninstall utility (if it has one) or Add/Remove Programs in the Windows Control Panel to remove it. Otherwise, you end up with out-of-date entries in the Registry that can slow down system performance and cause error messages to appear.

As far as Windows' Add/Remove Programs applet is concerned, there are two types of Windows programs: those that come with Windows itself (referred to as **Windows components**) and those that are separate. The procedures for adding and removing them are different, so let's look at each individually.

Adding and Removing Applications

Adding a new program that comes on CD-ROM is usually just a matter of popping the CD in the drive and following the onscreen prompts. If nothing happens when you insert a CD, browse its contents in My Computer and double-click on SETUP.EXE.

Most programs you can download from the Internet come in executable form (with an .exe extension), so you just double-click the file after downloading it and the setup program runs. If a downloaded program comes in ZIP format (with a .zip extension), use an unzipping program to extract the files to a folder on your hard disk and then run the Setup program from there. One popular unzipping program is WinZip (www.winzip.com). Windows XP has zip support built in, so no unzipping program is required; so does America Online.

Some applications come with their own Uninstall program, which you'll find next to the program itself on the Start menu:

Other programs must be removed from Add/Remove Programs in the Control Panel. The look-and-feel is different between Windows versions, but basically you select the program and then click the Remove button and follow the instructions.

Adding and Removing Windows Components

When you do a default install of Windows, some accessory programs are installed too, such as Calculator, Notepad, and so on. A few of the less popular ones are not installed by default, however, so you might want to add them later. You can also remove any of the installed accessories that you don't use, freeing up disk space.

To check out the assortment of Windows components to be installed or removed:

◇ In Windows 95, 98, or Me, double-click Add/Remove Programs in the Control Panel and then click the Windows Setup tab.

◇ In Windows 2000 or XP, double-click Add/Remove Programs in the Control Panel and then click the Add/Remove Windows Components icon.

From the window that appears, clear or mark the check boxes for the components—or entire categories of components—that you want to remove or add. Windows 9x has a huge array of programs to be added or removed, but Windows 2000 has only a few specialized tools there; all the mainstream end-user applications are non-removable in Windows 2000. Windows XP goes back to a more balanced list; there are both the end-user applications and the special tools and drivers.

The Details button becomes available when a category containing multiple items is selected; you can click Details to see a list of the individual items in the selected category. Notice that some check boxes have a gray background; this indicates that some—but not all—of the items in that category are selected.

Using a Command Prompt

Command-prompt commands and Windows menu selections are two different ways of accomplishing the same kinds of results. At a command prompt, a typical way of specifying settings for a command is to type **switches** following it. For example, FORMAT C: /Q means to format the C: drive using Quick Format mode, which does no physical checking of the disk and saves time. If this were a command in Windows, you might choose Format and be presented with a dialog box in which you chose which drive to format (C:) and what options you wanted (Quick Format).

Most of the time users find it easiest to interact with Windows' point-and-click GUI interface, but sometimes a command prompt will do a better job of an activity. For example, suppose you have a game that will operate in any of several video modes, and you sometimes want to use one mode, other times another mode. At a command prompt, you could type a switch following the command name that chooses the video mode you want. You can set up a shortcut in Windows for each video mode you want, but it's more involved to do so.

A PC technician should have a good grasp of a basic set of commands and their syntax, to be able to work confidently from a command prompt. Sometimes it's necessary to work with files from a command prompt when preparing a new hard disk, for example, or when recovering from a system disaster that requires repartitioning and/or reformatting.

Displaying a Command Prompt

There are two ways to execute command-line commands in Windows. One is with the Run command. Choose Start ➢ Run and then type the complete command and click OK. This works well when you need to run a program that doesn't have a Windows shortcut set up or when you want to specify switches along with the command.

The other way is to open a command-prompt window, which is like running a mini version of MS-DOS from within Windows. To do that, choose MS-DOS Prompt or Command Prompt (depending on the Windows version) from the Start ➢ Programs menu (or Start ➢ Programs ➢ Accessories in some Windows versions). This is useful when you need to see text-based results of the command you are executing, like with the IPCONFIG command shown in the figure. To close a command-prompt window, type **EXIT** and press Enter or close the window with its Close (X) button.

Switch
A code typed following a command-prompt command that further defines how the command should be executed.

290

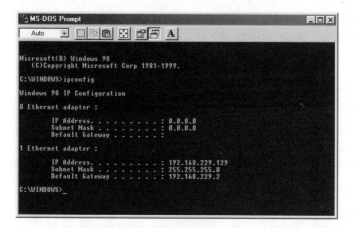

You can also boot to a command prompt rather than to the Windows GUI interface at startup, as you learned in Chapter 15, "Starting Up a PC."

Navigating Between Locations at a Command Prompt

When working with a command prompt, folders are known as **directories**. Only one directory is active at once; it's known as the **current directory**. The current directory's name appears in the command prompt. For example, a prompt like this:

    C:\Windows>

means that the Windows directory on the C: drive is current. Whatever commands you issue apply to the current directory unless you specify otherwise. For example, if you type this command (the part in bold below):

    C:\Windows>**COPY *.* A:**

it will copy all the files from the current directory to the A: drive. The asterisk (*) represents "all", so *.* means "all files, all extensions." It's the same as selecting the entire contents of a folder in Windows Explorer.

TIP

The asterisk (*) is called a **wildcard** because it can stand for anything. An asterisk stands for any number of characters. A question mark (?) is used as a wildcard to represent a single character.

Directory
Same thing as a folder. The term Directory is often used rather than folder when referring to work at a command prompt.

Current directory
The directory (folder) specified in the command prompt, to which any commands will apply that are not specifically directed at some other location.

Wildcard
A character that represents any value. Two standard wildcards are * for any number of characters and ? for a single character.

You could specify a different location, such as the C:\Backup folder, by changing the command to something like this:

```
C:\Windows>COPY C:\Backup\*.* A:
```

To change the current directory, you use the CD command (which stands for Change Directory). For example, to change to the Backup directory, you would type:

```
C:\Windows>CD \Backup
```

And the prompt would then change to:

```
C:\Backup>
```

To change to a different drive, you don't need any command; just type the drive letter and a colon. So, for example, to change to the A: drive:

```
C:\>Backup>A:
```

The prompt would then change to look like this:

```
A:\>
```

To make a new directory, use the MD command. The new directory is placed as a subdirectory of the current directory unless you specify otherwise. For example, the following command would create a new directory called Files as a subdirectory of C:\Backup:

```
C:\Backup>MD Files
```

To remove a directory, it must be empty first, so you must delete everything from it with the DEL command (discussed later). Then use the RD command like this:

```
C:\Backup>RD Files
```

Working with Files at a Command Prompt

If you are accustomed to working with files in Windows using Windows Explorer or My Computer, you'll find the command-prompt method of managing files slow and awkward. It's much better to do your file management from within Windows whenever possible.

However, sometimes you might not have a choice. Therefore, you should have a good grasp of the commands necessary for manipulating files at a command prompt.

Let's start with the most basic command: DIR. It's short for Directory, and it lists the contents of the current directory. So, for example, this command:

```
C:\Windows>DIR
```

would produce a listing of the files and subdirectories (folders) within C:\Windows. You can get a directory of other locations by specifying them in the command. For example, this command would give you a listing of what's on the A: drive's floppy disk:

```
C:\Windows>DIR A:
```

A couple of useful switches for the DIR command: /W displays the listing in a "wide" (multi-column) format, and /P displays them in a page-by-page format (one screenful at a time).

Another useful command is COPY, which copies files from place to place. For the syntax, just remember COPY *What Where.* For example, to copy everything from the root directory of the A: drive to C:\MYFILES, use this command:

```
C:\Windows>COPY A:*.* C:\MYFILES
```

Yet another command you will need to know is DEL, short for Delete. It deletes the specified file(s). For example, to delete the file TEXT.DOC from the A: drive, you would use this command:

```
C:\Windows>DEL A:\TEXT.DOC
```

As usual, you don't have to type the location if the file is in the current directory. So, for example, to delete all the files in C:\Backup, first change to that directory (CD \BACKUP) and then delete the files like this:

```
C:\Backup>DEL *.*
```

One last command: REN, short for Rename. Its syntax is REN Oldname Newname. So to rename the file APRIL.DOC to MAY.DOC, use this command:

```
C:\Backup>REN APRIL.DOC MAY.DOC
```

This chapter's discussion barely scratched the surface of the commands a good technician should be able to use at a command prompt, but by now you should have a sense of what command prompt work is about. For more information, pick up a basic book on MS-DOS or an advanced book on Windows that covers command prompts.

Review Questions

1. Name three different methods of copying a file to the Clipboard in Windows.

2. Which Windows utility fixes performance slowdowns caused by noncontiguous file storage?

3. Which Windows utility allows you to turn off individual startup items for troubleshooting purposes?

4. How would you run the utility you wrote down in Question 3?

5. What is the danger involved in editing the Registry?

6. What is a switch?

7. What Windows feature can you use to execute a single command-prompt command without opening a full command-prompt window?

Terms to Know
- ❏ File
- ❏ Folder
- ❏ Windows Clipboard
- ❏ Recycle Bin
- ❏ File extension
- ❏ Noncontiguous
- ❏ Windows components
- ❏ Switch
- ❏ Directory
- ❏ Current directory
- ❏ Wildcard

8. What command would you use for copying the file OLD.TXT in the current directory to the RETIRE directory on the E: drive?

_____

9. What command-prompt command deletes a directory?

_____

Chapter

17

Working
with Devices
in Windows

This chapter is all about devices—those various pieces of hardware inside and outside the main box of the PC. This includes modems, network adapters, sound cards, drives, scanners—just about everything except the motherboard, memory, and CPU. We've dealt with some of them specifically in other chapters, but this chapter focuses on what they all have in common: how they interact with Windows and with one another.

This chapter covers the following topics:

 Introduction to device resources

 Viewing resource assignments

 Installing new devices

 Removing devices

 Resolving resource conflicts

Introduction to Device Resources

Device resources
Pathways or memory addresses that help a device communicate with the CPU and the operating system.

A resource is a tool or commodity that helps you get something done. For example, when you want to go out to a movie but you don't have enough money, you might say you "don't have the resources."

In a computer, **device resources** are resources that help devices do their jobs—that is, communicate with the CPU and the operating system. A device can use four types of resources. Not all devices use all four of these types.

IRQ
Interrupt Request. A system resource assigned to a device so it can signal to the CPU that it is ready to communicate.

Interrupt Requests (IRQs)   IRQs are lines of communication to the CPU. There are 16 of them in a PC, numbered 0 through 15, but many of them are reserved for built-in system devices such as the keyboard and the IDE interfaces. They are necessary because the CPU must initiate all conversations with devices, but sometimes the devices need to "raise their hands" to ask for a conversation to be initiated. They do so by sending a signal on the interrupt request line, and the CPU responds by initiating a conversation.

I/O address
Input/Output addresses in memory where devices place data for pickup by the operating system, and where the operating system places data for pickup by the device.

I/O addresses   I/O addresses are memory addresses, expressed in hexadecimal. They define areas of memory reserved for transferring data to and from the device. They are usually written using only the last four digits of the full address like this: 03E8. They are usually expressed as a range of addresses, such as 03E8–03EF.

Memory addresses   Memory addresses are also defined addresses in RAM. They define areas of memory reserved for the device's use. They are usually written with eight digits of hexadecimal, such as 00A0000, and they are usually expressed as a range, such as 00A0000–00BFFFF.

Direct Memory Access (DMA) Channels   These are pathways from a device directly into memory, bypassing the CPU. They are not popular anymore because of advances in hardware technology, but they used to be employed by devices like the keyboard and the sound card to improve their reaction time.

Each built-in I/O port in a system has resources preassigned to it. For example, COM1 uses IRQ4 and I/O addresses 03F8 through 03FF. The port uses those resources whether or not anything is actually plugged into it (unless you disable it in the BIOS Setup program, that is). This is true for both COM (serial) and LPT (parallel) ports.

In contrast, the expansion slots in a motherboard do not get any resources when they're empty. Instead the system waits until you plug an expansion board into one of them, and then it assigns resources to that expansion board. For example, you might have four PCI expansion slots, and one of them is occupied by a modem. That modem uses an IRQ and an I/O address range. If the motherboard is **Plug and Play** capable, its chipset communicates with that modem, finds out what resources it needs, and assigns them.

Some older expansion boards have jumpers on the board for setting the I/O address and IRQ. These are non–Plug and Play models; you choose the resources they will get, and then the chipset takes its cue from the expansion board. Most cards these days, however, are Plug and Play and, therefore, jumperless. Some expansion boards that were manufactured during the changeover period can operate either way—they have jumpers, but one of the jumper positions is Plug and Play rather than a specific assignment.

Of the four resource types listed here, the most critical is the IRQ. That's because there is a limited number of them and almost every device requires one. Older systems with lots of ISA devices would run out of IRQs and no more devices could be installed in them. One of the advantages of the PCI interface over ISA is that PCI devices can share IRQs; each expansion board need not have a unique IRQ assigned to it.

There are other interfaces that help devices share resources too. Certain device types—such as SCSI, USB, and FireWire—work off a central controller that handles resource assignments for multiple devices. The controller requires an IRQ (and other resources too), but the individual devices do not.

Viewing Resource Assignments

To check out the current resource assignments of a device, use Device Manager in Windows. To open Device Manager:

1. Right-click My Computer and choose Properties. The System Properties box appears.

2. In Windows 9*x*, click the Device Manager tab. In Windows 2000, click the Hardware tab and then click the Device Manager button.

3. To open a device category, click the plus sign next to it.

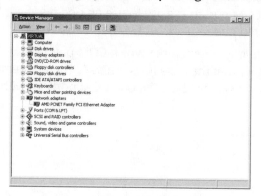

Plug and Play
A standard for detecting new devices and installing drivers for them automatically. To work, it must be supported by the device, the motherboard chipset, and the installed operating system.

4. To see the resources assigned to a particular device, double-click it and then click its Resources tab.

5. Check the Conflicting Device List to make sure there are no conflicts with other devices. (If the device is working, there are probably no conflicts.)

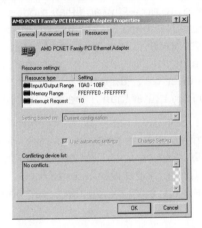

6. When you are finished, close all open dialog boxes.

If you decide to take the A+ exam, you will need to memorize the default IRQ assignments for all devices. Table 17.1 summarizes them. Here are a few notes about them:

◇ IRQs 2 and 9 cascade (i.e., connect) to one another, and they are, in fact, a single IRQ going by two different names. This connection is necessary because there are actually two banks of IRQs: 0 through 8 and 9 through 16.

◇ Most systems do not have an LPT2, but there is a default assignment for it anyway (IRQ 5). If there is no LPT2, IRQ5 is free. This point often shows up on the A+ exam, so make sure you remember the default assignment for LPT2.

◇ COM ports 2 and 4 share an IRQ, as do COM ports 1 and 3. However, they don't always share very gracefully, so if you ever have a choice of which COM port to use, try to use an odd-numbered one and an even-numbered one rather than two odd or two even.

◇ When trying to remember which COM port goes with which IRQ, first remember that they use IRQs 3 and 4. Then remember that odd and even don't go together. The odd COM ports go with the even IRQ (4).

Table 17.1: Default IRQ Assignments

IRQ	Device Commonly Assigned
0	System timer (system crystal)
1	Keyboard
2	Connector to IRQ 9
3	COM2 and COM4
4	COM1 and COM3
5	LPT2 (if present)
6	Floppy drive controller
7	LPT1
8	Real-time clock
9	Connector to IRQ2
10	Available
11	Available
12	PS/2 mouse
13	Math coprocessor
14	Primary hard disk controller (IDE1)
15	Secondary hard disk controller (IDE2)

You can also display a list of all the IRQs and their current assignments. In Windows 9x, double-click the computer at the top of the tree in Device Manager. Then click the IRQs option button. In Windows 2000, in Device Manager choose View ➢ Resources by Type and then click the plus sign next to IRQs. Here it is in Windows 2000:

Notice in the above figure that the IRQs used by ISA are listed first, with the PCI ones second. No shared IRQs are shown here because no sharing is needed—there are enough IRQs to go around. However, if any sharing were necessary, the PCI IRQs would do it.

NOTE

For more detailed information about resource usage, check out the System Information utility in Windows. To run it, choose Start ➢ Programs ➢ Accessories ➢ System Tools ➢ System Information.

Installing New Devices

Installing new hardware used to be a great big production in early Windows versions, because Plug and Play didn't work very well (if it worked at all) and because not all motherboards and devices were Plug and Play compatible. Nowadays, however, almost everything is Plug and Play compatible, so installing new hardware is basically a matter of plugging it in and turning on the PC.

WARNING

Most types of hardware are not **hot-pluggable**. In other words, you must turn off the PC before you hook them up. Damage can result if you try to connect a device while the PC is running. If in doubt, you should assume that you need to turn off the PC. Hot-pluggable devices are those that connect via USB, FireWire, or **PCMCIA** only.

Read and follow the instructions that came with the device to install it. In many cases, Windows may be able to detect the new device automatically but the instructions will say that you should run the software on the CD-ROM that came with the device. That's because the device might have its own application software or extra driver files that provide added functionality over the driver built into Windows for the device. If the instructions contradict what's in this chapter at any point, go with what the instructions say.

Plug and Play Devices

If Windows detects the new device at startup, one of two things may happen:

- ❖ A message may flash briefly on the screen about detecting new hardware and installing the drivers for it, and then the new device will start working automatically.

◇ A New Hardware Wizard may appear onscreen walking you through the process of identifying the location of the driver for the device. Point the wizard to the driver (probably on a disk that came with the device) or let the wizard search for the best driver available for it. The latter is the best way to go in most cases because it compares all the available drivers (such as the one that came with the device on disk versus the one that came with Windows for it), decides which one is most recent, and uses that one.

If the instructions that came with the device prescribe that you should run a Setup program on a disk provided, it's perfectly okay to click Cancel instead of running through the wizard. Clicking Cancel will enable Windows to finish loading and then you can run the Setup program from the disk. You might also want to cancel the wizard if no driver is available for the device; then after Windows finishes loading, you can use the Internet to locate a driver for it (or at least you can try).

If Windows does not detect the new device automatically at startup, one of these things is true:

◇ The device is not fully Plug and Play compatible. See the next section for guidance.

◇ The device is malfunctioning or not correctly installed. Check the install instructions and try to correct the problem.

◇ There are resource allocation problems. See the section "Resolving Resource Conflicts" later in this chapter.

To confirm that a device has been installed, open up Device Manager as described earlier in the chapter and look for the device. Double-click it to open its properties, and check its status. If it reports that the device is working properly, it should be good to go.

Non–Plug and Play Devices

If the device, the chipset, or the operating system is not Plug and Play compatible, Plug and Play won't work. As long as you are using Windows 95 or higher, you should be fine on the operating system front, but the chipset and the device may be another matter. If you have other Plug and Play devices installed in Windows, you can eliminate the motherboard chipset as the source of the problem as well. That leaves the device itself.

Windows' New Hardware Wizard (or Add/Remove Hardware Wizard in some Windows versions) has a feature in it that tries to detect non–Plug and Play hardware, and it actually works fairly well. But it doesn't notice the new device automatically; you have to manually start up the wizard. It can't assign system resources to a non–Plug and Play device; it merely reads the resource information that is hard-wired into the device (or set by its jumpers) and reports it to Windows. Windows then tries its best to rearrange the resource assignments of the Plug and Play devices to avoid conflicts.

To run the New Hardware Wizard, go to the Control Panel and double-click the Add New Hardware icon (or Add/Remove Hardware in some Windows versions). Then just follow the prompts. I won't run through the steps here because they're different for each Windows version and because they branch off into all sorts of different directions depending on your choices. Here's a sample screenshot from the Windows 2000 version.

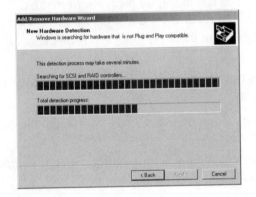

Removing Devices

To remove a piece of hardware, shut down Windows (unless it's a USB, FireWire, or PCMCIA device) and physically remove it. The next time you start Windows, there should be no trace of the device in Device Manager if it was a fully Plug and Play device.

If you do see the device's driver in Device Manager after it has been physically removed, delete it from there by clicking on it and then pressing Delete or clicking Remove.

If software came with the device, as is the case with some scanners, modems, digital cameras, and so on, you can remove it from Add/Remove Programs, as you learned in Chapter 16, "Essential Windows Tools and Skills."

Resolving Resource Conflicts

Plug and Play is not perfect, and sometimes it can't find free resources to assign to a device. This is especially true when other non–Plug and Play devices are installed or when there are many ISA expansion cards.

A device with a yellow-background exclamation point next to it in Device Manager may be having problems with resource assignments, as shown here:

To check out the device's resources, double-click it and look on the General tab for a status message. For example, the message in the following figure says there is not enough of one of the resource types available.

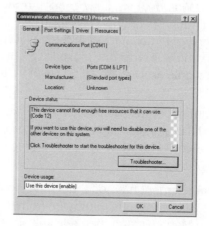

A look to the Resources tab shows that the resource in short supply is an IRQ.

To resolve the conflict, you could try a different setting from the Settings Based On drop-down list or click Interrupt Request and then click the Change Setting button to try to pick a different IRQ manually.

Resource troubleshooting can be much more complicated, but you've just seen 90 percent of the job right here. The essential steps are

1. Check Device Manager.
2. Identify the source of the conflict.
3. Manually reassign resources until you resolve the conflict.

TIP

Windows 2000 and XP are fairly good at resolving resource conflicts on their own through Plug and Play, so in real life you will seldom see a resource conflict. I "manufactured" the conflict I used as an example here, just so you could see what one looked like, but in a normal system COM1 and COM3 would likely share an IRQ with no problems.

If the problem is occurring because there are no free IRQs, you might try disabling one of the legacy serial or parallel ports that you aren't using. Remember that these ports use resources even when nothing is plugged into them; you can disable them in BIOS Setup.

Another resource management method that I have occasionally found helpful is to physically remove all nonessential hardware from the PC and make sure it is removed from Device Manager, and then reinstall all of the ISA and non–Plug and Play hardware first. Then reboot Windows and make sure all devices have resources they need. Then add the PCI Plug and Play hardware, one piece at a time and rebooting Windows after each installation. Sometimes this will coax Windows into managing the resources better.

Review Questions

1. Which type of resource is numbered 0 through 16 and provides lines of communication from a device to the CPU?

   _____

2. Which type of expansion slot requires a separate IRQ for each one?

   _____

Terms to Know

- ❑ Device resources
- ❑ IRQ
- ❑ I/O address
- ❑ Plug and Play
- ❑ Hot-pluggable
- ❑ PCMCIA

3. Name two types of interface that use a single set of resources for the controller and then allow multiple devices to be connected to that controller.

   _____

4. Name two types of interfaces that are hot-pluggable.

   _____

5. Which IRQs are connected to one another and are actually a single IRQ going by two different names?

   _____

6. Which COM port shares an IRQ with COM4?

   _____

7. Which IRQ does the keyboard connector use?

   _____

8. How do you start the New Hardware Wizard?

   _____

9. How can you tell whether Windows has successfully installed the needed drivers for a particular device?

   _____

10. What does a yellow circle with an exclamation point mean next to a device in Device Manager?

   _____

Chapter

18

Troubleshooting Windows Problems

Even though only a few questions on the A+ exam cover this topic, it's a big one in real life. Most PC technicians spend a large majority of their time troubleshooting problems that people have with Windows. The problems usually fall into one of four categories: virus infection, problems with devices, problems with applications, or problems with Windows itself. We looked at device issues in the last chapter; now let's turn our attention to the other three.

This chapter covers these topics:

 Avoiding and removing viruses

 Correcting problems with Windows

 Understanding application error messages

 Navigating Windows when the mouse won't work

 Doing a controlled Windows shutdown

 Looking for the underlying cause of Windows problems

Avoiding and Removing Viruses

Virus
A program designed to spread itself from one PC to another and (usually) to cause damage to the PCs or annoyance to the user.

Computer **viruses** have become a real problem in recent years because of the free exchange of files over the Internet. The results of having a virus vary depending on the virus. Some simply display a harmless message or play a sound. Some activate only on certain dates. Others destroy the master boot record on the disk, erase certain files, corrupt the FAT, or even flash-erase the EEPROM. Other viruses, especially those that spread via e-mail, send themselves to everyone in your address book without your permission.

NOTE

A Trojan horse is a variant of a virus. The name comes from the old myth about the big wooden horse that hid the Trojan soldiers. A Trojan horse program pretends to be something useful, like a game or a video clip, but harms your PC.

There are only two ways to get a virus:

◇ Boot from an infected disk
◇ Run an infected program

It's simple to avoid the first one—just don't boot from an unchecked floppy disk.

WARNING

If you accidentally leave a floppy disk in your drive and see an error at startup that says to remove the disk and press any key to continue, don't do that. Instead, press the Reset button on the PC. If that floppy contained a virus, the virus will have already transferred itself into memory by the time you see that message. By resetting the PC, you dump the memory contents and start over.

It can be more complicated to avoid running infected programs, however, because not all programs look like programs on the surface. For example, some viruses spread as Visual Basic scripts (with a .vbs extension) or as Word macros. When you open a document that contains a macro virus, the macro runs and infects your system. To further camouflage themselves in e-mail attachments, some viruses have double extensions, such as goodtimes.jpg.vbs. The "real" extension is the last one—it's a .vbs script, and probably a virus. If your PC is set up to hide extensions for known file types, it'll suppress the .vbs extension in the display and appear as goodtimes.jpg. Tricky, eh?

Viruses cannot infect nonexecutable files, so a virus cannot hide in a text or graphic file unless it contains a macro. However, viruses can destroy text and graphics files as part of their damage.

Precautions to Avoid Viruses

You can do several things to prevent virus infections on a PC:

- ◇ Buy and install an **antivirus program** such as Norton Antivirus, and keep it updated by downloading the latest **virus definitions** regularly. Some programs check for updates automatically at certain intervals. An antivirus program cannot catch the latest viruses if it has out-of-date definitions.

- ◇ Do not open e-mail attachments received from people you don't know. Even if it comes from someone you do know, scrutinize it carefully before opening. If the message has odd wording, or if it just doesn't "sound" like your friend the sender, it's probably a virus. Remember that some viruses e-mail themselves to everyone in an address book, so your friend might himself be a virus victim.

- ◇ If possible, use an antivirus program that scans incoming e-mail.

- ◇ So you can accurately see the extensions of all files, turn the file extension display back on in Windows. From a file management window, choose Tools ➤ Folder Options, click the View tab, and clear the Hide Extensions for Known File Types check box.

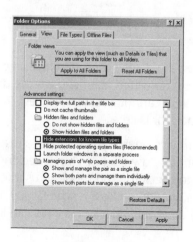

Antivirus program
Software that monitors files for specific strings of characters that are associated with viruses and then quarantines and offers to repair or delete the affected files.

Virus definitions
A data file containing the text strings that the antivirus program searches for to determine whether virus infection exists.

Do not boot from an unknown floppy. If you accidentally leave a floppy disk in the drive at startup, try to catch your mistake as soon as possible, and turn the computer completely off. Then remove the floppy and reboot. An infected floppy transfers its infection to RAM immediately, even before it displays an error message onscreen about the disk not being bootable. If you simply remove it and press a key to continue, as suggested onscreen, the virus is already in RAM.

Detecting and Removing Viruses

Windows does not have any antivirus capability; you must rely on third-party programs for this. The two biggest sellers are Norton Antivirus and McAfee VirusScan. Both are full-featured and easy to use, and both offer automatic updating via the Internet.

I use Norton Antivirus 2002, and it pretty much takes care of itself. It downloads new definitions whenever they are available and installs them automatically, and it performs a full system scan for viruses every week (in the middle of the night when I'm not using the PC anyway.) I recommend it to all my clients.

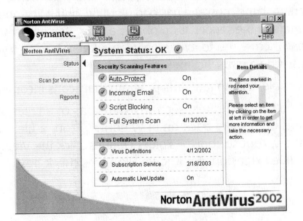

When an antivirus program detects a virus, a message pops up on the screen asking what you want to do with it. Your choices are usually Quarantine (move the file to a folder where it cannot infect other files), Repair (get rid of the virus but keep the file in place), or Delete.

Most antivirus programs also enable you to make a rescue disk, which is a floppy disk containing a stripped-down set of virus checking tools. You can boot a system with this disk to check for and repair virus infections in the event that Windows won't start. If you do make a rescue floppy disk, make sure you write-protect it immediately after making it so no virus can infect it.

Correcting Windows Problems

"It doesn't work right." That's 90 percent of what you'll hear, day after day, if you become a professional PC technician. Your challenge is to figure out what the customer means by that, and to fix it.

In working with computers, a fix is always possible—it's just a question of how drastic you have to get to fix it. No matter how badly a Windows installation is screwed up, you can always reformat the drive and start over with a fresh install, and just about any hardware piece that breaks can be replaced. The difference between a mediocre PC technician and a really great one is not that one gets the job done and the other doesn't—anyone can get the job done eventually. The really great technician can do it faster and avoid overkill by trying the simple solutions first before resorting to the big time-consuming solutions like reinstalling everything.

In the following sections, I'll list some of the most common things that go wrong in Windows and provide some suggestions for troubleshooting them. The best teacher for this stuff is everyday experience, though, so I encourage you to dive into fixing as many PCs as you can to hone your skills. Just put the word out to friends and relatives that you are interested in fixing their computers for free, and soon you'll have more dinner invitations than you can handle.

NOTE

Sometimes distinguishing between a problem with Windows itself and a problem with an individual application can be tough. The line between them is rather fuzzy, especially with programs that load automatically at startup. The following sections do not draw a sharp dividing line between the two because you won't always know which is the problem in real-life troubleshooting.

System Lockup with Frozen Mouse Pointer

When Windows locks up completely, such that you can't even move the mouse pointer, there's not much hope for a normal shutdown. The only thing you can do is press the PC's power button to shut it off, and then restart. This type of error is more common in Windows 9x than in Windows 2000/XP because Windows 2000 and XP run each 32-bit application in its own separate space.

After an abnormal shutdown, you should run Scandisk (or Check Disk) to make sure no file system errors have been created. Some versions of Windows run Scandisk automatically when starting up after an abnormal shutdown.

Once you're back in, look for the underlying problem causing the error. Some reasons for this type of problem might include:

Corrupt or incompatible video driver   Download and install the latest version.

Conflicting or poorly written programs loading at startup   This is a problem I have quite often with my beginner-level clients—they're suckers for any "free offers" they see on the Internet, many of which download little programs that load at startup and clog things. Clean out the Startup folder on the Start menu, and use Add/Remove Programs to remove as many of the nonessential installed programs as possible. If needed, use MSCONFIG to turn off certain programs from starting automatically to figure out which is causing the problem.

Overheating   If the system locks up after somewhere between 5 and 30 minutes of operation, and it seems to be random, I suspect a faulty cooling fan on the CPU. Make sure the fan is spinning and firmly attached to the CPU. Also make sure there are no missing backplates or drive bay covers that could be changing the airflow through the case.

Bad or incompatible RAM   The wrong kind of RAM (wrong speed, non-ECC in an ECC system, etc.) can cause random lockups, as can bad RAM. Check the motherboard's RAM requirements, and use a hardware diagnostic program to check the installed RAM for errors.

System Lockup with Operational Mouse Pointer

If you still have control over the mouse pointer but nothing else seems to be working, you might be able to do a controlled shutdown and restart. This is advantageous whenever possible because it minimizes the possibility of file system errors. See the section "Doing a Controlled Shutdown" later in this chapter.

As for fixing the problem, it may be a one-time thing. Just go about your business, and see if it happens again. If it does, refer to the troubleshooting suggestions in the preceding section. If it happens only when you run a certain application, try removing and reinstalling that application, or checking the manufacturer's website to see whether a patch is available for it.

Application Quits with Error Message

If you're using an application (or you have just attempted to start it) and the program quits with an error message, the problem is either that application directly or its relationship to some other program that was running at the same time. Some error messages you might see include:

General Protection Fault (GPF)   A **GPF** happens when an application tries to do something that Windows can't allow it to do because it would cause a problem with Windows itself or with other running applications. For example, the application might try to use memory space that is already in use or try to access hardware directly. This type of error usually occurs with 16-bit applications, and it can be solved by removing and reinstalling the program. If you see it on a 32-bit application, there is probably an internal flaw in the program itself, and you will need a patch from the manufacturer to correct it.

Illegal Operation   An **illegal operation** error occurs when the application requests an operation that Windows cannot carry out. It is not necessarily one that would harm anything else, as with a GPF. It could result from an internal flaw in the program or from a corrupted file. Typically, you'll see a message such as "This program has performed an illegal operation, and will be shut down." Click the Details button to see more information about it. Rebooting the PC may solve the problem; if not, remove and reinstall the program. If the problem still occurs, look for a patch on the manufacturer's website.

Invalid Working Directory   Each program needs a working directory (folder) in which to store temporary files as it operates. Some programs use the same folder that the application itself uses; others use C:\Windows\Temp or some other location. You might see this error if the working directory is located on a network that's temporarily down. You can change the working directory for the program by right-clicking the shortcut that starts the program and choosing Properties, and then changing the Start In location.

Nothing Happens
When Starting Application

Sometimes when you start an application, Windows acts as if nothing happened. Restarting the PC usually clears this up. If it doesn't, remove and reinstall the application (see Chapter 16, "Essential Windows Tools and Skills").

GPF

General Protection Fault. A type of program error that occurs when Windows protects itself against a program's request to do something that would cause problems. Usually results in program termination.

Illegal operation

A program error that occurs when an application asks Windows to do something that it cannot comply with. Usually results in program termination.

Working without a Mouse

You might occasionally run into a situation where the mouse pointer disappears (not freezes), but the keyboard still works. When this happens, you must rely on shortcut keys to get yourself out of the mess. It might affect only one program, such that when you terminate that program the problem goes away—or it might affect Windows in general.

Table 18.1 provides some essential key combinations you will need when trying to feel your way around Windows without a mouse. Two of them, the Windows key and the Menu key, are found only on Windows-style keyboards.

Table 18.1: Keyboard Navigation in Windows

Keys	Purpose
Alt+F4	Closes the active program window. If no program window is active, brings up the Shut Down dialog box for Windows itself.
Ctrl+Alt+Delete	Opens a Task Manager window (may have a different name in some Windows versions) from which you can select and terminate individual running programs or choose Shut Down to shut down Windows in general.
Windows key	Opens the Start menu. Then you can use the arrow keys to move around on it and press Enter to select a command.
Menu key	Same as right-clicking an object; brings up a shortcut menu for whatever item is at the mouse pointer location. (Of course, if you can't see the mouse pointer onscreen, this isn't all that useful.)
Alt+letter	Pressing Alt makes underlined letters appear in menu names if they don't appear already. Then following that up with a typed letter opens the menu with that letter underlined in its name. You can then use the arrow keys to move up or down the menu, and press Enter to select a command.
Alt+Tab	Switches between the open windows. Press and release to move one-by-one, or hold down Alt and tap Tab to see a box with icons for them and move among those icons.
Alt+Enter	Switches between the open windows by bringing the currently active one to the bottom of the pile and moving the next one up. Press this multiple times until the window you want comes to the top.

Doing a Controlled Shutdown

Usually when one error occurs, it starts a domino effect of other errors, so the best thing to do is to shut down and restart to clear the slate. Here's a procedure for shutting down when the system is acting a little (or a lot) iffy:

1. Try to shut down as many running applications normally as possible, especially those with unsaved work that you want to save. Switch to the program and save your work, and then shut it down with File ➤ Exit or by clicking its Close (X) button.

2. Try the Start ➤ Shut Down command. If the mouse isn't working, try pressing Alt+F4.

3. If that doesn't work, try shutting down from the Task Manager. Press Ctrl+Alt+Delete. In Windows 9x and XP, this brings up a list of running programs; in Windows 2000, you must then click Task Manager to see the list. From that dialog box, click Shut Down. Depending on the Windows version, Shut Down might be a button, or it might appear in the menu bar as shown here.

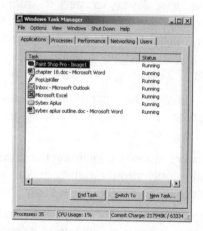

4. If you can't shut down from the Task Manager, try to terminate the nonresponsive program that is preventing shutdown. To do so, press Ctrl+Alt+Delete. Click the nonresponsive program, and then click End Task. Repeat for each program that reports Not Responding next to it. Then try Shut Down again.

Correcting the Underlying Problem

Think back—what was the last thing you did to the PC before the problem started happening? If it's not your PC, ask the person who uses it the most. Maybe there was a new piece of hardware installed or a new program loaded? It's a good bet that the new item is part of the current problem. Try removing it. If it's hardware that came with its own software, remove the software too. See Chapter 16 for help.

If you can't get the system back the way it was by normal means (i.e., by using Add/Remove Programs), try the System Restore utility (Windows Me and XP only). This is not covered on the A+ exam because it came out after the exam was written, but it's really handy. You'll find it in the System Tools subfolder on the Start menu. It lets you restore an earlier copy of the Registry, wiping out any bad edits that the errant program might have made to it.

There's a possibility that the problem is being caused by a corrupt or outdated driver for a certain hardware device, so check the manufacturers' websites for all your hardware and make sure you have all the latest drivers. There's also a possibility that two or more devices are causing the problem together by conflicting with one another, so check your device resource allocations in Device Manager (see Chapter 17, "Working with Devices in Windows").

If nothing works and you're still having problems, try reinstalling Windows. There are several ways to go about this, and it can be a crapshoot to determine which one is appropriate for a given situation.

- ⬥ Reinstalling over the top of an existing Windows installation is fairly easy to do and takes only about a half-hour. You keep all your installed programs. However, it doesn't always solve the problem.

- ⬥ Reinstalling Windows in a different folder on the hard disk gives you a fresh Windows installation but you must reinstall all your Windows applications. It's about 95 percent sure to fix the problem, but it requires that you have adequate hard disk space to support two separate installations of Windows temporarily. (You can delete the old installation once you've confirmed that the new one works.)

- ⬥ Reformatting the hard disk and reinstalling Windows is about 99.9 percent sure to correct the problem. However, this is a tremendous amount of work because you have to back up all your data files first, format the drive, reinstall Windows, reinstall each application, and then restore the data files. That's a whole-day project.

So, are you wondering about that last 0.1 percent of problems that a complete reinstall won't fix? In some situations, hardware can be incompatible with Windows or with some other piece of hardware. In those cases, all the reinstalling in the world won't fix the problem; what you need is a device driver update. You'll kick yourself if you do a complete reinstall of Windows only to find out that all you needed was an updated driver for your sound card to solve the problem, so always check the easy solutions first!

Review Questions

1. What are the two ways of getting a computer virus?

_____

2. Name two precautions for preventing virus infection.

_____

3. True or False: Windows Me has an antivirus utility built into it.

_____

4. How could you check for virus infection on a PC that won't start Windows?

_____

5. After an abnormal Windows shutdown, what utility should you run to make sure there are no file system errors?

_____

6. What key combination closes the active window or shuts down Windows if there is no active window open?

_____

7. What key do you press to activate the underlined letters in menu names?

_____

8. What versions of Windows include the System Restore utility?

_____

9. True or False: You must reinstall all your Windows applications if you reinstall Windows in a different folder.

_____

10. What is the purpose of the Windows key on a keyboard?

_____

Chapter

19

Setting Up
Internet
Connections

In only a decade, the Internet has gone from a specialized geek tool to a mainstream community with millions of members. Nearly everyone, from kids to seniors, is on the Internet these days. As a PC technician, you will need to know how to set up and configure Internet connections of various types. I won't explain how to use the Internet here—that's a subject for a whole 'nother book and besides, you probably know already. Instead, I'll cover the following topics:

 Understanding Internet connectivity

 Types of Internet connections

 Understanding Internet protocols

 Setting up an Internet connection

 Internet connection sharing

Understanding Internet Connectivity

The **Internet** is a huge network of computers all over the world. Some of those computers are connected 24/7; others connect only when needed.

All the computers on the Internet can be divided into two broad categories, just like on a LAN: clients and servers. An **Internet client** is one where an end user sits, surfing the Web, reading e-mail, and so on. An **Internet server** is one that either offers client PCs an access point for tapping into the Internet or stores Internet content for client PCs to retrieve, such as web pages and e-mail.

Sometimes the line between an Internet client and Internet server can be fuzzy. For example, a home PC user with a full-time cable or DSL connection to the Internet might host a small website on his PC or might share that connection with several PCs in his home. In those cases, his PC is serving both as a client and a server. However, when people talk about Internet servers, they usually mean large, powerful corporate servers such as those owned by **ISPs** and **web hosting companies**.

Large corporations sometimes have their own web servers and provide their employees with full-time access to the Internet through the corporate LAN. Individuals who want to connect to the Internet, however, must sign up with an ISP, a company that provides Internet connectivity for a fee. The services provided by ISPs vary, but the average package includes a username and password for connecting, at least one e-mail account, and a small amount of space for storing a personal website.

Types of Internet Connections

Until a few years ago, only clients connecting through a corporate network had high-speed Internet access; everyone else struggled along with dial-up modems. This has changed dramatically lately, however, and high-speed access is available to almost any home user who wants it.

There are different ways of breaking down the various connection types into categories. Table 19.1 lists the major players along with some pertinent details about them, such as connection speed, telephone usage, and whether or not they use Windows **Dial-Up Networking** (DUN). The alternative is for them to be always on, so you don't connect each time.

As far as Windows is concerned, there are only two kinds of Internet connections: those that require Dial-Up Networking and those that don't. All the rest is just details. I'll explain how to set up DUN and non-DUN connections later in the chapter.

Internet
A global network of interconnected computers that share data.

Internet client
A computer that uses Internet services.

Internet server
A computer that provides Internet services to other computers.

ISP
Internet Service Provider. A company that charges people money to help them connect to the Internet.

Web hosting company
A company that charges people money to store their websites and keep them available at all times to other clients.

Dial-up networking
A Windows feature that enables clients to log into a remote network via telephone.

Table 19.1: Internet Connection Types

Service	Phone Line?	DUN?	Speed	Notes
Modem	Yes	Yes	56Kbps	Available everywhere there is telephone service. Slowest type. Ties up phone line when in use.
Integrated Digital Subscriber Network (ISDN)	Yes (special digital line required)	Yes	64Kbps to 200Kbps	Expensive, and speed not much faster than modem. Requires special digital type of phone line.
Cable	No	No	512Kbps to 2Mbps	Uses cable TV line but does not interfere with TV watching. Residential service only.
One-way satellite	Yes	Yes	56Kbps upload, 512Kbps download	You need modem service too; the satellite is for downloading only. Dish can also be used for TV.
Two-way satellite	No	No	512Kbps to 1.5Mbps	Requires a special two-way satellite dish (expensive) and professional installation. Dish can also be used for TV.
T1	No	No	1.5Mbps	T1 line comes from phone company, but it is not a normal phone line. Suitable for small or medium-sized companies.
T3	No	No	44Mbps	Like a T1 but faster. Expensive. Suitable for large companies with many simultaneous Internet users.
Frame Relay	No	No	56Kbps to 1.554Mbps	An inexpensive alternative to T1 for small companies.
ATM	No	No	155Mbps	Fiber optic connection. Fast and expensive. For large companies only.

Understanding Internet Protocols

Protocol
Generically, a set of rules governing a situation. When referring to communications, a set of rules that specify how the data is sent and received.

There's a veritable alphabet soup associated with Internet connectivity, but you don't have to memorize all of the acronyms and **protocols** to set up an Internet connection—thankfully! However, if you decide to take the A+ exam, you will want to study them. Here's the briefest of overviews.

TCP/IP

TCP/IP
Transmission Control Protocol/Internet Protocol. A set of communication standards for sending and receiving data over a network.

A lot of other standards fall under the big tent of **TCP/IP**, because it's not actually a single standard, but rather a whole collection of standards, and they apply not only to the Internet but to networking in general. Here are some of the key points involved in TCP/IP.

IP Addresses

Fixed IP address
An IP address that never changes, assigned permanently to a specific client.

The "IP" part of TCP/IP stands for Internet Protocol. You may have heard of IP addressing before—it's a way of assigning a unique numeric address to a particular PC or network resource so that other PCs can access it from anywhere in the network. An IP address is a string of four three-digit numbers separated by periods, like this:

```
207.150.192.12
```

Each number does not necessarily have to be a full three digits; leading zeros are assumed (i.e., 012 is the same as 12).

An IP address is actually four eight-digit binary numbers. For example, 207.150.192.12 is 11001111.10010110.11000000.00001100 in binary. But just try typing that into a web browser! That's why IP addresses are normally converted to decimal. It just makes them easier to read and remember.

TIP

You can use the Windows Calculator to convert numbers between binary and decimal. To do so, choose View ➢ Scientific and then click the Dec button. Type in the decimal-base number, and then click the Bin button. The binary equivalent appears.

When you set up an Internet connection on a PC, you can handle IP addressing in two ways. One is to enter a **fixed IP address** for it. Such an address would be assigned by your ISP. Most ISPs, however, do not assign fixed IP addresses because there are only a limited number of them to go around and not every customer will be connected to the Internet at the same time. Therefore, whenever you connect, the ISP assigns a **dynamic IP address**. You keep this IP address for as long as you're connected, and when you terminate the connection, it goes back into that ISP's pool of addresses. You don't decide this yourself; your ISP tells you what settings to use. Almost all dial-up connections use dynamic IP addressing. Always-on connections such as cable or DSL can use either.

DNS

Even with the decimal numbering system and the separators, IP addresses are not exactly catchy, and remembering them can be difficult. A **DNS** server, therefore, is used to translate IP addresses into text-based addresses called **URLs** that have familiar words in them that people can remember.

DNS servers are all over the world. These specialized servers have the job of translating each address that a client requests in URL form into an IP address and sending that IP address back to the client for its use. All the DNS servers share information with one another, so they all contain the same data (although sometimes when there's a change, it takes a day or so for that change to filter out to all the DNS servers in the world).

For example, suppose the client types www.sycamoreknoll.com. The DNS server comes back with the information that this address translates to 207.150.192.12, and the web browser software uses that information to connect to the website. This is called a DNS lookup. If you ever see a DNS Lookup Error in a web browser, it means the DNS server has failed to provide a translation for the address you entered. It could be because there is no information available or because the DNS server is not working.

When you set up an Internet connection, you can enter the IP address of a specific DNS server that your ISP has instructed you to use, or you can set it up to automatically find a DNS server. Again this is not a decision you make yourself; your ISP tells you how to set it up.

Subnet Masks

When you set up an Internet connection with a static IP address, you also have the opportunity to enter a subnet mask. This is usually something involving 255s and 0s, like this: 255.255.255.0. The easy answer here is to just enter what your ISP instructs and leave it at that. Those of you who are curious about how things work can read the next few paragraphs; the rest of you can skip them and not be any less prepared for the A+ exams.

Dynamic IP address
An IP address that is assigned from a pool of available addresses upon connection, and released upon disconnection.

DNS
Stands for Domain Name System. A method of translating numeric IP addresses to text-based URLs.

URL
Stands for Uniform Resource Locator. The text-based name of a network (usually Internet) resource that maps to an IP address through a DNS server, expressed in http:// format.

327

Earlier I said that IP addressing was not just for the Internet, but for corporate LANs as well. In a TCP/IP network, each IP address can be broken down into two parts. The first part tells what domain the PC belongs to, and the second part is the unique identifier of that device within that domain. It's sort of like area codes and prefixes in a telephone number except in that case there are three levels of division rather than two.

The dividing line between the first and second parts of the IP address is not a fixed point; it can vary depending on the way the network is set up. This is great for people designing networks because it gives them lots of flexibility. You could have lots of domains with a few addresses each, a few domains with lots of addresses each, or anywhere in the middle between those extremes. The subnet mask defines where the separator line should be placed. In very simplistic terms, the separator comes at the point where the 0s begin. So, for example, in 255.255.255.0, the separator comes after the third group of digits.

In actual use, however, it becomes more complicated—at least from a human-understanding perspective—because an IP address is actually a 32-digit binary number, not decimal, as you'll recall. Each number between the periods is an 8-digit binary. So the address 255.255.255.0 is actually 11111111111111111111111100000000. So the breaking point between 1 and 0 is actually after the 24th digit. It doesn't necessarily need to break on an even 8, so you could potentially have a subnet mask such as 255.255.248.0, which would break after the 21st digit.

If you ever take a course on networking, or study for the Network+ exam, you will spend a lot of time learning how to calculate subnet masks. But for our purposes in this chapter, all you need to know is how to type one into a dialog box.

Connection Protocols

In the early days of the Internet, several different connection protocols were used to establish a TCP/IP Internet connection: SLIP (Serial Line Interface Protocol), CSLIP (Compressed SLIP), and PPP (Point to Point Protocol). Today, however, PPP is the dominant connection protocol, to the point where it is the default and hardly anybody ever needs to change it. Many specifications are associated with each of these, but you don't need to know about them for the A+ exam.

Communication Protocols

Once you get an Internet connection established, then what? Then you need some TCP/IP communication protocols to send and receive data.

Several different protocols are standard on the Internet. In earlier days, you needed separate applications on your PC to work with each one of them, but today some programs can handle multiple protocols. Here are the most important ones to know:

Hypertext Transfer Protocol (HTTP)   This is the protocol for the **World Wide Web** (or Web for short). You use a **web browser** such as Internet Explorer to view **web pages**. A web page's address usually starts with `http://`. Pages written to be viewed with the HTTP protocol are written in a text-only programming language called **HTML** (Hypertext Markup Language). Within an HTML document, there might be additional commands that run mini-applications that produce the animation and other bells-and-whistles associated with the fancier web pages. These mini-applications are usually written in a system-independent programming language such as **Java**, so they will run on any computer.

> **NOTE**
>
> HTML uses only the characters found on a normal keyboard. It embeds codes within the text to represent different kinds of formatting. For example, the code <p> starts a new paragraph.

File Transfer Protocol (FTP)   This is a protocol for file **uploading** and **downloading**. For a long time, it was the only protocol for this purpose, but today many web pages integrate file transfer too. You use an FTP program to connect to an **FTP site** and upload or download files from an FTP server. Some web browsers enable you to connect to FTP sites through them—without a special FTP program—by preceding an IP address with `ftp://`.

Telnet

Telnet is a very old protocol, used for making a direct connection to a computer network. You log in as a remote user through Telnet and have access to the text-based operating system on the server (usually Unix). You can use a separate Telnet program or you can make a telnet connection from within a web browser by preceding the IP address with `Telnet://`.

E-mail protocols   These protocols are used on mail servers for picking up and sending e-mail. The most common one is Post Office Protocol (POP); a close second in popularity is Internet Message Access Protocol (IMAP). Both of these require separate e-mail programs, such as Outlook Express or Eudora. Each of these receives mail only; they use a third protocol called Simple Mail Transfer Protocol (SMTP) to send mail. Depending on your ISP there might be an alternative web access to your POP or IMAP e-mail account as well. In addition to these "normal" e-mail protocols, there are e-mail accounts that are entirely web based and use only the HTTP protocol (for example, those free e-mail accounts you can get through Yahoo!, Hotmail, and other services).

World Wide Web
A network of web pages available for public display on the Internet.

Web browser
A program that displays web pages.

Web page
A text document with embedded HTML codes that make it appear to be formatted and/or to contain pictures and other elements when viewed with a web browser.

HTML
Hypertext Markup Language. A text-based programming language used to create Web content.

Java
A platform-independent programming language for creating applications that users using any type of PC can run through a web browser interface.

Upload
To transfer a file from your PC to another PC.

Download
To transfer a file from another PC to your PC.

FTP site
A server that provides FTP access for a hard disk that accepts uploading or downloading operations.

Setting Up an Internet Connection

I introduced all those terms and protocols earlier so that when it comes time to fill in the blanks to set up a connection, you'll understand what the various blanks are requesting. So now that you're fully armed with that knowledge, let's get down to business!

First, make sure you have the information you need from the ISP. For a dial-up connection, you will need:

Username   The name you will use when establishing the dial-up connection. This might or might not be the same as your e-mail username.

Password   You'll need the password for establishing the connection.

Phone number   The phone number that your modem should call to connect to your ISP.

E-mail server information   You will need the names of the incoming and outgoing mail servers, the server type (probably POP), and your e-mail username and password.

TIP

If you don't have the e-mail server information, you might be able to guess it. For example, if your ISP is Acme.com, your incoming mail server is probably either mail.acme.com or pop.acme.com, and your outgoing mail server is probably mail.acme.com or smtp.acme.com.

Newsgroup server information   Some ISPs provide a news server. This is another protocol we haven't talked about yet in this chapter; it enables you to read newsgroups via a newsreader program. It's probably the ISP name with "news." tacked on in front, as in news.acme.com.

DNS server   If you are supposed to set up a specific DNS server to use, an address will be provided. They might provide two addresses: one primary and one secondary (to be used as a backup).

For a non–dial-up connection, you will need all of the items listed above except the username, password, and phone number, and you might also receive a static IP address to use.

Once you've assembled the information you need, go on to the next applicable section.

Setting Up a Dial-Up Connection

A dial-up connection necessarily involves Windows Dial-Up Networking (DUN). Most versions of Windows include some type of wizard that walks you through setting up a dial-up networking connection, so it's not difficult.

> **NOTE**
>
> The dial-up connection described in the following sections is for a regular ISP, not for America Online. AOL does use dial-up connection, but it has its own software and uses its own proprietary connection protocol. It sets itself up automatically when you install the AOL software. You can also set up AOL to use an existing Internet connection, which can be handy if you already have **broadband** service but want to continue to be a member of AOL. To set that up, set the connection type in AOL to TCP/IP.

Broadband
High-speed connection to a network resource (usually refers to the Internet).

Windows 95/98/Me

If using Windows 95, you must manually install Dial-Up Networking (from the Windows Components tab of Add/Remove Programs; see Chapter 16, "Essential Windows Tools and Skills") and TCP/IP (from the Network Properties box; see Chapter 13, "Introduction to Networking"). In Windows 98 and Windows Me, both are installed by default.

If Dial-Up Networking has been installed, an icon for it appears in My Computer. One way of setting up a dial-up Internet connection is to create a new DUN connection in the Dial-Up Networking window. To do so, double-click Dial-Up Networking from My Computer. If there are existing dial-up networking connections, the Dial-Up Networking window appears; double-click Make New Connection to start the New Connection Wizard. Then just follow the prompts to create the new connection.

Another way (Windows 98 and Windows Me only) is to try to open up Internet Explorer or Outlook Express. If no Internet connection has been set up, the Internet Connection Wizard will run and walk you through the process of creating the DUN connection and creating your e-mail account at the same time.

If you choose not to set up an e-mail account during the Internet Connection Wizard, you can do it later from within the e-mail program. Windows 95 comes with a program called Internet Mail. The first time you start it (from the Start menu), it walks you through a setup wizard in which you enter your mail server, e-mail ID and password, and so on. In Windows 98, the program is called Outlook Express, and it too configures itself the first time you run it, prompting you for the needed data. This data will include your e-mail username, your e-mail password, and your incoming and outgoing mail servers.

Once you've gone through either process, you will have a default-configured dial-up connection. It appears in the Dial-Up Networking window as an icon. You can establish the connection any time you like by double-clicking it from there. You can place a shortcut for the connection on the Desktop as well.

You might want to check the connection's properties against the settings list that your ISP provided. To do so, right-click the connection and choose Properties. Some of the properties you can change include these:

Phone number   Update this on the General tab if it ever changes. Clear the Use Country Code and Area Code check box if it's a local call.

Connect using   Choose a different modem on the General tab if desired.

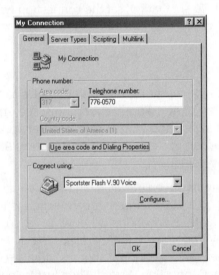

Log on to network   You can clear this check box on the Server Types tab to shave a few seconds off the connection time if you're making an Internet connection; leave it marked if you are dialing into a corporate network.

Allowed network protocols   Make sure TCP/IP is marked on the Server Types tab; all other protocols are optional.

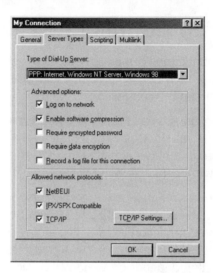

TCP/IP Settings   Click this button to open a dialog box in which you can specify a fixed IP address and/or a DNS server address.

Windows 2000

Windows 2000 automatically installs dial-up networking and TCP/IP, so you're all set on that front. Windows 2000 also has enhanced Internet connection setup features; its Internet Connection Wizard walks you through the setup process painlessly. Not only does it set up your dial-up connection, but it also configures your e-mail program for you (if you use Outlook Express or Outlook).

To start the Internet Connection Wizard, choose Start ➢ Programs ➢ Accessories ➢ Communications ➢ Internet Connection Wizard. Then choose I Want To Set Up My Internet Connection Manually… and click Next. Work your way through the wizard by answering the questions.

Just as with Windows 9*x*, you can place a shortcut for the connection on your Desktop. You can also right-click it and choose Properties to adjust its settings.

To set the TCP/IP properties for the connection, right-click the connection icon in Dial-Up Networking and choose Properties. Then click the Networking tab and double-click Internet Protocol. From the dialog box that appears, you can set up a static IP address and/or DNS server address or fine-tune any other settings.

Non–Dial-Up Connections

Most non–dial-up connections come with their own setup software. Your cable, DSL, or satellite service provider will probably give you a CD-ROM or specific instructions for setting up the connection.

Cable and DSL connections aren't usually fussy about settings–they simply work, right out of the box in most cases. When I had cable access for a while, for example, it connected to a network card in my PC, and my PC saw the Internet connection as a network connection in My Network Places.

To test the settings for a non–dial-up connection, try viewing a web page. If it appears, the connection is working. If it doesn't work, try rerunning the Internet Setup Wizard (or New Connection Wizard, depending on the Windows version). To do this, you can select it from one of the Accessories submenus off the Start menu (the exact location depends on Windows version) or by opening the Internet Properties from the Control Panel and clicking the Setup button on the Connections tab. The wizard asks how you connect to the Internet; specify that you have a network connection.

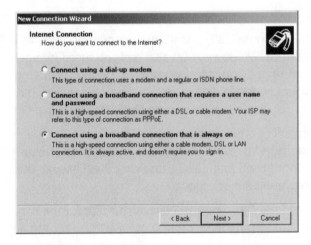

Satellite access is a little trickier and quirkier. To set it up, you must run the software that comes with the hardware and follow the instructions to the letter. I currently have two-way satellite Internet service on my PC, and it consists of two external modem-like boxes that connect to my PC via USB. They are each connected to a coaxial cable that leads to my satellite dish. To establish the connection initially, I had to go through a long and involved software setup process that involved using a dial-up modem to download some files.

Internet Connection Sharing

Windows 98 Second Edition, Windows Me, Windows 2000, and Windows XP all have a feature built in called Internet Connection Sharing (ICS) that allows a LAN-connected computer to share its Internet connection with other PCs on the LAN. This makes it possible for a family to have a single broadband Internet connection with multiple PCs able to access the Internet simultaneously. The PCs that will be using the shared connection do not necessarily have to have a particular Windows version, as long as they have at least Windows 95, because the wizard that sets up the feature can make a configuration floppy disk to take to each PC that enables it to access the shared connection.

In a nutshell, here's how it works. The main Internet-connected PC has a single IP address by which it is known on the Internet for the duration of its connection. That's the "real" IP address. When another PC on the network wants to use that connection, the sharing PC assigns it a separate IP address using a set of private IP addresses for local use. Then whenever traffic comes in or out, the sharing PC shuttles the data off to the internal IP address for the requesting PC. This is known as **virtual private IP addressing**. It's kind of like when a group of people are at a restaurant and one person orders for the entire table. Each person tells the orderer what he or she wants, and then the orderer speaks in a single voice to the waiter, conveying all the orders.

Windows 98 Second Edition has a special wizard that sets this up; it is found on the Accessories menu. In Windows Me, its setup is built into the Internet Connection Wizard. In Windows XP, the setup is built into the New Connection Wizard. When you set up the connection, you are asked whether you want to share it or not.

To turn the sharing feature off or on after the initial configuration, display the properties for the shared connection. In Windows 98 and Me, a Sharing button opens a dialog box where you can turn it on or off. In Windows XP, a check box for Internet Connection Sharing appears on the Advanced tab.

Another way to share an Internet connection is with a router. If you have cable or DSL Internet service and a home network, you can hook the incoming cable or DSL line to a router and then hook up each PC in the network to that router. The router will then provide the internal IP address translation needed to share the connection. You don't need any special version of Windows in order to do that, but you may find that the router costs as much as a Windows upgrade would cost. Some ISPs frown on this sharing, and they even explicitly forbid it in their member agreements and terminate your service if they find out you are doing it. Others don't mind and will even help you set it up.

Virtual private IP addressing
Assigning internal IP addresses to PCs that are separate from their external IP addresses in order to share an external IP address among multiple PCs. Private IP addresses begin with 192.168 and range from 192.168.0.1 to 192.168.255.254.

Troubleshooting Internet Connections

Here are a few of the most common problems encountered and some suggestions for solving them.

Modem won't dial   Make sure the correct modem is identified in the properties for the DUN connection, and make sure that the correct COM port has been assigned to the modem in Modem Properties.

Modem won't stay connected   This can happen sometimes because of problems with the ISP, so don't assume it's your PC's fault unless the problem is persistent and the connection has never worked right. If it hangs up after less than a minute, check to make sure the TCP/IP protocol is installed in Network Properties. If it hangs up at random intervals, try a different access phone number for your ISP or a different phone cord. Also make sure that you have the phone cord plugged into the correct jack on the modem. You could also ask the phone company to test your phone line for quality.

Can't view web pages   If you can establish a DUN connection (or if you are sure that your broadband always-on connection is working) but you can't view web pages, your web browser is probably having problems contacting a DNS server for IP address translation. Check the recommendations of your ISP for using a specific DNS server address versus automatic addressing and make sure the correct settings are chosen in the connection properties.

Can't send or receive e-mail   If you can view web pages but you can't get your e-mail, and you have never been able to get your e-mail from this PC, the problem is likely bad e-mail settings. Edit the properties for your e-mail account in your e-mail program. If you have been able to get your e-mail in the past but can't at the moment, and you have not made any recent changes to your settings, it is almost certainly a mail server problem and there is nothing you can do anything about. Just wait for your ISP to get it fixed.

Much more is involved in troubleshooting problems with TCP/IP than the few hints provided here; entire books are devoted to the subject. If you find yourself spending a lot of time with TCP/IP, you might want to review some Network+ study materials.

Conclusion

Congratulations, you have reached the end of this book! By now you have a thorough grasp of the basic concepts involved in A+ certification and in day-to-day life as a PC technician. If you decide to continue your studies toward this career, I suggest the following books to help you prepare further:

A+® Complete Study Guide
by David Groth; Dan Newland
ISBN: 0-7821-2802-5

A+® Complete Study Guide, Deluxe Edition
by David Groth; Dan Newland
ISBN: 0-7821-4052-1

A+® Certification Kit
by David Groth et al.
ISBN: 0-7821-2805-X

A+® Complete Exam Notes™
by David Groth; Dan Newland; Todd Haplin
ISBN: 0-7821-2803-3

Review Questions

Terms to Know

❏ Internet
❏ Internet client
❏ Internet server
❏ ISP
❏ Web hosting
   company
❏ Broadband
❏ Dial-up networking
❏ TCP/IP
❏ Protocol
❏ Fixed IP address
❏ Dynamic IP address
❏ DNS
❏ URL
❏ World Wide Web
❏ Web browser
❏ Web page
❏ HTML
❏ Java
❏ Upload
❏ Download
❏ FTP site
❏ Virtual private IP
   addressing

1. What is the difference between an ISP and a web hosting company?

2. True or False: DSL and cable do not require telephone line access.

3. Which is faster: a T1 line or a T3 line?

4. What would be the binary equivalent of 192.168.1.1? (If necessary, use the Calculator in Windows set to Scientific mode to do the conversion.)

5. What is the purpose of a DNS server?

6. What protocol is used for displaying web pages?

7. What is DUN?

8. Which versions of Windows include Internet Connection Sharing?

9. True or False: A PC running Windows 95 cannot use a shared Internet connection over a LAN.

10. True or False: Intermittent problems sending and receiving e-mail are usually problems with the ISP's mail server rather than with the client PC.

Appendix

A

What's in a PC Technician's Toolkit?

If you plan to take apart, repair, and reassemble PCs, a good toolkit is an essential investment. The right tools can save you a lot of time, and help you avoid damage to your equipment or injury to yourself.

Most computer stores sell toolkits of various sizes. You don't need the largest, fanciest one, as long as you have the few basic tools you need for the PCs that you'll be working on. For example, Compaq laptops happen to use a small Torx screw (T-8 size), so if you work on those, you'll need a T-8 screwdriver; otherwise, you probably won't need one.

Generally speaking, a good toolkit should contain:

At least two sizes of Phillips head screwdrivers   You'll need a medium-sized one for large screws such as those on the cover of the computer case, plus a small one for tiny screws such as those holding a disk drive in place. Most screws in a typical computer are Phillips (a four-prong star) rather than regular flathead screws (a straight line).

WARNING

Do not use a magnetized screwdriver inside the computer. Some technicians enjoy the convenience of using a screwdriver with a magnetized tip to fish dropped screws out of crevices, but it's easy to damage disks by touching them with a magnet. If the only screwdriver you have available is magnetized, exercise extreme care not to touch its tip to any part of the PC except the screws themselves.

At least two sizes of flathead screwdrivers   Although flathead screws are less common in computer equipment, you will occasionally encounter them.

Needle-nose pliers   These are useful for grasping small items and for removing and replacing circuit board jumpers.

Tweezers   Or even better, a part retriever, which is like a tiny set of retractable claws with a spring-loaded handle.

The above constitutes the basic set; you might also want the following tools:

Wire snips   A pair of wire snips for cutting wire and stripping insulation.

Small flashlight   This is useful to see small areas inside the computer, for example, the pin 1 marking on a connector.

3/16-inch nut driver   This tool helps place 3/16-inch hexagonal nuts into the computer. The nuts are useful for mounting hardware on motherboards as well as serial and parallel ports.

Torx screwdrivers or bits   A six-pointed star-shaped screwdriver head. Torx screws are often used to secure the covers on places where the manufacturer does not want the average consumer to venture, because most people do not have this type of screwdriver.

Knife   A cutting blade or utility knife of some sort.

Windows 98 or Me startup disk   Windows 95 startup disks do not contain real-mode CD-ROM drivers so that your CD-ROM drives will work from the command prompt. You must manually edit the CONFIG.SYS and AUTOEXEC.BAT files on a Windows 95 startup disk to add CD-ROM support. It's a good idea, therefore, to have a Windows 98 or Me startup disk in your troubleshooting toolkit. It can be used on Windows 95 systems.

Besides your toolkit, you will also want to carry a bag containing these useful items:

Antistatic wrist strap   A safety device that greatly reduces the chance of static damage to components by channeling any static electric charge to the ground instead of through computer components.

Roll of black electrical tape   Helpful for wrapping wire ends and insulating components.

Can of compressed air   For cleaning components without using any hazardous liquids.

Soft, lint-free cloth   For cleaning the monitor and other components.

Digital multimeter   A meter that measures multiple types of electrical specs (ohms, amps, and volts).

Finally, it is a good idea to accumulate a stockpile of spare parts if you do many PC repairs. Some suggestions are as follows:

Screws   A supply of various sized screws.

Expansion card backplates   Save the metal inserts that you take out of the back of a case when you put a modem or other card into the PC. You may need them again later.

Drive faceplates   Save the plastic faceplates that you remove from the front of cases so you can replace them later if needed.

Mounting kits   These are sometimes supplied with retail hard disks and allow you to put a 3.5-inch drive into a 5.25-inch bay. They are useful when your case has more free 5.25-inch bays than 3.5-inch bays.

Cables   Save any power, IDE, floppy, CD-ROM, or other cables that you may accumulate.

Keyboard, mouse, and 3.5-inch floppy drive   Keep an extra one of each of these components to help with troubleshooting problems.

Alcohol and Swabs   A small vial of denatured alcohol and some cotton swabs can come in handy for cleaning the corona wires on laser printers.

Monitor cleaner   Because monitor screens should not be cleaned with ordinary glass cleaner, you might want a supply of premoistened monitor cleaner towelettes on hand.

Information   Make a notebook you can carry around to work sites that lists information you are likely to need. This might include the toll-free support numbers for various brands of hardware, a list of hazardous materials disposal sites in various towns, and so on.

Appendix

B

Answers to
Review Questions

Chapter 1

1. Batteries, circuit boards, monitors, cleaning chemicals, and toner cartridges

2. Electrostatic discharge

3. Wear an antistatic wrist strap, use a grounding mat, touch the PC frame periodically as you work, wear rubber-soled shoes and cotton socks, and keep the room's atmosphere humid.

4. Separate cables from one another; use shielded cables; and use short cables.

5. False. A keyboard does not contain any magnetism-susceptible parts. Disks are the primary components that need to be kept away from magnets.

6. True. An online UPS supplies power through the battery full-time, but a standby power system uses the battery only when it is needed.

7. Joules

8. False. Clean a circuit board with compressed air. You should never use water on a circuit board because it might not dry completely and might cause a short circuit.

9. The mouse pointer might jump or stutter onscreen instead of moving smoothly where you wanted it to go.

10. Run the head cleaning utility by pressing buttons on the printer itself or by using its Windows driver.

Chapter 2

1. IDE connector

2. You can return the keyboard and get a model designed for an AT system, or you can get an adapter to convert to the correct plug type.

3. A serial mouse

4. The female one

5. A sound card

6. A monitor

7. Random Access Memory

8. CD-ROM, hard disk, and floppy disk

9. The disk is the removable cartridge; the drive is the read/write unit that remains inside the PC.

10. It steps down the voltage to the level needed by the motherboard and various components, and it converts AC to DC.

Chapter 3

1. AT

2. ATX

3. AT

4. AT

5. A pathway between two or more components on the same circuit board.

6. Because the expansion bus is much slower than the local I/O bus. There are other reasons too, but they were not covered in this chapter.

7. PGA

8. 168

9. AGP and PCI. It probably will not have ISA.

10. It marks pin 1, which must align with the red stripe on the cable that plugs into the connector.

Chapter 4

1. Registers

2. System crystal

3. Forcing the CPU to operate at a higher speed than the speed for which it is rated.

4. The address bus

5. Dual Inline Pin Package (DIPP)

6. Slot A

7. Real mode and protected mode

8. Virtual memory and Virtual 8086. An answer of 386 Protected Mode is also acceptable.

9. L2 cache

10. It was slower than a regular Pentium when running 16-bit applications, and it did not support MMX.

Chapter 5

1. ROM is read-only, and it can be changed only under special circumstances (if at all). RAM can be freely written to and read from.

2. Dynamic

3. Static

4. Because the system bus width was greater than the width of a single stick of the RAM. The two numbers must be equal.

5. DIMM

6. They are both physically the same size. However, parity memory has an extra chip on it.

7. 64-bits

8. 32MB

9. You can't tell from the information given; PC100 refers to the speed of the RAM, not its capacity.

10. SDRAM

Chapter 6

1. 640×480 and 16 colors

2. 65,536 (2 to the 16th power)

3. 8MB

4. A set of standards that programmers can use to access the features of a piece of hardware in their programs.

5. AGP

6. Red, Blue, and Green

7. Thin Film Transistor (TFT)

8. 100Hz

9. Check all connections for snugness. Check the monitor's brightness and contrast settings. Make sure the monitor is turned on. You could also try a different monitor and/or try a different video card.

10. Adjust the controls on the monitor itself to increase the height and width of the picture.

Chapter 7

1. Floppy drive

2. False. The charge of an individual particle has no relationship to a 1 or a 0 of data.

3. Track. (Cylinder is also an acceptable answer.)

4. Cylinder

5. Pits and land

6. A transition between a pit and land

7. It heats the metal and dye in certain spots to create areas of less reflectivity that the laser sees as pits.

8. Hard disks only

9. Three

10. Low-level formatting

Chapter 8

1. SCSI

2. False. You need an 80-wire ribbon cable.

3. Update the BIOS.

4. Use FDISK to delete the current partitions and create a single new one.

5. The CD-ROM drive must be set to Slave, and the new hard drive must be set to Master.

6. Buy and install a SCSI interface card.

7. Velocity

8. Power cable from the power supply and ribbon cable from the motherboard or IDE interface board.

9. Incorrect jumper settings

10. Scandisk (Windows 9*x*) or Check Disk (Windows 2000/XP)

Chapter 9

1. Any drive can be installed in a large external bay, although it might require a mounting bracket if the drive is small (such as a floppy or hard drive).

2. A floppy ribbon cable has only 34 rather than 40 wires/pins, and it has a twist in some of the wires at one end.

3. An audio cable between the CD-ROM drive and the sound card

4. 3.5-inch 1.44MB

5. It allows playback of DVD movies.

6. True

7. To save money, or to use the disks on a Macintosh or other non–IBM-compatible PC.

8. The tab is open, so you can see through the hole.

9. The red stripe on ribbon cable is not oriented to Pin 1 on one or both ends of the cable.

10. It does not change or examine the data area of the disk; it only rewrites the File Allocation Table.

Chapter 10

1. Jumpers for setting the IRQ and I/O address

2. It converts the digital computer data into analog sounds that can be sent over analog telephone lines. Then at the other end, another modem converts the sounds back into data again.

3. An ISA internal modem or an external modem

4. There are no special operating system requirements for a hardware modem. A hardware modem will work with any operating system, including MS-DOS, Windows, or Linux. A software modem, on the other hand, is limited to a particular operating system (usually Windows).

5. The incoming telephone line coming from the wall. The other jack, Phone, is for a telephone.

6. It is not a Plug and Play card.

7. Check that there is a working phone line attached to the Line jack on the modem.

8. A song on an audio CD, an MP3 clip, and a sound clip you record with a microphone are all examples. Any sound file that originated as a real sound rather than a computer-generated one is waveform.

9. Recorded clips of musical instruments for use in MIDI playback, stored in the ROM of the sound card.

10. Speaker

Chapter 11

1. An ergonomic keyboard. You might also suggest a consultation with a physician to rule out more serious problems.

2. The Keyboard options in the Control Panel

3. False. An optical mouse has no rolling ball. It may or may not have a cord.

4. ATX

5. Because they can potentially have more drives installed than a smaller case, and each drive has wattage requirements

6. Ohms

7. Amps

8. 9.5 watts

9. Red

Chapter 12

1. Because it's a page printer, it must form the entire page in RAM before it can print the page. An inkjet printer is a line printer, and it needs to store only one line at a time.

2. Dot matrix

3. They are scaleable to any size, and they work with any Windows printer and any Windows application.

4. Open the Fonts window and then choose File ➢ Install New Font. Navigate to the location containing the fonts, select the font, and click OK.

5. Dots per inch, or dpi

6. 720dpi

7. Dot matrix

8. Developing

9. Parallel, USB, serial, or network

10. Check to see whether the printer is out of a certain color of ink. If not, run the head-cleaning utility to unclog the ink jets.

Chapter 13

1. A Wide Area Network, which is a network that is stretched out geographically rather than being located in a defined area such as a single building

2. True

3. Bus, ring, and star

4. TCP/IP

5. Two—one for each PC. A network consists of a minimum of two PCs.

6. Ethernet

7. Category 5 or Category 6 Unshielded Twisted-Pair (UTP).

8. A gateway

9. File and Printer Sharing for Microsoft Networks

10. The Add Printer Wizard

Chapter 14

1. An operating system with a graphical user interface (GUI) is one that the user interacts with using pictures and a pointing device rather than typing and a command line.

2. Cooperative multitasking processes only one program at a time, but it allows programs to take turns. Preemptive multitasking enables multiple programs to use the CPU at the same time.

3. Upper memory

4. eXtended Memory Specification (XMS)

5. HIMEM.SYS. An alternative answer might be EMM386.EXE, which allows extended memory to simulate either XMS or EMS memory as needed.

6. SYSTEM.DAT and USER.DAT

7. Windows NT, Windows 2000, and Windows XP

8. Windows 2000

9. 133MHz Pentium CPU and 64MB of memory

10. The one that does not support dual-booting directly. This would include MS-DOS, Windows 95, Windows 98, or Windows Me.

Chapter 15

1. IO.SYS, MSDOS.SYS, and Command.COM

2. CONFIG.SYS and AUTOEXEC.BAT, in that order

3. USER.DAT and SYSTEM.DAT

4. NTLDR and NTOSKRNL, in that order

5. BOOT.INI

6. F8

7. BOOTLOG.TXT

8. Add/Remove Programs

9. The Recovery Console

10. You cannot use most CD-ROM drives in Safe mode.

Chapter 16

1. Edit ➤ Copy, right-click and choose Copy, press Ctrl+C, or click the Copy button on the toolbar.

2. Disk Defragmenter

3. System Configuration Utility (MSCONFIG)

4. Start ➤ Run and type **MSCONFIG**, and then click OK.

5. You might accidentally make changes to the Registry that would prevent Windows from starting or cause errors to occur.

6. A code that is typed following a command-prompt command that further defines how the command should be executed

7. The Start ➤ Run command

8. `COPY OLD.TXT E:\RETIRE`

9. RD

Chapter 17

1. Interrupt Requests, or IRQs

2. ISA

3. SCSI, USB, and FireWire

4. USB, FireWire, and PCMCIA (PC Card)

5. IRQs 2 and 9

6. COM2

7. IRQ 1

8. From the Control Panel, double-click Add New Hardware or Add/Remove Hardware, depending on the Windows version.

9. Look for the device in Device Manager, and then double-click it to view its properties.

10. The device has a problem. This is most often—but not always—due to a resource conflict.

Chapter 18

1. Booting from an infected disk and running an infected program

2. Possible answers include installing an antivirus program, downloading virus definition updates, not opening unknown e-mail attachments, not booting from untested floppy disks, and displaying file extensions.

3. False

4. Create a rescue disk using an antivirus program on a working PC, and then use that disk to start the nonworking PC and check for viruses.

5. Scandisk (in Windows 9x/Me) or Check Disk (in Windows 2000 or XP)

6. Alt+F4

7. Alt

8. Windows Me and Windows XP

9. True

10. Opens the Start menu

Chapter 19

1. An ISP provides Internet connectivity, and a web hosting company rents space on a web server for posting web pages. A single company could perform both functions, or you could contract separately for the services.

2. False. DSL requires phone access; however, it does not tie up the phone line for telephone calls during Internet access.

3. T3

4. 11000000.10101000.00000001.00000001

5. To convert between IP addresses and URLs

6. Hypertext Transfer Protocol (HTTP)

7. Dial-up networking, a system for enabling a Windows-based computer to connect with another computer via telephone and modem

8. Windows 98 Second Edition, Windows Me, Windows 2000, and Windows XP

9. False. Any PC running Windows 95 or higher can use a shared connection. The version restriction is only for the PC that is doing the sharing; it must have a version of Windows that supports ICS.

10. True

Appendix
C

Glossary

286 protected mode   An operating mode for an 80386 CPU that emulates an 80286 CPU.

386 protected mode   An operating mode for an 80386 CPU that takes advantage of the 80386's advanced features, but is incompatible with programs written for earlier CPUs.

3D video acceleration   Memory buffers on a video card that give it better performance when displaying graphically intense programs that draw images with depth perspective.

Active matrix   A type of LCD monitor that uses a separate transistor for each pixel.

Actuator   The arm on which the read/write head is mounted, which moves the head in and out on the disk surface.

Address bus   The portion of the system bus that transports data between the CPU and RAM. Also called *frontside bus*.

Amps   Short for amperes. A measurement of electrical current or rate of flow.

Antivirus program   Software that monitors files for specific strings of characters that are associated with viruses and then quarantines and offers to repair or delete the affected files.

Aperture grille   A system of vertical wires that help guide the electrons so they hit the correct phosphors on a CRT.

API   Application Programming Interface. A set of standards that programmers can use to access the features of a piece of hardware in their programs.

ATA   AT Attachment. A standard for IDE drives in PCs that makes it possible for PCs to share IDE devices without compatibility problems.

Audio cable   A cable that runs from a CD-ROM drive to a sound card and enables the CD-ROM drive to play audio CDs through the sound card and its attached speakers.

AUTOEXEC.BAT   A file that lists the programs that should automatically be run at startup.

Back probing   Testing electricity while the device is on by sticking the multimeter probes down the back of the connector.

Backplate   A plate at the back of an expansion slot to keep the dust out of the PC case when that slot is not being used. You remove the backplate before you install an expansion card in that slot. Can also refer to the metal plate attached to the expansion card itself that fits into the same spot that the blank backplate occupied.

BNC   Stands for British Naval Connector. The type of connector used on coaxial cable (the kind used with cable TV). Some dictionaries show BNC as an abbreviation of different words, including Bayonet Neill-Concelman or Bayonet Nut Coupler.

Boot sector   A reserved sector on the disk for commands that load an operating system when the PC starts up.

Broadband   A high-speed connection between computers.

Broadband   High-speed connection to a network resource (usually refers to the Internet).

Bus   A pathway between two or more components on the same circuit board.

Cache   A temporary holding area for data that needs to be kept close at hand for reuse.

Cache on a Stick   A type of SRAM that serves as an external CPU cache, found mainly on older systems.

Cathode Ray Tube (CRT)   The technology behind the box-type display monitors sold today. It consists of a vacuum tube that sends electron rays to charge photosensitive phosphors on the monitor screen. The phosphors light up, creating the display picture.

Chipset   The set of chips built into the motherboard that collectively control its operation.

Client   A computer that uses network resources as an end user.

Client/server network   A network that includes both client and server PCs.

Clock cycle   One "beat" or "tick" of the system crystal's oscillator.

Clock multiplier   The number of times by which the internal speed exceeds the internal speed.

Color depth   The number of unique colors that a particular video mode supports.

Command line   A line onscreen where user-typed text appears.

CONFIG.SYS   A file that lists the drivers that should automatically be loaded each time the PC starts.

Conventional memory   The first 640KB of a PC's RAM. Used for running programs.

Convergence   The ability of the electron guns in a monitor to align precisely on each triad. If one of the guns is slightly off, it will result in a green, red, or blue tinge to the screen, either overall or in certain areas.

Cooperative multitasking   Multiple virtual machines taking turns using the main CPU one at a time, with each application being in charge of releasing the CPU when it is finished with it.

CPU   Also called the processor, this large, powerful silicon chip takes in data, performs calculations on it, and spits it out again into memory. The CPU is sometimes called the "brain" of a PC, but the "calculator" of the PC is actually more accurate because it does not think or reason for itself.

CRT   Cathode Ray Tube. A type of monitor that uses a large vacuum tube and electrons to light up phosphors on a glass screen.

Current   The volume of electricity flowing through a circuit. Measured in amps.

Current directory   The directory (folder) specified in the command prompt, to which any commands will apply that are not specifically directed at some other location.

Cylinder   The same head position on a stack of platters in a multiplatter disk such as a hard disk.

Desktop case   A PC case designed to sit with its largest side flat on a desk.

Device resources   Pathways or memory addresses that help a device communicate with the CPU and the operating system.

Dial-up networking   A Windows feature that enables clients to log into a remote network via telephone.

DIMM   Dual Inline Memory Module. A modern type of RAM packaging with 168 pins.

Directory   Same thing as a folder. The term Directory is often used rather than folder when referring to work at a command prompt.

DMA   Direct Memory Access. A way of increasing data transfer rates by enabling the device to bypass the CPU and access memory directly.

DNS   Stands for Domain Name System. A method of translating numeric IP addresses to text-based URLs.

Dot pitch   The measurement of the distance between one colored dot in a triad and the same color in an adjacent triad.

Double-click speed   The speed at which one click must follow another in order for the PC to perceive it as a double-click rather than two single clicks.

Double-scan passive matrix   An improved passive matrix display that divides the screen into separate sections and has one transistor for each row and column in each section.

Download   To transfer a file from another PC to your PC.

Dpi   Dots per inch, a measurement of printer output quality.

DPMI   DOS Protected-Mode Interface. Like an MS-DOS command prompt interface except it's in Protected mode rather than Real mode.

Drive timing   The amount of time that passes between reading one bit and reading the next bit on a drive.

D-sub   A type of connector with asymmetrically arranged pins or holes in multiple rows. The outer ring looks sort of like a capital *D*, which is where the term D-sub comes originates.

Dual-boot   A system on which two (or more) operating systems are installed, each on a separate partition. At startup the user can choose which one should run.

Dynamic IP address   An IP address that is assigned from a pool of available addresses upon connection, and released upon disconnection.

Dynamic RAM   RAM that requires constant electricity to retain its data. Abbreviated as DRAM.

Electromagnetic   A magnetic field created by electricity.

Electromagnetic interference (EMI)   The corruption of a signal by the magnetic field of another nearby electrical device.

Electrostatic discharge (ESD)   An electrical shock that occurs when two objects of uneven charge come in contact with one another. Otherwise known as static electricity.

EMM386.EXE   A memory management utility that allows the operating system to use extended memory to supply either EMS or XMS support to an application as needed.

EMS   Expanded Memory Standard. The industry standard specification for expanded memory usage.

Encoding method   The pattern that determine the distance between each bit of data on a disk.

Ergonomic keyboard   A keyboard designed t minimize the stress placed on the users' hands and wrists.

Expanded memory   Additional memory over 1MB supplied via an expansion board for 80286 PC

Expansion bus   The bus used by ISA expansio slots. Slow and old; soon to be obsolete.

Extended memory   Additional memory abov 1MB on a motherboard.

External data bus   The bus that transfers dat from outside the CPU to inside and then back out again.

External speed   The system crystal speed, which controls the CPU's speed.

Female   A female connector is one that has hol rather than pins.

File   A collection of computer data stored under single name.

File Allocation Table (FAT)   A table that keeps track of the content of each sector of the dis The operating system consults the FAT whenever it needs to open or save a file.

File extension   A code (usually three characters) following a file's name that indicates the file type. For example, in MYFILE.DOC, the doc extension indicates a document.

Fixed IP address   An IP address that never changes, assigned permanently to a specific client.

Flux   The direction of the flow of the magnetic field.

lux transition   A spot where the flux changes
irections.

M synthesis   A method of computer simulating
ne sounds of various musical instruments. Results in
rtificial-sounding MIDI music.

older   An organizing container for holding com-
uter files, residing on a disk.

ont   Strictly defined, a particular typeface at a
articular size. However, *font* has lately come to be
nonymous with *typeface*.

orm factor   The size and shape of a device. Most
ommonly applied to motherboards, but it can also
pply to other devices that come in a variety of sizes.

ormatting   Laying down guide tracks for the
ad/write heads on a disk in a drive.

PM   Fast Page Mode. An older type of RAM in
hich the speed does not correspond to the system
is speed. Speeds are measured in nanoseconds.

TP site   A server that provides FTP access for a
ard disk that accepts uploading or downloading
perations.

ateway   A network box that can translate and
ansfer data between two unlike network systems.

eometry   A drive's organizational structure,
cluding the number of cylinders, number of read/
rite heads, and number of sectors.

PF   General Protection Fault. A type of program
ror that occurs when Windows protects itself against
program's request to do something that would cause
oblems. Usually results in program termination.

raphical User Interface (GUI)   An
perating system that provides a picture-based
terface with which the user interacts.

round   To bleed off electrical charge to a safe
cation where it can dissipate, such as to the earth
elf.

Hardware modem   A modem that contains
everything it needs to operate within its own
hardware, so it can work with any operating system.

Heat sink   A porcupine-like block that channels
heat away from the CPU.

High memory   The first 64KB of RAM above the
1MB mark. Also called High Memory Area (HMA).

High-order bits   The second four bits in a
byte (reading from right to left), representing the
instructions for processing the data.

HIMEM.SYS   A memory management driver
loaded at startup that allows programs to use
extended memory under the XMS specification.

Hot-pluggable   Able to be connected and
disconnected without shutting down the PC.
Sometimes called *hot-swappable*.

HTML   Hypertext Markup Language. A text-based
programming language used to create Web content.

I/O address   Input/Output addresses in memory
where devices place data for pickup by the operating
system, and where the operating system places data
for pickup by the device.

IDE   Integrated Device Electronics. A type of
drive connector provided on the motherboard for
interfacing with hard drives and CD-ROM drives.

IDE   Integrated Drive Electronics. A drive with a
built-in controller.

Illegal operation   A program error that occurs
when an application asks Windows to do something
that it cannot comply with. Usually results in program
termination.

Internal speed   The maximum speed at which
a particular CPU can operate.

Internet   A global network of interconnected
computers that share data.

Internet client   A computer that uses Internet services.

Internet server   A computer that provides Internet services to other computers.

IRQ   Interrupt Request. A system resource assigned to a device so it can signal to the CPU that it is ready to communicate.

ISP   Internet Service Provider. A company that charges people money to help them connect to the Internet.

Java   A platform-independent programming language for creating applications that users using any type of PC can run through a web browser interface.

Joule   A unit of electrical energy. Surge suppressors are rated in joules, such as 800 or 1,300 joules.

Jumper   A cap that fits over a pair of pins, changing the electrical flow through a circuit board.

Jumper   A metal and plastic cap that fits over two pins on a circuit board, completing an electrical circuit between them and changing the flow of electricity through the board.

Key matrix   The grid of keys on a keyboard.

Keyframes   A set of still images that represent the start, middle, and end points of an animation; the computer can then generate the additional frames between the points.

L1   Stands for Level 1. A cache that holds data that is waiting to enter the CPU. Sometimes called a front-side cache.

L2   Stands for Level 2. A cache that holds data that is waiting to leave the CPU. Also called a back-side cache.

Land   An area of an optical disc that is unpitted, resulting in a full measure of light reflecting back from it.

LCD   Liquid Crystal Display. A type of monitor that sends an electrical charge through liquid crystals to bend their reflectivity, changing the light passing through them.

Line printer   A printer that prints one line of a page at a time.

Local Area Network   A network in which all the resources are located near one another.

Local I/O bus   A bus for connecting certain types of high-speed expansion slots to the system bus.

Logical drive   A section of a physical hard disk that's identified by a unique drive letter, such as C:, D:, etc.

Low-order bits   The first four bits in a byte (reading from right to left), representing data to be processed.

LS-120   An IDE-based floppy drive that accepts both normal floppy drives and 120MB super disks.

Machine language   The set of codes that the CPU understands for accepting numbers and instructions for calculating them.

Male   In computer jargon, a male connector is one that has pins rather than holes.

Master   The drive designated to handle all the data traffic on the IDE cable.

Math coprocessor   An extra chip that provides additional registers with which the CPU can process complex math calculations more quickly and efficiently.

MBR   Master Boot Record. Information stored on a drive about its partitions and boot capabilities.

MIDI Musical Instrument Digital Interface. An interface and method for creating sound and music files entirely digitally, with no analog origin.

MMX Stands for Multimedia Extensions. Built-in CPU functions that applications designed for MMX can take advantage of to streamline the processing of graphics-intensive commands.

Modem A device that converts digital data to analog sound and vice-versa so data can be transferred between computers via telephone line.

Monitor A display panel that shows the results of the PC's activities or processing.

Monochrome Consisting of only one color. A monochrome monitor shows a single color on a black or white background (usually black).

MS-DOS kernel The portion of MS-DOS that gets loaded into memory at startup and remains resident there while the PC is running.

Multimeter A meter that is capable of taking several electrical measurements, including voltage, amperage, and resistance.

Multitask To execute more than one program at once.

Network Two or more computers connected together to share resources.

Network Operating System (NOS) An operating system designed to help a server PC provide access to files, printers, and other network resources to client PCs.

Network topology The physical layout of a network.

Noncontiguous Not physically located together.

NTFS NT File System. The file storage system native to Windows NT, offering efficiency and feature improvements over FAT16.

Ohms The unit of measurement for resistance.

OLE Object Linking and Embedding. A standard for sharing information between applications that allows data to maintain a link with its data file and/or application of origin.

Operating system (OS) The system program that runs on the PC all the time and makes it possible for other programs to execute and for the user to issue commands.

Optical mouse A mouse that uses light sensors instead of a ball to record movement.

Overclocking Operating a CPU at a higher clock speed than the speed for which it is rated.

Packet A piece of data packaged for network transit, including the data itself plus addressing information. Also called a frame.

Packet writing A feature that enables a CD-RW disc to be treated as a regular disk, and to be written and rewritten multiple times.

Page frame The 64KB area in upper memory used to swap data into and out of expanded memory.

Page printer A printer that waits until it has a whole page of data in its memory and then prints the entire page at once.

Paging file The file on the hard disk that stores the data in virtual memory. Also called a swap file.

Parity An error checking mechanism in RAM that uses an extra bit to ensure data accuracy.

Partition A formattable section of a physical hard disk.

Passive matrix An inexpensive type of LCD display that uses one transistor for each row and each column.

PCMCIA   Also called PC Card. A standard for credit-card size devices that plug into a notebook PC. There are three sizes: Type I (for memory), Type II (for most devices), and Type III (for drives).

Peer-to-peer network   A network that consists only of clients, with no central server.

PGA   Pin Grid Array. A type of CPU with a grid of pins on its underside that fit into a motherboard socket.

Physical drive   The entire physical hard disk, encompassing all partitions and logical drives.

Piezoelectric inkjet printer   An inkjet printer that moves the ink through the print nozzles by applying electrical charges to piezoelectric crystals.

Pit   An area of an optical disk that is indented, resulting in less light reflecting back from it.

Pixel   A dot with a separately described color from the surrounding dots on the display.

Platen   The roller bar behind the ribbon on an impact printer that absorbs the impact and keeps the paper in place.

Plug and Play   A standard for devices to talk to operating systems to report their specifications and driver requirements so the operating system can set them up without user intervention.

Plug and Play   A standard for detecting new devices and installing drivers for them automatically. To work, it must be supported by the device, the motherboard chipset, and the installed operating system.

Polarity   The positive or negative aspect of an electrical voltage. A charge can have either a positive polarity or a negative polarity.

POST   Power-On Self Test. A set of low-level hardware diagnostics that confirm the basic operability of the motherboard, memory, CPU, and some other essential components.

Power sag   Occurs when the power supply doesn't get enough power. It's also called a brownout. You may have experienced this in your home when the lights dim and buzz for a moment but don't go out completely.

Power surge   A power surge occurs when the power supply gets too much power. It can cause the PC to reset, the power supply to burn out, or circuit boards to go bad. A power spike is like a surge only more so. Power spikes are even more likely to permanently damage hardware.

Power_Good Wire   Also called Power_OK wire. The wire from the power supply to the motherboard that tests the power supply's performance before the rest of the system starts up.

Ppm   Pages per minute, a measurement of printer output speed.

Preemptive multitasking   Multiple applications taking turns using the main CPU with the CPU itself being in charge of how much time each application gets at once.

Primary corona wire   A negatively charged wire in a laser printer that applies a uniform −600v charge to the drum in preparation for writing a page image to it.

Print resolution   The number of individual dots that make up a printed image, measured in dpi.

Print spooler   A program that holds print jobs in a queue while they are waiting to be printed. The spooler takes the pressure off the operating system, freeing it to work on other tasks.

Printer driver   A piece of software that acts as a translator and traffic director between a printer and the operating system.

Product activation   An anticopying measure in Windows XP and some other Microsoft applications that makes it nearly impossible to install the software on additional PCs once it has been installed and activated on another PC.

rotected mode   A mode of operation for an
0286 CPU that enables it to take advantage of
dvanced features not available in the 8088 CPU.

rotected mode   A PC operating mode
ompatible with 80286 and higher CPUs, addressing
ultiple megabytes of RAM.

rotocol   A language or set of rules for trans-
itting data between devices.

rotocol   Generically, a set of rules governing a
ituation. When referring to communications, a set of
les that specify how the data is sent and received.

S/2 port   A small round port used for
onnecting some keyboards and mice. The name
erives from a model of IBM PC that used this type
f connector. The PS/2 computer is long obsolete,
ut the plug type is still around.

Quick format   A faster than normal way of
eformatting an already-formatted disk that just
ipes out the FAT contents rather than physically
eformatting the data area.

RAM   Chips that store data using electrical
mpulses that are constantly refreshed by the power
upply. When the power goes off, the data is erased.
lso known as memory, although memory actually is
 broader term encompassing more than just RAM.

RAM   Random Access Memory. Memory that you
an both read from and write to.

RAM depth   The number of rows that the RAM
an simultaneously store. Analogous to a column on
 spreadsheet.

RAM disk   A temporary virtual hard disk created
ut of RAM.

RAM width   The number of bits that the RAM
can simultaneously accept. Analogous to a row on a
spreadsheet.

Random access   Able to jump to and access
any part of the data just as easily as any other part.

Read/write head   The recorder/reader unit on
a drive that reads data from the disk and writes data
to the disk.

Real mode   A mode of operation for an 80286
CPU that makes it compatible with applications
written for the 8088 CPU.

Real mode   MS-DOS mode, in which only a
single task can be performed at once. MS-DOS
operates in Real mode; Windows does not.

Real mode   A PC operating mode compatible with
8086 CPU operation, addressing only 1MB of RAM.

Recovery Console   A command line interface
for troubleshooting problems with a Windows 2000
or XP installation.

Recycle Bin   A temporary storage area for files
and folders that have been deleted.

Refresh rate   The rate at which pixels are
refreshed on a monitor, expressed in hertz (Hz).

Register   A work area inside the CPU that holds a
numeric value while the CPU performs a calculation
upon it.

Registry   A configuration file that specifies how
Windows 95 and higher will look and act in relation
to users, applications, and hardware.

Resident font   A font that is stored in the printer's
ROM and is available at all times, regardless of what
PC is connected to it.

Resistance   The amount of obstacle in an
electrical path.

Resolution   The number of pixels across and
down in a particular video display mode.

Ribbon cable   A cable consisting of several
wires laid out in a flat, side-by-side arrangement and
encased in plastic. It gets its name from the fact that
the flat, wide cable looks something like a piece of
ribbon.

RJ-45   A type of connector that looks like a wider-than-normal telephone plug. Used for network cables and ISDN phone lines.

ROM   Stands for Read-Only Memory. A memory chip that can be read but not written to.

ROM Shadowing   Copying the data from a ROM BIOS chip into RAM for quicker access to it.

Root directory   The top-level or main storage area on a disk, not associated with any particular folder.

Router   A traffic director box on a network that allows data addressed to a PC on a network segment to pass through to that segment while blocking other traffic from entering.

Safe mode   A limited-functionality Windows troubleshooting mode in which only essential drivers are loaded.

SCSI   Small Computer Systems Interface. An interface for connecting drives and other devices to a PC that allows chaining of up to seven devices together. An alternative to IDE.

SDRAM   Synchronous Dynamic RAM. RAM in which the speed is the same as the system bus speed. Speeds are measured in megahertz (MHz).

SEC   Single Edge Contact cartridge. A type of CPU mounted on a circuit board inside a plastic casing.

Sector   A section of a track created by straight lines cutting across the diameter of the disk platter.

Server   A computer that serves data to other PCs and provides access to network resources.

Shadow mask   A grid of perforated metal with holes that guide electron placement to ensure that the correct phosphors are illuminated on a CRT.

Sheet fed   A paper feed system that uses individual pre-cut sheets of paper.

SIMM   Single Inline Memory Module. An older type of RAM packaging with either 72 or 30 pins.

Slave   The drive that receives all its data through the drive designated as master.

Slot 1   A motherboard slot that accepts an Intel SEC cartridge CPU.

Slot A   A motherboard slot that accepts an AMD SEC cartridge CPU.

Slot mask   A hybrid technology combining shadow mask and aperture grille.

Software font   A font provided to the printer via software stored on the PC.

Software modem (Winmodem)   A modem that relies on a Windows application to team with its hardware in order to work. Software modems work only with a specific operating system (usually Windows).

Sound card   An expansion board that functions as a converter between analog sound and digital data, enabling the computer to generate and receive audio output and input.

Splash screen   The graphic that appears while Windows or some other program is loading. It usually lists the program name and version number.

Standard VGA   VGA stands for Video Graphics Array; it's the standard for basic operation of all modern monitors. Standard VGA is 640×480 pixels of resolution and 16 colors.

Startup disk   A bootable floppy disk containing command line utility programs for troubleshooting.

Static RAM   RAM that retains its data until new data is received. Abbreviated as SRAM.

Stick   A small circuit board on which is mounted multiple RAM chips. SIMMs and DIMMs are both sticks.

Switch A code typed following a command-prompt command that further defines how the command should be executed.

System bus The bus that carries data between the CPU and memory. Also called the external bus. "External" refers to the fact that the bus is outside the CPU; the CPU also has its own internal bus.

System crystal A quartz oscillator on the motherboard that sets the pace for movement of data into and out of the CPU.

TCP/IP Stands for Transmission Control Protocol/Internet Protocol. A communications protocol used in the Internet and in many LANs.

TCP/IP Transmission Control Protocol/Internet Protocol. A set of communication standards for sending and receiving data over a network.

Terminate To close the SCSI chain at the end, letting the system know that there are no other SCSI devices in the chain.

TFT Thin Film Transistor. A type of LCD display that uses multiple transistors for each pixel, resulting in a very bright and high-quality display.

Thermal inkjet printer An inkjet printer that heats the ink to create vapor bubbles that force the ink out.

Tower case A PC case designed to stand upright.

Trackball A mouse alternative in which the body stays stationary and the user rolls the ball manually.

Tracks Concentric bands on a disk platter, like the rings on a tree.

Tractor fed A paper feed system that uses continuous paper (where one sheet is attached to the next at top and bottom) and pulls the paper through the paper path with gears that grab onto perforated holes on the sides of the pages.

Transfer corona wire A wire in a laser printer that applies a positive charge to the paper on which the image will be printed.

TrueType font A software-based outline font that works with any Windows-supported printer and application. TrueType fonts are also used on Macintosh computers.

Typematic The quick repetition of a typed character, such as holding down the period key to make a row of dots. Also called character repeat.

Upload To transfer a file from your PC to another PC.

Upper memory The last 360KB of a PC's first megabyte of RAM. Reserved for system use.

URL Stands for Uniform Resource Locator. The text-based name of a network (usually Internet) resource that maps to an IP address through a DNS server, expressed in `ttp://` format.

VGA display A display mode consisting of 640480 resolution and 4-bit color depth (16 colors).

Video card An expansion board that adds a port into which a monitor can be connected. Also called *video board* or *video adapter*.

Video driver A file that translates instructions from the operating system into commands that the video card understands.

Virtual 8086 Using a single CPU to simulate multiple 8086 CPUs so several tasks can run concurrently.

Virtual machine A simulated separate CPU that runs programs independently of other activities occurring on the same physical system.

Virtual memory Using the hard disk to simulate RAM.

Virtual private IP addressing Assigning internal IP addresses to PCs that are separate from their external IP addresses in order to share an external IP address among multiple PCs. Private IP addresses begin with `92.168` and range from `92.168.0.1 to 192.168.255.254`.

Virus A program designed to spread itself from one PC to another and (usually) to cause damage to the PCs or annoyance to the user.

Virus definitions A data file containing the text strings that the antivirus program searches for to determine whether virus infection exists.

Voice A channel in the sound card that plays a single note by a single instrument. A typical sound card might have 64 voices, so 64 different sounds could be played at once.

Volts The measurement of the strength of a positive or negative electrical charge.

Volume label An internal identifier for a formatted disk. It appears under the drive icon in My Computer in Windows and at the top of a file listing from a command prompt. It has no relationship to any physical label on the outside of the disk.

Wattage The amount of electricity a device uses, determined by multiplying volts by amps.

Wave table synthesis A method of storing waveform clips of various musical instruments in the sound card's memory and then playing them back when playing MIDI music. Results in much more natural sounding MIDI music.

Waveform A sound that originates in the real world, rather than being originated by a computer.

Web browser A program that displays web pages.

Web hosting company A company that charges people money to store their websites and keep them available at all times to other clients.

Web page A text document with embedded HTML codes that make it appear to be formatted and/or to contain pictures and other elements when viewed with a web browser.

Wide Area Network A network in which resources are separated physically from one another (not in the same building).

Wildcard A character that represents any value. Two standard wildcards are * for any number of characters and ? for a single character.

Windows Clipboard A tool for copying and moving data between Windows applications.

Windows components Programs, utilities, and add-ons that come with Windows itself rather than being purchased separately.

World Wide Web A network of web pages available for public display on the Internet.

Write-protect To make a disk read-only so that nothing can be changed, added, or deleted on it.

XMS Stands for eXtended Memory Specification. A standard for using extended memory in applications.

ZIF Zero insertion force. A type of socket into which you can insert a chip without applying any pressure to it. ZIF sockets are advantageous when you're working with a chip that has many "legs" or pins because it reduces the chance of bending one of them.

Index

377

TELL US WHAT YOU THINK!

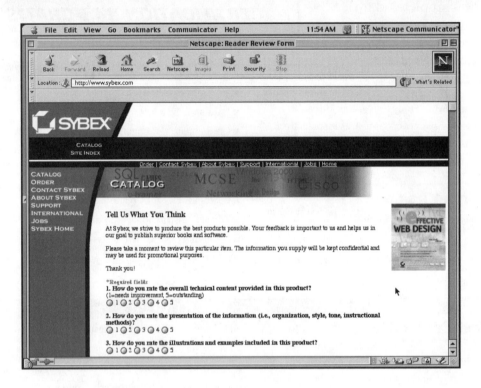

Your feedback is critical to our efforts to provide you with the best books and software on the market. Tell us what you think about the products you've purchased. It's simple:

1. Visit the Sybex website
2. Go to the product page
3. Click on **Submit a Review**
4. Fill out the questionnaire and comments
5. Click **Submit**

With your feedback, we can continue to publish the highest quality computer books and software products that today's busy IT professionals deserve.

www.sybex.com

SYBEX Inc. • 1151 Marina Village Parkway, Alameda, CA 94501 • 510-523-8233